# THE
# PARTY
# FAITHFUL

How and Why
Democrats Are Closing the God Gap

AMY SULLIVAN

SCRIBNER
New York London Toronto Sydney

SCRIBNER
A Division of Simon & Schuster, Inc.
1230 Avenue of the Americas
New York, NY 10020

First Scribner hardcover edition February 2008

SCRIBNER and design are trademarks of Macmillan Library Reference USA, Inc.,
used under license by Simon & Schuster, the publisher of this work.

For information about special discounts for bulk purchases,
please contact Simon & Schuster Special Sales at 1-800-456-6798
or business@simonandschuster.com.

Manufactured in the United States of America

1   3   5   7   9   10   8   6   4   2

Library of Congress Control Number: 2007038162

ISBN-13: 978-0-7432-9787-5
ISBN-10:     0-7432-9787-3

# CONTENTS

# CONTENTS

# AUTHOR'S NOTE

This is a book about the Democratic Party's relationship with religious voters, specifically white Catholics and evangelicals. The religious do not have a monopoly on morality, nor are they the only voters who care about the values that motivate candidates and politicians. But in the United States they are an overwhelming majority. How these voters perceive and react to the two major political parties is therefore of significant interest. Trying to understand American politics without looking at religion would be like trying to understand the politics of the Middle East without paying attention to oil.

Within the community of the faithful, there are obviously a multitude of various traditions and denominations. I have focused on white Catholics and evangelicals. Together they represent slightly more than 50 percent of the American electorate. Both are communities that became newly active and engaged in the political system starting in the 1970s, and their gradual alignment with the Republican Party has shaped American politics in the decades since. The ways in which Republicans and Democrats have reached out to mainline Protestant and Jewish voters, African-Americans and Hispanics, Muslims and Buddhists, and members of other religious traditions are vast and often fascinating. They could fill a book of their own. But as they have not yet altered the outcomes of presidential elections, they are not the subject of this one.

It can be tempting to use political and religious terms as material for constructing straw men, so I have made a particular effort to take care with my words. When I use the term *Democrats,* I try to make clear whether the subject is the party as a whole, or whether it refers instead to Democratic politicians, voters, or operatives. In some instances, I also describe attitudes shared by "political liberals" in order to avoid ascribing to the entire party a set of views held by a subset of members.

*Religious liberals* is a phrase that has long been misunderstood. Its use should be theological; the label refers to those who hold liberal (less orthodox and doctrinal) theological beliefs. But it is often conscripted as a catchall term for all politically liberal people of faith. I use the phrase to refer to theological liberals, who are usually politically liberal as well. Additionally, I write about religious progressives and religious moderates—the two groups are largely theologically orthodox, but the former has traditionally leaned Democratic while the latter has leaned Republican. They are both, broadly speaking, socially liberal and morally conservative.

Over the past three decades, journalists, liberals, and conservatives have all—for different reasons—conflated the religious label *evangelical* with *political conservative.* Here it has a religious meaning, referring to those Protestants who emphasize four main beliefs: spiritual conversion, a personal relationship with God through Jesus Christ, a biblically centered faith, and the importance of sharing the Gospel. Evangelicals are also often called born-again Christians. *Fundamentalists* and *Pentecostals* are important subsets of the evangelical community, but they are each small minorities.

Up through the late 1800s, most Protestants in America were evangelicals, as a result of the revivals that brought Baptists and Methodists to prominence in the eighteenth and early nineteenth centuries. The development and popularity of a more theologically liberal Protestant strain led some formerly evangelical denominations to become *mainline Protestants.* Some of the remaining evangelicals reacted by reasserting traditional doctrines, what they called the fundamentals, and came to be known as *fundamentalists* in the early part of the twentieth century. In the 1930s, *neo-evangelicals* reclaimed the label *evangelical* to distinguish themselves from fundamentalists. The neo-evangelicals were, in turn, referred to as *establishment evangelicals* by the movement of *young evangelicals* that emerged in the 1960s. Those young evangelicals grew into the constituency I refer to as *liberal evangelicals* or *progressive evangelicals.*

Finally, the phrase *conservative evangelicals* refers to those who are both theologically orthodox and politically conservative. Many conservative evangelicals were mobilized by the *religious right,* but that political designation has expanded to include politically conservative Catholics and Jews and is not a religious label.

Today, white evangelicals are between 25 and 30 percent of the U.S. population. With the addition of Hispanic and African-American evangelicals, that total rises to around 35 percent. Approximately 40 percent of evangelicals are politically moderates, another 10 percent are liberal, and the remaining 50 percent are conservative. Nearly all are theologically orthodox.

# THE
# PARTY
# FAITHFUL

# CHAPTER 1

# JESUS BUMPS
# AND GOD GAPS

## INTRODUCTION

In the summer of 2004, my dad had a heart attack. My sister and I flew home to Michigan immediately, and because I didn't have to start a new job for another month, I stayed on to help my parents adjust to their new medication-filled and cheeseburger-free existence. It turned out that I was hardly necessary. Nothing showcases Midwestern pragmatism like a crisis, and our friends and neighbors rallied. Former colleagues drove my dad to cardiac rehabilitation appointments. Relatives came over with stacks of low-cal, low-fat, heart-healthy cookbooks, while the chef who lives next door whipped up a red-wine-and-portobello risotto for the rest of us. And the good folks at the First Baptist Church of Plymouth did what they do best—they prayed.

On Sunday morning, I drove down leafy, tree-lined Penniman Avenue to the Baptist church where I spent my childhood. I wanted to worship with the people who had been my second family. When it was time to share praises and prayer requests, I took the cordless microphone from the roving usher, thanked them all for their prayers, and reported that Dad was making good progress. "Amen!" came the response from around the sanctuary. Sitting back down in a cushioned pew that still bore the remnants of some Silly Putty that got away from me during a particularly dull sermon twenty-five years earlier, I let my mind drift while the pastor took to the pulpit.

I grew up in this church, singing the rollicking tune "Happy Birthday, Baby Jesus" on Christmas mornings and learning my Bible stories from a Sunday school teacher who talked about getting "Jesus bumps" instead of goose bumps. At age ten, I walked up the aisle to the altar one morning at the end of a service and announced (although it came out as more of a squeak) my desire to be baptized. The event took place a few weeks later in the baptistery high above the choir loft, a dunking that was celebrated afterward with cake and orange sherbet in the church gym. I was a nerdy mess of orthodontics, peach plastic eyeglasses, and half-damp hair, but the congregation at First Baptist welcomed me with open arms as a child of God.

Now, at the end of what had been a gut-wrenching week, in which I had been strong for everyone else, I needed to be wrapped in that faith again. I felt comforted in this church. I felt at home. I felt as if I were finally catching my breath. I tried to remember why it had been so long since I had visited. And then I tuned back into Pastor Mike's sermon just in time to hear him declare that it wasn't possible to be a good Christian and a Democrat.

The pronouncement, and the matter-of-fact tone in which it was delivered, knocked the wind out of me. My liberal politics were, after all, due in large part to the Gospel lessons I had absorbed at First Baptist, over years of Sunday sermons, Wednesday-evening church clubs, youth retreats, and devotions. A painfully literal kid, I took seriously Jesus' instructions in Matthew 25 on how to be righteous: "For I was hungry and you gave me something to eat, I was thirsty and you gave me something to drink, I was a stranger and you invited me in." At a young age, that meant constantly worrying that I wasn't doing enough for the "least of these," that I might inadvertently have snubbed Jesus-in-disguise by failing to share my fruit roll-ups with a classmate who forgot his lunch. Over time this impulse developed into a more concrete political conviction that citizens—and governments—had a moral obligation to take care of the poor, the sick, the marginalized.

By the time I graduated from high school, however, those Gospel lessons had been subsumed by a different kind of politics at my church. An assistant pastor rebuked me for taking a course on Zen philosophy and the writings of Emerson ("The Bible says to beware of false religions"). Antiabortion messages found their way into the occasional Advent sermon. I heard less about the inherent failings of humankind and more about the moral turpitude of liberals. As a result, I sought out different church homes in other cities. But First Baptist retained a special distinction as the place that had formed my faith, and it was still the congregation I turned to in this time of crisis.

With Pastor Mike's words still ricocheting inside my head, I bristled at his implication. The God of Abraham and Isaac, the God who created the heavens and the earth, the God I was taught to trust and obey, could not be squeezed into the narrow confines of partisan politics. He wasn't anybody's campaign surrogate, and He certainly didn't do endorsements. Baptists believe in an active and engaged God. But there is a difference between believing that the hand of God occasionally intervenes in human events and that it pulls the lever for Republican candidates.

Pastor Mike was hardly the only one reading out of the New Republican Standard Version (NRSV) of the Bible during the 2004 campaign season. Back in January, before the first party primaries, Pat Robertson informed his *700 Club* viewers that he was "hearing from the Lord it's going to be like a blowout election in 2004" and that "George Bush is going to win in a walk." In dioceses around the country, Catholic parishioners were warned not to present themselves for Communion if they supported pro-choice Democrats (pro-choice Republicans, on the other hand, were almost never singled out). Several weeks before the election, the pastor of East Waynesville Church in western North Carolina told members of his flock that if they planned to vote for John Kerry, they needed to repent of their sins or else leave the congregation. Every news outlet, it seemed, had an interview with some voter explaining that she didn't really agree with George W. Bush on the war or the economy or environmental policy or stem-cell research or, come to think of it, much at all—but she planned to vote for him anyway because he was a good Christian man. Come Election Day, so many churchgoing Americans cast their votes for Bush that pundits created a new phrase—"the God gap"—to explain their voting patterns. The more often you attended church, the more likely you were to vote Republican.

The arrogant assumption of conservatives that they had a patent on piety was bad enough. But what really took me aback was that Democrats seemed to buy into this conventional wisdom as well, believing that religious Americans were all conservative. The Kerry campaign turned down opportunities to reach out to Catholics in Ohio because, as one adviser put it, "We don't do white churches." A leading Democratic pollster proclaimed all evangelicals "unreachable," insisting that such voters line up with Republicans on every single issue. In the Democratic glossary of terms, *religious voters* were Catholics and evangelicals who only cared about abortion. They were, in other words, lost causes.

That conclusion would surprise a lot of Democratic voters who are themselves practicing Catholics and evangelicals. National polls consistently show that two-thirds of Democratic voters attend worship services regularly. Yet the people who run the Democratic Party largely believe that the "God gap" is an immutable law of the political universe. Most forget the legacy of William Jennings Bryan, the populist evangelical who ran as the Democratic presidential nominee three times around the turn of the twentieth century. Or Dorothy Day, the social-justice activist who founded the Catholic Worker Movement in the 1930s and who devoted her life to promoting pacifism. They endlessly cite the work of Dr. Martin Luther King Jr. but forget that he was "Reverend King" before he was a national icon. The few who do remember the Democratic Party as a once-proud home to religious voters believe the emergence of abortion as a political lightning rod made their defection to the GOP inevitable.

I wrote this book because my personal experience told me these assumptions about religion and the political parties simply weren't correct. I didn't believe that Kerry's rout among religious voters was really preordained. I didn't believe that evangelicals and Catholics had set up a permanent home in the Republican Party. And I certainly didn't believe that Pastor Mike and other religious conservatives had a right to be so smug in their pronouncements about which issues and values qualified as genuinely religious. I was raised to honor God, my parents, and the Kennedys—and not necessarily in that order. As a young bona fide Jesus geek, I spent Friday nights playing a card game called Bible Daughters with my sister (think Go Fish, but with Mary Magdalene and Esther) and Saturday afternoons knocking on doors for Democratic candidates. And I wasn't some weird outlier. Although they didn't necessarily advertise their religious leanings, many of the people I met in Democratic politics knew their way around a church potluck as well as a committee markup. They were liberals because of, not despite, their religious beliefs.

Sadly, however, my experience also taught me that our fellow liberals and Democrats weren't completely blameless for the popular assumption that only conservatives were religious. After graduating from college, I worked for a series of congressional Democrats because I shared their belief that government can play an important role in protecting the most vulnerable among us. But many colleagues didn't share my belief that people of faith had an important role to play in these causes. At times, they took an actively hostile view toward religion, as though it were an obstacle to progress. I lost track of the number of times Democratic aides—and even the rare congressman—wielded public opinion polls about evolution as triumphant conversation-enders in private meetings. If these people were too stupid to believe in evolution, they argued, how were we supposed to work with them on progressive political issues?

I last worked in Democratic politics more than ten years ago and am now a journalist whose reporting is informed by my time spent in the worlds of religion and politics. The intersection of the two is a professional interest of mine, but also inevitably personal. Although I left the Baptist Church long ago, I'm still very much Baptist and an evangelical. For me, that has meant that my faith is rooted in biblical authority instead of church tradition, it depends on a personal relationship with God, and it requires me to share my beliefs with others, although my "witnessing" is focused not on converting others but on presenting a different face of evangelicalism to my fellow liberals.

I don't much like being told that my faith is called into question because of my political views. But neither do I like hearing that my ability to participate in political debate is suspect because of my religious convictions. So while this book is primarily a response to Pastor Mike and my conservative religious friends who wonder how it is possible for Christians to support liberal politicians, it is also a plea for understanding from those Democrats who look embarrassed for me when I tell them I'm an evangelical, and who wonder how it is possible for political liberals to worship side by side with Republican values voters. And finally, of course, this book is an offering for people just like me. For the people I meet in every corner of the country who are angry with Republicans for claiming a monopoly on faith and disappointed with Democrats for giving it to them.

So how was it that the Democratic Party lost its faith in faith? The most obvious explanation is that conservatives and Republicans have spent thirty years telling us that Democrats aren't religious. Conservative religious leaders have relentlessly promoted the idea that there is a liberal war on people of faith (or Christmas or the Bible), a mantra that Republican politicians have lustily repeated. However, this marriage of convenience between religious and political conservatives has been ably chronicled elsewhere—and it's only part of the story.

The tale that has remained untold involves the left's response to the rise of the religious right. That story is largely one of fear, ignorance, and political deafness. For while the political, religious, and cultural forces that gave rise to the religious right formed a perfect storm that was bound to have a significant impact on American politics, Democrats and liberals weren't just passive nonactors who stood by helplessly on the sidelines while it all happened. Instead of pushing back, they chose to beat a retreat in the competition for religious voters and the discussion of morality, effectively ceding the ground to conservatives. The emergence of the God gap represents a failure of the left as much as it does an achievement of the right.

As recently as the late 1960s, religion was a decidedly nonpartisan affair in the United States. Presidents of all political stripes sprinkled their speeches with references to the Almighty. Religious Americans led political movements to battle communism and poverty, to promote temperance and civil rights. If anything, the contours of the religious landscape favored Democrats: their voters were evangelical Southerners and ethnic Catholics, while Republicans appealed to wealthier Northeastern WASPs and Catholics who were more private about their faith.

The relationship between religion and politics changed abruptly in the turbulent decade that spanned the mid-1960s to the mid-1970s. The twin disappointments of Vietnam and Watergate led to widespread disillusionment with traditional institutions, and the cynicism tainted religious authority as well. The postmodern argument that advanced societies would progress beyond the need for religious practice or belief in a higher power took hold in educated circles and further deepened the divide between secular elites and religious believers that had broken open during the Scopes trial decades earlier. The women's movement and civil rights struggles led to greater opportunities, but in an era marked by assassinations and fear of nuclear annihilation, it seemed to many that the pace of change was out of control.

This country is a better place for the enhanced freedoms and tolerance that the women's and civil rights movements delivered. That Democrats paid a hefty political price for championing these causes was by no means a reason to sit them out. The question is whether the price needed to have been as steep as it turned out to be. I believe that it did not.

It's hard to imagine today, but it was, after all, the Democratic Party that first successfully responded to the disillusionment of religious voters. Jimmy Carter, the party's nominee in 1976, was the first politician to recognize that voters now wanted to know more about a candidate than simply his position on energy policy or taxes; they cared about the moral fiber of their president as well. And those voters increasingly saw religious faith as a proxy, an efficient way to size up a candidate's character. With an evangelist sister and his own background as an organizer for Billy Graham crusades, Carter talked openly about his religious faith, not just in the generic "God bless America" sort of way that politicians had previously favored. When he used the phrase "born-again" to describe himself, Carter connected with millions of evangelicals who had previously stayed away from politics. And his promise "I'll never lie to you" was—in the wake of Richard Nixon's resignation—a potent statement for Americans of all faiths and no faith at all.

But while Carter was the right candidate for the new politics of values, his party was rapidly moving in the other direction. Educated elites, particularly on the left, increasingly placed their faith in the tangible power of political action rather than the unfathomable might of a divine being. Carter's own advisers begged him to tone down the God talk. "We're reassuring people Jimmy won't turn the White House into a Billy Graham Bible class," adman Jerry Rafshoon told reporters at one point during the 1976 campaign. But they misread the direction of the country. Far from becoming less religious in a postmodern age, Americans remained strongly devout, with 80 percent or more consistently reporting that religion was an "important" part of their lives.

Instead of finding another way to talk about character and values, Democratic leaders rejected the Carter model altogether, effectively opting out of a conversation with evangelicals. Later, as debate over abortion laws heated up in the 1980s, Democrats compounded the mistake by ending their dialogue with Catholic audiences as well. When Michael Dukakis ran at the head of the ticket in 1988, his campaign turned down all requests for appearances at Catholic institutions. Democratic politicians with national ambitions quickly learned that they needed to renounce their pro-life positions to attract money and support from powerful interest groups. And as the Catholic Church began to put pressure on Democrats who supported abortion rights, Catholic politicians also stopped publicizing their religious affiliation, further cementing the image of the Democratic Party as secularist.

The GOP, meanwhile, aggressively courted faith voters. Ronald Reagan famously told religious conservatives, "You can't endorse me, but I can endorse you." Republicans never missed an opportunity to paint Democrats as secular heathens who would ban the Bible if given half a chance. The party also built an extensive infrastructure to mobilize and connect with religious voters, a strategy that reached its zenith in 2004.

When Bill Clinton came along, he defied the stubborn conventional wisdom that had formed about the two parties' relationship to religion. A Southern Baptist who could literally quote chapter and verse, Clinton freely talked to religious publications like *Christianity Today*. He made the protection of religious freedom a key focus of his domestic agenda and insisted his staff work with conservative evangelical leaders in addition to progressive religious allies. Liberal leaders chalked up Clinton's religious fluency to his general political skill, the ability to be everything to everyone. Conservatives saw him as a fake who exploited religion for political purposes and pandered to voters. The actual voters, however, responded favorably to Clinton, rewarding him with a greater share of the evangelical and Catholic electorate than any other Democrat since Carter.

But the lesson didn't take. In many ways, Clinton's personal comfort with religion and his extraordinary ability to act as his own religious liaison masked the ongoing problems of the Democratic Party, which still had no inclination or ability to reach out to religious communities. Democrats were all too happy to let Clinton meet with religious leaders and sermonize in black churches. They did not, however, go so far as to change their approach on abortion to reflect his "safe, legal, and rare" mantra. Nor did they alter the party infrastructure so as to make it more hospitable to people of faith: there were no

9

religious outreach efforts, no strategists who focused on religious voters. By the time Clinton left the White House in 2001, the Democratic Party was as disconnected as ever from religious voters. And George W. Bush got away with arguing that his White House would protect religious organizations that had been "discriminated against" by the antireligion Clinton administration.

So it should not have surprised anyone that Democrats found themselves so outmatched in the presidential campaign of 2004. That year, the Bush-Cheney operation did more with religious outreach than any other campaign in history, employing a massive parish- and congregation-level mobilization effort. In Florida alone, the Bush-Cheney campaign employed a state chairwoman for evangelical outreach who appointed a dozen regional coordinators around the state and designated outreach chairs in each of Florida's sixty-seven counties. Every county chair, in turn, recruited between thirty and fifty volunteers to contact and register their evangelical neighbors. In September, the Republican National Convention had all the characteristics of a four-day revival meeting, featuring popular acts from the Christian music world and screenings of the documentary *George W. Bush: Faith in the White House.* And in November, 3.5 million white evangelicals who had not voted in 2000 turned out to the polls.

The Kerry campaign, meanwhile, hired one junior staff aide with no national campaign experience to oversee religious outreach and allowed her one intern—the two had a single telephone between them with which to recruit and contact volunteers. Kerry's top advisers decided not to publicly defend their candidate against charges from some Catholic bishops that his support for abortion rights meant he could not truly be a Catholic. While Kerry did give a remarkable speech about his faith and values, it took place little more than a week before the election. And because of staff concerns about abortion protesters, the senator gave his faith talk not at a Catholic university in Ohio as originally scheduled, but at a Jewish senior center in Florida with little fanfare. Nine days later, Kerry lost the Catholic vote in Ohio by a margin of 44 to 55. It was a six-point drop from Al Gore's showing among Catholics in that state four years earlier—if Kerry had matched Gore's percentage of the Catholic vote in Ohio, he would have captured the state by 41,000 votes. Instead, he came slightly more than 118,000 votes short, losing Ohio and, with it, the election.

When I sat slightly stunned in that Baptist pew during the summer of 2004, listening to Pastor Mike utter what were essentially GOP talking points, it took all of my self-control not to leap up and stomp out of the church. As it was, I scribbled furious notes in my bulletin, sang the closing hymn on autopilot, and prepared to march on over to the pastor and lecture him on the history of religious progressives. I couldn't do much about the fact that this same scene was playing out in churches around the country, but I could at least remind this particular religious leader that he was preaching to a choir with diverse views.

Fortunately for Pastor Mike, I was intercepted on my way out of the sanctuary by a retired minister who wanted to know if I was the Sullivan girl who wrote about politics. Pleased to learn that he had the right sister, Reverend Younge launched into a reflection about Harry Truman, and the influence his faith had on the decisions he made in the Oval Office. As he talked, my anger and frustration rapidly dissipated. Reverend Younge came from the Billy Graham mold of ministers, more probing and thoughtful than fire-and-brimstone. I'd never seen him wearing anything other than a proper Sunday suit; he wouldn't have been caught dead in casual worship attire. He was a Republican voter, in part because of the party's acknowledgment that values inevitably shape public policy—but he certainly didn't think it was his Christian duty to support the GOP. And he was a figure from an earlier era, when religion wasn't yet such a divisive political element, when it wasn't assumed that evangelicals were cut from one partisan cloth.

As we talked, I found myself wondering what had happened to evangelicals like Reverend Younge. There had to be a story about why they left the Democratic Party for the GOP—and, for that matter, about why Catholics made the leap as well. If Democrats were to have a chance of leveling the praying field again, they would first need to understand their own history.

Reverend Younge seemed to read my mind as we shook hands before I wove my way through the pews and headed home. Tossing in one last historical example about Franklin Roosevelt's speeches, he reminded me that politicians of all kinds have drawn on theological language and ideas to support their causes. "Isn't it strange," he mused, "that we tend to forget all that now?"

# CHAPTER 2

# "THE GODDAM CHRISTIANS"

## HOW DEMOCRATS LOST EVANGELICALS

Late in the fall of 1973, an eclectic group of left-leaning evangelicals gathered in Chicago to begin charting a way forward in the aftermath of President Nixon's crushing defeat of George McGovern a year earlier. It was a curiously optimistic occasion. Many of the forty or so mostly young ministers and social activists who assembled that Thanksgiving weekend in a shabby YMCA hotel on South Wabash Avenue had supported McGovern and shared both his opposition to the Vietnam War and his support of women's rights, racial equality, and economic justice. Like most political progressives, they were disheartened by the magnitude of the Republican victory. Nixon had beaten McGovern by a 61 to 38 margin, carrying every state except Massachusetts and drawing 80 percent of the evangelical vote. It was a dramatic reversal of the 1964 election when 63 percent of evangelicals supported Lyndon Johnson over Republican Barry Goldwater in a landslide of similar proportions.

But what concerned those attending the Chicago gathering more than the election results was the apathy they perceived among their coreligionists toward the most pressing issues of the day. Too many evangelicals had sat out the civil rights movement in the 1960s—or, worse, had opposed it—and now they were tacitly tolerating the misguided militarism of the Vietnam War despite a growing antiwar chorus emanating from other religious communities. It appeared that evangelicals were indeed part of Nixon's "silent majority"—quiescent backers of the status quo. The Chicago activists were determined to change that.

Going into the meeting, no consensus existed on a precise course of action. The evangelical movement, after all, was broad and politically diverse. It comprised some 60 million Americans who shared a generally conservative outlook on theological and social issues but who, when it came to partisan politics, were scattered across the board. Some participants—such as Jim Wallis, a mop-haired seminary dropout and peace activist who would go on to found the liberal Sojourners community in Washington, D.C., and Ron Sider, a recent Yale Ph.D. graduate who had helped organize Evangelicals for McGovern—had visions of unleashing a biblically motivated political force to promote progressive causes. Others had less specific goals. Two older representatives of the evangelical establishment, Carl F. H. Henry, a revered theologian and founding editor of *Christianity Today* magazine, and Vernon Grounds, president of the prestigious Denver Seminary, had come to Chicago simply to urge their fellow evangelicals, as they had been doing for years, to shake off the isolationist proclivities of their fundamentalist past and fully engage the American mainstream. Yet overarching the sometimes intense discussions was a shared conviction that on matters of social justice evangelicals could no longer remain silent.

Out of that weekend gathering came "The Chicago Declaration on Evangelical Social Concern," a five-hundred-word manifesto that its signers hoped would prick the evangelical social conscience and launch a new era of religious activism. Part mea culpa and part prophetic exhortation, the statement acknowledged evangelical complicity in the national sins of racism, sexism, militarism, and materialism and called on evangelicals "to demonstrate repentance in a Christian discipleship that confronts the social and political injustice of our nation. . . .

14

We must attack the materialism of our culture and the maldistribution of the nation's wealth and services. . . . We must challenge the misplaced trust of the nation in economic and military might—a proud trust that promotes a national pathology of war and violence. . . . We acknowledge that we have encouraged men to prideful domination and women to irresponsible passivity. So we call both men and women to mutual submission. . . . By this declaration, we endorse no political ideology or party, but call our nation's leaders and people to that righteousness which exalts a nation.

The statement struck a chord that seemed to resonate favorably throughout the evangelical movement. Within days of the Chicago gathering, a number of high-visibility evangelical leaders who had not attended the meeting eagerly added their names to the document—from Republican senator Mark Hatfield of Oregon to Leighton Ford, Billy Graham's brother-in-law and a noted evangelist in his own right. Even leaders of mainline Protestantism, who traditionally had little to do with the theologically conservative and often standoffish evangelicals, were impressed: the National Council of Churches (NCC) fired off a congratulatory letter to the Chicago organizers, declaring, "We are moved by the Holy Spirit to express a deep feeling of kinship with that statement and with our fellow Christians who issued it."

The Chicago activists went home brimming with optimism. The opportunity for a broad-based coalition that united evangelicals and mainline Protestants behind progressive political causes was hovering in the air. The historic moment was not lost on two journalists who had covered the event. Marjorie Hyer of the *Washington Post* wrote at the time that the Chicago Declaration "could well change the face of both religion and politics in America." And *Chicago Sun-Times* religion writer Roy Larson wrote, "Someday American church historians may write that the most significant church-related event of 1973 took place last week at the YMCA hotel on S. Wabash."

But it was not to be. By the end of the decade, the founding of the Moral Majority by fundamentalist preacher Jerry Falwell and the election of Ronald Reagan to the White House would give birth to the religious right and push millions of newly energized evangelical voters into the eager arms of the Republican Party. "We wanted to get evangelicals politically engaged," Sider recalled with irony many years later. "We never expected that the Moral Majority would be the result." Several of the Chicago participants continued to meet during the mid-seventies and in 1978 organized Evangelicals for Social Action, a nationwide group headed by Sider to promote the principles of the Chicago Declaration. Faced with a growing tide of Republicanism, the organization would never gain more than marginal evangelical support. At the same time, attempts to establish a working alliance with mainline Protestants fell through after a few exploratory conversations. "We wanted to garb the progressive social agenda in orthodox biblical language, and they weren't interested in that," Sider recalls of the failed discussions with NCC leaders. Long-standing rivalries and theological differences between the two Protestant branches proved too difficult to overcome.

By 2004, with the reelection of George W. Bush, conservative evangelical voters had become a core Republican constituency, accounting for 36 percent of the winning presidential vote. In the public mind, and in much of the media coverage that year, *evangelical* and *religious right* had become virtually synonymous, and a handful of hot-button sexual issues—abortion, homosexuality, and pornography—had come to define the evangelical social agenda. The dream of the activists in Chicago for a revival of progressive social concern, it seemed, had been reduced to little more than that—a dream. The "Republicanization" of the evangelical movement appeared complete.

It need not have turned out that way. Indeed, for most of the nation's history it had not been that way at all.

In the early days of the republic, religion was hardly a partisan affair. Religious language and sensibilities infused the founding documents and the debates that produced them, beginning with "the Laws of Nature and of Nature's God" and the "Creator"—endowed rights delineated in the Declaration of Independence. At the height of the Civil War, Abraham Lincoln bathed his second Inaugural Address in references to the Almighty and His will. In 1902, Theodore Roosevelt declared to the nation that the true gospel—a "gospel of hope"—lay in one's works and not just in one's words. A few decades later, the second President Roosevelt described the New Deal as an effort to enact the Sermon on the Mount and declared, "There is not a problem—social, political, or economic—that would not find full solution in the fire of a religious awakening." And on the morning of his inauguration, John Kennedy brought his remarks to a close with this charge: "Let us go forth to lead the land we love, asking His blessing and His help, but knowing that here on earth God's work must truly be our own."

None of these statements were crafted by political consultants seeking to woo religious voters. Nor were they intended to suggest that those who uttered them were more pious than their political opponents. Republicans and Democrats alike wove religious allusions into their speech because religion was, after all, a natural part of civic and political life. "I do not know whether all Americans have a sincere faith in their religion," wrote that keen observer of the American psyche Alexis de Tocqueville, in 1835, "but I am certain that they hold it to be indispensable to the maintenance of republican institutions. This opinion is not peculiar to a class of citizens or to a party, but it belongs to the whole nation and to every rank of society."

Religion's pervasive presence in the public square had been no accident. Out of the two Great Awakenings—religious revivals that swept the country in the early eighteenth and early nineteenth centuries—American Protestantism emerged as a powerful culture-shaping force, and its character was overwhelmingly evangelical. While there were pockets of liberal dissent, most of the major Protestant denominations in the nineteenth century were evangelical, adhering to an orthodox theology that emphasized the necessity of conversion, biblical authority, missionary outreach, and benevolent activism—all hallmarks of classic evangelicalism.

Yet this evangelicalism bore little resemblance to the socially conservative and narrowly partisan movement that would materialize a century later under the banner of the religious right. This evangelicalism was infused with a decidedly progressive mind-set that deemed social reform an important part of the church's mission. By both saving souls and fighting social ills, evangelicals believed they could establish the Kingdom of God on earth and usher in the Second Coming of Christ. Their outlook was called postmillennial, in that it reflected the belief that Christ would return after the biblical millennium—a thousand years of peace and righteousness described in the book of Revelation.

Prodded by that social-reforming impulse, evangelical Protestants organized hundreds of voluntary charitable organizations in New England in the early 1800s to help the poor, widows, and orphans. As the century wore on, many churches in the North joined the abolitionist crusade and campaigned for prison reform, child labor laws, and other progressive causes. In the South, meanwhile, evangelicals tended to be staunch defenders of slavery, and as the Civil War approached, several denominations split along sectional lines. In contrast to their culturally engaged Northern counterparts, when war finally erupted, embattled evangelicals in the South turned increasingly inward, embracing an insularity that foreshadowed changes awaiting the broader evangelical movement a few decades later.

With the end of the Civil War, a triumphal spirit swept the Northern churches. Some Protestant preachers exulted that the Union victory had brought vindication—confirming, as one Presbyterian put it, that "we as individuals, and as a nation, are identified with the kingdom of God among men, which is righteousness, and peace, and joy in the Holy Ghost." As religion historian George Marsden has observed, while there were "many Roman Catholics, sectarians, skeptics, and non-Christians [who] had other views of the matter . . . evangelicals considered their faith to be the normative American creed."

But neither the postmillennial optimism nor the cultural dominance of evangelicalism would last. Within a few decades, industrialization and accompanying waves of immigration would dramatically alter the nation's social and economic landscape, bringing both new diversity and intractable social problems. For evangelicals, it would also create a theological crisis. By the 1880s, notes Columbia University professor Randall Balmer, "teeming, squalid tenements populated by immigrants, most of them non-Protestant, hardly looked like the precincts of Zion" that evangelicals thought they were building to usher in the biblical millennium. They had little choice but to adjust their theology to reflect the more pessimistic reality.

From the 1870s onward, evangelicals increasingly embraced a belief system known as premillennial dispensationalism. Based on the teachings of English theologian John Nelson Darby, it held that history is divided into seven ages, or dispensations, leading to the Second Coming, the Final Judgment, and the end of the world. The Second Coming, according to Darby, would occur *before* the biblical millennium and could, therefore, happen at any moment. Until then, world conditions would only get worse.

The doctrine would gain prominence among evangelicals in the twentieth century and become popularized in the best-selling *Left Behind* novels in the 1990s. But late in the nineteenth century it had a twofold impact. Belief in an imminent Second Coming spurred a new evangelical passion for missions and evangelism—it was important to save as many souls as possible before time ran out. And believing that the world's problems were beyond human repair and destined to multiply made social reform seem futile. Consequently, many conservative churches began shifting their resources and energy away from battling social ills to the more urgent business of winning converts.

Meanwhile, more theologically liberal Protestants responded to the wrenching cultural changes much differently. Rather than abandoning social reform, some Northern critics of evangelical revivalism saw the dismal plight of the cities as reason for churches to redouble their efforts on behalf of the downtrodden. In their view, fighting illiteracy, supporting refugees, working for passage of child labor laws, providing settlement houses, and offering food and health care services for the poor were supreme acts of Christian service in direct obedience to Jesus' admonition to care "for the least of these."

By the end of the century, liberal Protestants had developed a full-blown theology that emphasized social progress over spiritual conversion. Walter Rauschenbusch, a Baptist theologian and professor at Rochester Theological Seminary in New York, popularized the idea that Jesus' radical politics had been lost in a narrow focus on saving souls. "Such a conception of present life and future destiny," Rauschenbusch wrote in his famous 1907 book *Christianity and the Social Crisis,* "offered no motive for an ennobling transformation of the present life." The book sold more than fifty thousand copies to ministers and laypeople and was a prime example of Protestantism reconciling itself to secular modernity. The phrases "laws of social development," "scientific comprehension of society," and the "evolution of social institutions" were liberally sprinkled throughout the text; the teachings presented were less Jesus and Paul than Darwin and Marx.

The Social Gospel, as this new theological directive became known, attracted a strong following in New York and other major Northern cities, giving voice to a growing liberal movement that would soon challenge the evangelical dominance of most Protestant denominations. The liberal churches became known as "mainline" Protestants, a reference to the cluster of prominent churches along the main commuter railway line of suburban Philadelphia.

Yet even before the rise of the Social Gospel movement, the stage had been set for a clash between liberal and conservative Protestants by two important developments in Europe. The publication of Charles Darwin's *Origin of Species* in London in 1859, and the concurrent rise of higher criticism—a body of mainly German scholarship that used methods of scientific inquiry to challenge the origins and historicity of the Bible—had begun to stir heated debate in European churches. American churchmen had been too consumed by the approach of the Civil War to pay much notice. After the war, however, the theological implications began to sink in. Many evangelicals quickly came to view both Darwin's theory and the arguments of the higher critics as a direct assault on the authority of Scripture and its accounts of creation and miracles.

But among more liberal Protestants, the antiliteralist and anti-supernaturalist views of the European scholars found a growing audience. More important, they recognized that secularization was taking hold in the institutions—from higher education to the legal world to journalism—that formed the American establishment. Eager to maintain their respected place in society, the major liberal denominations responded in true Darwinian fashion by adapting to the new intellectual worldview. Europeans may have seen their options as sticking with old-fashioned churches or abandoning faith altogether, but the American religious marketplace was based on constant innovation. For liberal Protestant leaders, that meant developing a theological justification for their concerns about industrialization and modernity.

Evangelical leaders were increasingly incensed by the liberalizing trend. By the 1880s, conservative theologians were rising up to defend the Bible—and their denominational institutions—against the growing ranks of "modernists" who were seen as questioning not only the Bible's inspiration but such core Christian beliefs as the divinity of Jesus, the Virgin Birth, and the Resurrection. Liberals at several prominent seminaries were brought up on heresy charges and some were dismissed. Efforts to enforce orthodoxy at such places as Methodist-run Vanderbilt University in Nashville and the Southern Baptist Seminary in Louisville, Kentucky, proved generally effective. But in the North, as historian Marsden observes, "Conservative victories turned out to be largely illusory. Liberalism continued to grow as if the trials had never taken place."

Within a few decades, most major Northern seminaries had restructured their curricula to reflect the new social theology. Nearly all of the major denominations had established commissions for social action. The Federal Council of Churches (the predecessor of the National Council of Churches) was organized in 1908 largely to help churches respond more effectively to the problems of a modern industrial society—one of the first acts of the new organization was its adoption of a "Social Creed of the Churches." Evangelical hegemony in Protestant America was fading fast.

But the conservatives were not about to give up. Between 1910 and 1915, with the financial backing of two California oil tycoons, evangelical churchmen published a series of pamphlets enunciating what they saw as essential Christian doctrines. Entitled *The Fundamentals: Testimony to the Truth,* the twelve-volume series vigorously defended the inspiration of Scripture and articulated conservative positions on such issues as the Virgin Birth, the Resurrection, the authenticity of miracles, and the Genesis account of creation. Some 3 million copies were distributed among influential Protestants throughout the English-speaking world.

By the end of World War I, those who subscribed to the conservative doctrines had taken upon themselves the label *fundamentalists* and were forging alliances to combat the drift toward liberalism. Through the early 1920s, fundamentalist preachers in Northern Baptist, Presbyterian, and other denominations railed against doctrinal error and moral laxity in their churches, singling out for special attention the "Great Apostasy" of Darwinism. The theory of evolution, the fundamentalists insisted, was a "lie of Satan" that encouraged moral degeneracy by denying the literal truth of Scripture that God created man in His image. If humans were nothing more than evolved apes, they argued, what need was there for God?

As the power struggles in the Northern churches intensified, and as the tide increasingly turned against them, fundamentalists began to rally around a nationwide campaign to prohibit the teaching of evolution in public schools. In state after state, conservative preachers mobilized their flocks to lobby their legislators, and the efforts appeared to pay off. Between 1923 and 1925 five Southern states enacted laws banning evolution from the classroom, and bills were introduced in at least eleven others. But the victories were short-lived. A dramatic legal battle was brewing that would finally topple fundamentalism from its influential cultural perch.

In the summer of 1925, inside a small Tennessee courthouse, a twenty-four-year-old public high school teacher named John Scopes was put on trial. He stood accused of violating a recently enacted state law prohibiting the teaching of "any theory that denies the story of Divine Creation of man as taught in the Bible." The "Monkey trial," as it became known, captivated the nation and became a full-fledged media circus. Owners of pet chimpanzees and monkeys made their way to the sleepy town of Dayton to provide photo ops, and reporters descended as well, clogging the streets with carriages and Model T Fords. Radio brought the trial into American homes, and moviegoers followed it via newsreels.

There was never any real doubt that Scopes had broken the law. He had done so deliberately at the urging of the American Civil Liberties Union in order to test the statute, which the ACLU—and many other people around the country—believed was unconstitutional. The trial pitted the famed orator and three-time Democratic presidential nominee William Jennings Bryan against Clarence Darrow, one of the nation's top defense lawyers.

For decades, Bryan had perhaps been the nation's most prominent evangelical, waging populist campaigns against the excesses of the Gilded Age and what he saw as the social Darwinism of wealthy capitalists. Their reasoning, as he saw it, was that if survival of the fittest was indeed a law of nature, then it applied to commerce as well. The strong would flourish and the weak would fall by the wayside. There was no need for government regulation. Let nature take its course. Bryan considered this a dangerous philosophy—one that could easily be used to justify eugenics and racial cleansing. As a biblical literalist, he also believed wholeheartedly in the Genesis account of creation. So he welcomed the opportunity to prosecute the Scopes case. Darwinism in all its forms had to be eradicated.

But Bryan had more than met his match in Darrow. An irreverent and acerbic litigator who had been recruited for the case by the ACLU, Darrow went into the trial knowing that he wouldn't win. Instead, his defense strategy was to put fundamentalism itself on trial and demonstrate the absurdity of literalistic beliefs and opposition to evolution.

For eight sultry days in a packed and stuffy courtroom, the two legal titans battled over the legitimacy of scientific inquiry and the literal interpretation of Scripture. Bryan himself unwittingly proved the defense's greatest asset. When the judge demanded that Darrow find a biblical expert to testify, Bryan volunteered his own services. On the seventh day of the trial, the courtroom audience watched the unusual spectacle of Bryan taking the stand to be questioned by Darrow about the historicity of the Bible. For two hours, the men engaged in a tense confrontation over the believability of biblical stories such as the creation of Eve from Adam's rib, Jonah living for three days in the belly of a fish, and the sun standing still in the sky.

Throughout the bizarre episode, Bryan, then in his sixties and in poor health, repeatedly became flustered and contradicted himself, insisting at one juncture that he believed in the literal truth of biblical stories and conceding later that those passages might just be metaphorical. The crowd snickered at his confused answers, and Darrow exploited the opportunity to paint Bryan as a naive religious dupe. "You insult every man of science and learning in the world because he does not believe in your fool religion," charged the defense attorney. When Bryan shot back that the questioning was intended "to cast ridicule on everybody who believes in the Bible," Darrow had the last word: "We have the purpose of preventing bigots and ignoramuses from controlling the education of the United States."

Although Bryan ultimately won the case, fundamentalists lost in the court of public opinion. A new breed of secular journalists, led by H. L. Mencken, mocked the religious "yokels" and "hookworm carriers." Their media reports heavily influenced the popular belief that the Scopes trial signified the triumph of science over faith. The memory of Bryan's career as a progressive political leader was effectively erased, confining him to the history books instead as an opponent of reason and progress, a bumbling man led astray by fundamentalist religion.

In the trial's aftermath the political momentum to ban the teaching of evolution collapsed. Having lost the denominational battles, and perceiving that the culture had turned against them, the humiliated fundamentalists retreated from the public square and from the Protestant mainstream.

But they did not disappear. For the next two decades they poured their creative energies and financial resources into building their own churches and denominations and a supporting infrastructure of Bible colleges, seminaries, publishing houses, and broadcast ministries—all apart from the Protestant establishment. They tended to avoid political involvement except for voting, and even that was frowned upon in some fundamentalist circles. Politics was widely regarded as a futile and "worldly" pursuit that could only distract from the more important business of winning souls to Christ. When they did cast their ballots, it was seldom as a bloc. In the South, fundamentalists voted overwhelmingly Democratic, as did most Southerners in the first half of the twentieth century. In the North, they were more evenly divided between the two major parties. For a half century from the 1920s onward, fundamentalists as a group exhibited few distinguishing political characteristics and had no discernible impact on national elections.

They had fallen off the public's radar screen. But they would be back. And when they reappeared, they would be a stronger and more sophisticated force than before.

By the end of the 1930s, discontent was brewing in some fundamentalist circles over the separatism and anti-intellectualism that now characterized the movement. While their churches and ministries had continued to expand, a growing number of churchmen saw fundamentalism's rigid and reclusive character as an impediment to spreading the gospel and a betrayal of the evangelical social conscience of the nineteenth century. The seeds of a countermovement had begun to stir.

As the nation headed off to war in Europe and the Pacific, a new generation of leaders from New England, Philadelphia, California, and the upper Midwest began to chart a more irenic and moderate course. Among them were the Reverend Harold Ockenga of Park Street Church in Boston, Baptist theologian Carl F. H. Henry, and a young evangelist named Billy Graham.

The neo-evangelicals—a moniker they chose to distinguish themselves from fundamentalists and to reconnect with nineteenth-century evangelicalism—were no less theologically conservative than their fundamentalist brethren. They, too, insisted on the necessity of personal conversion and the unquestioned authority and accuracy of Scripture. But they also insisted that conservative Christians needed to engage the culture socially and intellectually to save it. So they began to establish a new network of organizations and alliances that would lay the groundwork for an evangelical resurgence in the final third of the twentieth century.

Unwilling to accept the theological liberalism of their mainline neighbors, the neo-evangelicals rejected the idea of joining the Federal Council of Churches. Instead, in 1942 they formed the National Association of Evangelicals, with Ockenga as president, to act as a unified voice for conservative churches and to coordinate nationwide ministries. A decade later, they had their own journal, *Christianity Today,* edited by Henry, and a new constellation of accredited seminaries with flagship schools such as Fuller Theological Seminary in Pasadena, California, and Gordon-Conwell in Massachusetts. Several neo-evangelical leaders had spent their undergraduate years at Wheaton College, a small liberal arts school just outside Chicago, which was gaining the lofty reputation of "the evangelical Harvard" because of its academic rigor. Probably Wheaton's most famous graduate was Graham, who, by the early 1950s, was attracting nationwide media attention as a crusade evangelist, radio broadcaster, and acquaintance of U.S. presidents.

From the outset, neo-evangelicals professed a strong social concern. Graham, for example, stirred controversy in the South by refusing to allow segregated seating at his citywide services in the 1950s and '60s, and he later spoke favorably of both the Civil Rights Act of 1964 and Lyndon Johnson's War on Poverty. Henry had set the moral tone a few years earlier, writing in *The Uneasy Conscience of Modern Fundamental-*

*ism* that "there is no room . . . for a gospel that is indifferent to the needs of the total man nor of the global man." Christianity, Henry argued, should speak to the whole person—spiritually, intellectually, culturally, and politically. The neo-evangelicals had established a new identity and set a new direction for theologically conservative Protestants who had previously been lumped together under the fundamentalist banner. By the 1960s, they would be known simply as evangelicals—a label that would be embraced by all but a shrinking number of fundamentalist holdouts on the movement's fringes.

But the careful social conscience of Graham, Henry, and other neo-evangelical leaders was too timid for many young people in the movement who came of age in the 1960s and '70s. They were times to test faith—public assassinations of beloved leaders, the injustices that prompted the civil rights struggle, urban race riots, the unpopular war in Vietnam, and a countercultural revolution led many Americans to lose their trust in institutions. The old civil religion that had once united Americans, that declared unquestioning support for one's country to be of a piece with faith in one's God, now seemed naive, empty, and possibly corrupt.

While evangelicals had been struggling to define themselves and carve out room for their own institutions in the years following the Scopes trial, liberal mainline Protestants had flourished. The secular-religious amalgam they developed, with its emphasis on values and purposes instead of religious doctrines, became the foundation for a potent brand of civil religion that seized the country.

As families left cities for the suburbs in a national migration throughout the 1940s and '50s, they sought ways to establish community ties. Churches were an obvious anchor, and church membership shot up to record levels; in 1958, nearly half the population (49 percent) reported attending church weekly. The ongoing Cold War against "godless" communism inspired a conception of patriotism that was hard to disentangle from religious piety. The phrase "under God" was approvingly inserted into the Pledge of Allegiance by Congress. Even popular culture recognized the widespread embrace of religion, with Hollywood blockbusters such as *The Ten Commandments* and *Samson and Delilah*. In 1954, President Dwight Eisenhower held up religious faith as a civic virtue unto itself, declaring, "Our government makes no sense unless it is founded in a deeply felt religious faith. And I don't care what it is."

Despite Eisenhower's wonderfully ambivalent coda, America's civil religion looked very much like a specific kind of faith: mainline Protestantism. Liberal Protestants were the official religious voice of the establishment, with theologians such as Paul Tillich writing in the pages of the *New Republic* and Reinhold Niebuhr featured on the cover of *Time* magazine in 1948. Union Theological Seminary in New York City was widely considered the most influential religious training ground in the country. And *Christianity and Crisis* magazine, one of the two signal publications of liberal Protestantism, was read by everyone from journalist Walter Lippmann to Supreme Court justice Felix Frankfurter. The magazine's pronouncements had a ripple effect throughout elite culture—an editorial in *Christianity and Crisis* was often reported in the pages of the *New York Times* and then picked up by newspapers further down the journalism food chain.

Mainline Protestants seemed to have successfully navigated a tightrope, retaining both their religious faith and their position in elite society. Like their secular peers in the establishment, however, members of what could broadly be termed the religious left were so captivated by their perch that they failed to notice the ground beneath them was shifting as the country moved through the unruly 1960s. If the 1950s were all about God, family, and country, the decades to follow called into question traditional beliefs about all three.

Sociologist Martin Marty, America's own modern Tocqueville, has written, "Mainline churches always have the advantage that in years in which the official culture is secure and expansive, they are well off. . . . [But they] suffer in times of cultural crisis and disintegration, when they receive blame for what goes wrong in society but are bypassed when people look for new ways to achieve social identity and location." Indeed, during the 1960s, churchgoing declined with each passing year. And mainline Protestants fell off the pages of national newspapers and magazines, and out of political favor as a new generation of young Americans increasingly saw their civil religion as part of the problem, not as a source of spiritual comfort.

Like their secular peers, young evangelicals were disillusioned. However, they didn't react by discarding religion altogether. Instead, their faith motivated them to confront issues of war and poverty and race relations. One of the institutions they reacted against was the evangelical establishment. "We have found social concern among Establishment Evangelicals to be often merely an offering of pious words rather than a demonstration of prophetic action," a young sociologist, Richard Quebedeaux, wrote in his 1974 book, *The Young Evangelicals*. "For them, individual conversion is the precondition for revolutionary social transformation, yet conversion *by itself* is not enough to bring about such change." The younger and more liberal evangelicals wanted to save souls and save the world at the same time.

Intentionally or not, the growing network of neo-evangelical liberal arts schools played a key role in preparing the younger generation for political action. Unlike fundamentalist Bible colleges, schools such as Wheaton and Calvin College in Michigan encouraged students to explore vocations beyond missionary and ministry work. Just as their political consciousness was forming, young evangelicals were being encouraged to apply their faith to other causes. At the same time, professors fostered critical-thinking skills, critiquing, for example, the flawed geology in the fundamentalist view of "young earth" creationism, and seeking to reconcile the natural world with orthodox Christian beliefs. As a result, neo-evangelical colleges began forming the intellectual foundation for a more progressive approach to culture and politics.

Wheaton, which had been a proud purveyor of the fundamentalist subculture earlier in the century, underwent particularly radical changes during the 1960s. By the middle of the decade, long hair and informal clothing had replaced the traditional clean-cut church-kid look, and folk music had supplanted hymns at student-led worship services. The campus paper published full-page spreads of Wheaton students marching with civil rights workers in Selma, Alabama. And a young arts student named Wes Craven—later famous for his horror films, including the *Scream* trilogy—penned a stinging essay in the campus arts magazine about his fundamentalist upbringing.

National politics stirred increasingly robust debate on Wheaton's campus. Barry Goldwater's visit to the still predominantly conservative school in 1964 sparked a surprisingly vigorous student protest. While the Wheaton administration had refused to allow John Kennedy to rent the college gym for a campaign rally in 1960, it warmly welcomed George McGovern to address students and faculty in the campus chapel in 1972. Evangelicals for McGovern became the first organized effort by evangelicals to back a presidential candidate, with chapters across the country. "A rising tide of younger evangelicals," read one press release from the organization, "feels that the time has come to dispel the old stereotype that evangelical theology entails unconcern toward the poor, blacks, and other minorities, and the needs of the Third World."

The movement of young evangelical activists wasn't limited to Christian schools. Evangelicals had impressive reach into secular universities, thanks to a void left by mainline churches, which simply did not focus on campus ministry. From its first chapter at the University of Michigan, InterVarsity Christian Fellowship spread to 550 campuses by 1950, swamping the presence of liberal Protestant chaplains and ministries. As campus activism heated up in the 1960s, evangelicals were right in the middle, producing underground newspapers such as *Manna* at the University of Wisconsin and *The Fish* at Harvard, which were explicitly evangelical and leftist.

This new breed of politically liberal evangelicals might have found common cause with the mainline Protestants and Catholic activists who lent their voices and their bodies to the civil rights movement. The Reverend Jerry Falwell spoke for most fundamentalists when he declared in 1965, "Preachers are not called upon to be politicians, but

soul winners. Nowhere are we commissioned to reform externals."
This time, however, the fundamentalist pronouncement seemed less
about focusing on salvation and more about ignoring racial injustice.
It was the more liberal Protestant ministers from the North who
linked arms with African-American pastors in the South to sing "We
Shall Overcome." The National Council of Churches—the umbrella
organization of mainline Protestantism—provided defense lawyers for
those arrested in demonstrations and voter registration activities in
Mississippi, Alabama, and other states throughout the South.

The civil rights movement seemed like a vibrant, united religious
cause—and is still celebrated as such today. In fact, it was almost
exclusively a project of black churches, with outside support from a
few determined souls in the mainline world who bucked the prevail-
ing impulse of their congregations to refrain from getting too involved.
Support for the civil rights movement in the pews of mainline
churches was never as vigorous as that in national denominational
offices. The Vietnam War only deepened that divide. Legendary figures
such as Yale chaplain William Sloane Coffin thundered against the U.S.
government's military action in Southeast Asia. But until Vietnam took
a dramatic turn for the worse in the late 1960s, many Presbyterian dea-
cons and Methodist Sunday school teachers believed that opposition
to the war was unpatriotic. The last remaining believers in a civil
religion, they were put off by their denominations' statements against
the war. (Catholics faced similar problems, with the community split
between elite leaders such as Daniel Berrigan, who dipped draft cards
in blood to protest U.S. involvement, and lower-class, ethnic Catholics
who were deeply offended by such actions.)

The mainline churches were also beset by social debates that had
entered their own institutions and distracted them from external
political questions. Newly empowered women sought to serve their
churches by doing more than manning the flower guild or baking
casseroles for sick congregants. In response, many denominations
hunkered down for battles over whether women could be ordained as
clergy. (In the 1970s, the Episcopal Church, American Lutheran bod-

ies, and the Reformed Church of America all reversed long-standing policies against female ordination.) The Equal Rights Amendment also split mainline churches; the National Council of Churches supported ratification of the ERA and discouraged the debate more skeptical congregations wanted to have about the meaning of changing gender roles and family structures.

And in 1971, the United Presbyterian Church (later the Presbyterian Church USA) outraged its member churches when the national mission board contributed $10,000 to Angela Davis's defense fund. The onetime Black Panther had first gained notoriety when she was dismissed from her teaching job at UCLA because of her Communist Party membership. After being accused of abetting the murder of a judge during a courthouse escape, Davis went underground and ended up on the FBI's Ten Most Wanted list. The denomination's leadership soon discovered that many Presbyterians saw a significant difference between supporting the civil rights movement and giving money to a Communist, black-activist murder defendant. Local churches stopped sending money to the national organization—although local giving remained steady, contributions to the United Presbyterian Church dropped by 28 percent between 1967 and 1973. During the same period, the denomination was forced to eliminate three-quarters of its national staff positions and to sell off its eleven-story Witherspoon Building in Philadelphia. The most conservative congregations simply left the denomination altogether. Unable to reliably hold their own congregations together, mainline denominations were in no position to champion the liberal evangelicals who sought to bring about changes within their own religious tradition.

The 1976 election was a turning point for evangelicals and for a nation still dealing with the aftermath of Vietnam and Watergate. The divisive war and the White House scandal that followed it had bred a cynicism that was proving hard to shake. President Ford, though a decent and honorable man, still bore the political baggage of having pardoned Nixon two years earlier—which had caused his popularity to plummet more than twenty percentage points. What voters wanted most of all in 1976, it seemed, was someone they could trust. So when a soft-spoken peanut farmer named Jimmy Carter looked America in the eye and vowed, "I'll never lie to you," his assurance resonated. Although Democrats had been thoroughly routed just four years earlier, they looked to have a fighting chance this time around.

As the campaign unfolded, news coverage increasingly focused on the character of the candidates. Ford was a longtime fixture in Washington, having served twenty-four years in the House of Representatives, the last eight as Republican leader. Consequently, his public persona was fairly familiar. Carter, a one-term Southern governor, was more unknown, and journalists covering the campaign were eager to fill in the blanks. They knew early on that Carter, like Harry Truman, was a Southern Baptist and that he taught a weekly Sunday school class. But that was of little interest to reporters—a candidate's religion seldom was—until they made an amazing "discovery" midway through the primary campaign.

At an outdoor gathering in Winston-Salem, North Carolina, a few days before that state's primary election, Carter was taking questions from a group of supporters when someone asked him if he was "a born-again Christian." Candidates in the South often get that question, and Baptists are especially fond of asking it to sort out those they view as authentic Christians from nominal ones. To the members of the press corps who were tracking Carter, however, the query was surprising and unfamiliar. They leaned in close to hear the answer.

"Yes," Carter responded without hesitation. Though raised in the church, he had accepted Christ as an adult. "I recognized for the first time that I had lacked something very precious—a complete commitment to Christ, a presence of the Holy Spirit in my life in a more profound and personal way," Carter told the crowd regarding his conversion. "And since then I've had an inner peace and inner conviction and assurance that transformed my life for the better."

To the journalists' ears it all sounded rather bizarre. At a news conference the following day they pressed Carter to explain this "born-again" business. It wasn't a voice of God from heaven, Carter assured them. It wasn't mysterious. The term was drawn from the Gospel of John where Jesus tells a Pharisee, "Except a man be born again, he cannot see the kingdom of God." Anyone familiar with the New Testament knows this.

The national media would not, however, be put off so easily. They thought they were on to something, and for the next several days reporters on the coasts scurried to find out what this strange religious phenomenon from America's heartland was all about. "We have checked on the religious meaning of Carter's profound experience," NBC news anchor John Chancellor proudly announced to his audience that week. "It is described by other Baptists as a common experience, not something out of the ordinary." *Newsweek* weighed in some weeks later with a cover story that proclaimed 1976 "The Year of the Evangelical." The magazine attempted to explain born-again Christianity and analyze how it might influence a Carter presidency. Kenneth Briggs, then chief religion reporter for the *New York Times,* would later recall that the mainstream press "really didn't know what an evangelical was. And what they did know harkened back to the days of the Scopes trial and fundamentalism and a kind of backwoods yahooism that they found very distasteful. No one was sure a presidential candidate should be talking about such things as private 'born-again' experiences and conversions."

Evangelicals, on the other hand, were delighted—and more than a little surprised—to find their faith suddenly in the national spotlight. They seized the opportunity to publicize their message. In a nationally televised evangelistic service that spring, Billy Graham observed, "Everybody is asking, 'What does it mean to be born again?'" He then explained the phrase and invited viewers to partake. Convicted Watergate conspirator Charles Colson, who had become a believer in prison, rushed out a spiritual autobiography entitled *Born Again,* and it became an instant best seller. In evangelical pulpits around the country, preachers expounded on the subject with renewed vigor. *Born-again* was working its way into the cultural vernacular.

More important from a political perspective, evangelicals were thrilled to find one of their own on the verge of nomination for the presidency, and they rallied behind him. In a keynote address to some fifteen thousand Southern Baptist pastors and lay leaders, the denomination's future president, Oklahoma pastor Bailey Smith, proclaimed that the nation "needs a born-again man in the White House . . . and his initials are the same as our Lord's." Energized evangelicals flocked to the polls during the primaries, helping to hand Carter important wins not only in the Deep South but also in such key Northern states as Pennsylvania, Ohio, and Illinois.

There was no divorcing Carter's faith from his public persona. His religion was a central and natural part of his life—"like breathing," as he often said. "Like many southerners, he found no contradiction in mixing an earthy appreciation of the good, secular life with the harder demands of evangelicalism," one political analyst wrote. Perhaps better than any other presidential candidate before him, and certainly better than his own staff and other Democratic Party operatives, he saw his faith as a political asset. "There is a hidden religious power base in American culture which our secular biases prevent many of us from noticing," Michael Novak, a Catholic theologian and social critic, observed at the time. "Jimmy Carter has found it."

By the time the Democrats gathered in New York City for their national convention that July, Carter had the nomination sewn up. But rather than a coronation, the nationally televised proceedings in Madison Square Garden had the air of a revival meeting. From Texas congresswoman Barbara Jordan's rousing keynote exhorting Americans to embrace a "sense of national community," to the closing prayer of Martin Luther King Sr., the atmospherics of down-home religion were palpable. "Surely the Lord is in this place," Daddy King intoned at the end of the final evening. "Surely the Lord sent Jimmy Carter to come on out and bring America back where she belongs"—

and, he might have added, to lead his fellow evangelicals out of political exile.

Not everyone in the Democratic Party was happy about this new base of religious support. Some of Carter's campaign aides tried to tone down their candidate's religiosity and walk back some of his public statements. Stuart Eizenstat, Carter's chief adviser on domestic affairs, recalled that whenever Carter sat down to make a list of strengths to be incorporated into his basic stump speech, he included his Christian faith. "I kept striking that out in every draft and he kept putting it back in every draft," Eizenstat said. "He obviously had an intention—which I was unaware of at the time—of making that a fairly central focus in terms of appealing to some of the rural Southern white voters. I don't think it was a totally political decision. I think it's something he very deeply believed in. But in my previous discussions and conversations with him, he certainly didn't advertise that to me." Campaign communications adviser Gerald Rafshoon felt the need that summer to reassure secular Democrats, who were becoming increasingly skittish about all the God talk, that "Jimmy won't turn the White House into a Billy Graham Bible class."

Carter's notorious interview with *Playboy* magazine in the fall of 1976 was part of the campaign's effort to prove that the Georgia Democrat wasn't a moralistic Bible-thumper. "We did the *Playboy* interview to show that being a born-again Christian was not a threat to more secular Democrats and young people," Patrick Caddell, a Democratic pollster and Carter adviser, recalled later. In a lengthy and far-ranging conversation published just weeks before the election, Carter confessed that he had "looked on a lot of women with lust" and had "committed adultery in my heart many times"—odd-sounding statements that were widely reported in the national press. To his campaign staff, the interview seemed at the time like a smart move.

But the gambit backfired. To the magazine's hedonistic readers Carter came off sounding like a prude. Many evangelicals, meanwhile, were incensed, first, that he had spoken at all to the soft-porn magazine, and, second, that he had used coarse language in paraphrasing the Sermon on the Mount. "God forgives me" for having sinful thoughts, Carter said in the interview. "But that doesn't mean that I condemn someone who not only looks on a woman with lust but who leaves his wife and shacks up with somebody out of wedlock. . . . Christ says don't consider yourself better than someone else because one guy screws a whole bunch of women, while the other guy is loyal to his wife."

The reaction from conservative Christian leaders was predictably negative. W. A. Criswell, pastor of First Baptist Church in Dallas, Texas, the nation's largest Southern Baptist congregation at the time, announced that he was "highly offended" by Carter's remarks, and he subsequently endorsed Ford. TV preacher Jerry Falwell declared, "Like many, I am quite disillusioned. Four months ago, the majority of people I knew were pro-Carter. Today, that has totally reversed." Even Bailey Smith, the Oklahoma pastor who had spoken so highly of Carter a few months earlier, expressed disappointment. "We're totally against pornography," Smith told the *Washington Post*. "And, well, *screw* is just not a good Baptist word."

Despite some erosion during the campaign's closing weeks, Carter ended up winning nearly half of the evangelical vote—more than twice what Democrats had managed in the previous two elections—and won the presidency by three percentage points. Born-again Christians had provided the victory margin. They had done so not because they were courted and mobilized by the Democratic Party (which they were not), but because of the personal affinity they felt for Carter—even if they did disagree with him on some issues.

Once Carter took office, however, the disagreements seemed to multiply, and evangelical support for the Democratic president continued to plummet. Nearly four years after the Supreme Court's *Roe v. Wade* decision, abortion was becoming an increasingly prominent issue for evangelicals. Carter refused to support a constitutional ban on abortion and declared that even though he was "personally opposed to abortion," he had to enforce the law of the land. He also pushed for ratification of the Equal Rights Amendment, which many conservative evangelicals believed was an affront to the biblical ordering of male-female relationships. And he supported ending legal and cultural discrimination against homosexuals, which most evangelicals at the time did not. Meanwhile, his Justice Department's efforts to enforce racial desegregation at Bob Jones University, a fundamentalist school in Greenville, South Carolina, were viewed by many conservative Christians as a direct government incursion into the evangelical subculture.

Increasingly alienated by the policies of the Carter administration, evangelicals also found themselves sorely neglected as a constituency. None had been appointed to a top administration post. First Lady Rosalynn Carter pressed her husband to name a religious liaison—Robert Maddox, a Baptist pastor from Georgia—but White House aides dragged their feet. Finally, in May 1979, Maddox was brought aboard as a speechwriter.

Early in 1980, at Maddox's behest, Carter invited a small group of conservative evangelicals to breakfast at the White House. They included some of the top TV preachers at the time—Falwell, faith healers Oral Roberts and Rex Humbard, the PTL's Jim Bakker, pastors Charles Stanley and D. James Kennedy. Maddox hoped it would be an opportunity for fence-mending. He urged Carter to acknowledge the "political and moral power of the evangelicals" in his remarks to the group and let them "feel his identification with them as a Christian believer while still communicating that he is president of all the people." Carter declined to actually join his guests for the meal. He showed up after they'd eaten, and each guest was allowed one question, preapproved by Maddox. In a chilly and stilted atmosphere, Carter deflected their predictable questions on abortion, the ERA, and the dearth of evangelical appointees, giving answers the preachers found vague.

The evangelical broadcasters left the meeting feeling glum and disaffected. One of them, Tim LaHaye (who years later would coauthor the best-selling *Left Behind* novels), recalled thinking at the time, "We had a man in the White House who professed to be a Christian, but he didn't understand how un-Christian his administration was . . . and I prayed . . . 'God, we have to get this man out of the White House and get someone in there who will be aggressive about bringing back traditional moral values.'" A group of secular and religious conservatives would soon harness this frustration and create a powerful political movement known as the religious right. But in the meantime, Carter and other more moderate evangelicals were finding that they had problems on their left flank as well.

The problem for any progressive religious movement during the past fifty years has been that its most natural political allies—the New Left and the future leaders of the Democratic Party—largely threw religion overboard in the countercultural revolution of the 1960s. Years after the 1973 gathering of evangelical activists in Chicago, Jim Wallis, one of the meeting's organizers, bemoaned the fact that Democratic Party leaders at the time made no effort to reach out to progressive evangelicals. "The left by then had turned away from 'common good' politics and toward an identity politics, a rights politics" that had little in common with religiously motivated altruism, Wallis told me in 2006. "Had Democrats been in power who were open to religion, we would have been more visible. But the Republicans were in power and the Democrats were secular." As a result, he said, a historic opportunity was lost.

It had not been the first time. If ever there was an evangelical group that secular liberals should have found common ground with early on it was the Christian World Liberation Front. A small group of religious antiwar activists based in Berkeley, California, in the early 1970s, the CWLF was headed by an evangelical-missionary-turned-radical named Jack Sparks. Sparks was a former college professor from Pennsylvania who had come to Berkeley to minister to students at the University of California. On his first day in town in May of 1969, he was mingling with antiwar demonstrators on the edge of campus when police fired tear gas into the crowd, sending Sparks and dozens of others running for cover and choking for breath. The aggressive attack by police was a turning point for Sparks. Overnight he became "Daddy Jack," ditching his suit and tie, big glasses, and short hair for a beard, a shaggy mane, and overalls.

Although Sparks started the CWLF as an evangelistic outreach, the group quickly turned to political activism. A few months after moving into a house on Telegraph Avenue next to the Berkeley campus, CWLF members began producing and distributing a tabloid called *Right On* that preached spiritual liberation from "the exploiters." Later in 1969, at an antiwar march in San Francisco, the group distributed sixty thousand leaflets urging immediate withdrawal of U.S. troops from Vietnam. Berkeley was, not surprisingly, the center for secular antiwar activism as well, and members of the CWLF assumed they would be able to combine their efforts to bring about an end to the war.

But their fellow travelers in the New Left at Berkeley wanted nothing to do with Sparks and his followers. They associated evangelicals with bigots and Bible-thumpers, the kind of folks who threatened, spit on, and cursed student protesters at antiwar rallies. An editorial in the *Daily Californian,* the campus paper, complained that "around Berkeley . . . the tart spice of theology is doled out in shovelsfull. Like any overly-rich dish, it is often apt to make you puke." It wasn't religion in general that bothered the writer, however. The "Krishna Krazies" and "the little Buddhist ladies," he noted, were perfectly acceptable—"a manifestation of our time, like dope and rock music." Cool, unthreatening Asian religions were fine. "What riles me," the writer admitted, "is the goddam Christians!"

The secular revolution that had started a century earlier with the onset of industrialization became complete in the classrooms and lecture halls of American universities in the 1960s and '70s. A 1976 report by the Rockefeller Foundation found that fewer than half the graduates of the nation's top five divinity schools—Harvard, Yale, Chicago, Vanderbilt, and New York's Union Theological Seminary—went on to church work or to further study of religion, down from four-fifths who did so a few decades earlier. At secular universities, the study of religion was no longer seen as part of liberal education. When Harvard University designed its "Core" curriculum for undergraduates in the 1970s, with the express purpose of ensuring that students were "broadly educated," religion was not included, leaving students ill-equipped to assess such events as the Iranian revolution, the mass suicide at Jonestown, Guyana, and, ultimately, the rise of the religious right. (Thirty years later in 2006, when a Harvard task force recommended adding a required course on religion to the Core, an uproar from university professors over the idea of "forcing" students to study religion quickly quashed the proposal.) Following the lead of liberal theologians who proclaimed the "death of God" in the early 1960s, students and professors alike assumed that the nation was entering a postreligious age in which religion was at best irrelevant and at worst irrational.

Gone, it seemed, were the great public theologians such as Reinhold Niebuhr and Paul Tillich, Union Theological Seminary professors whose thoughtful cultural critiques often appeared in the *New Republic* and other influential journals in the mid-twentieth century. Theologians now were walled off in religion departments, writing arcane articles that went largely unread by the general public or the political and cultural elite. Instead of applying theological thought to contemporary social problems, religious academia was kept busy defending its right to contribute to public discourse at all. It seemed that the liberal intelligentsia, having lost all interest in religion, had bought the argument of John Rawls, an influential Harvard political philosopher, that setting aside one's religious views was the price of admission to the public square.

As a result, secular liberals not only pushed away potential allies in the religious community, they also rejected the use of religious language in pressing progressive causes. Eager to stay in the game, many mainline Protestants responded by filtering most religion out of their political rhetoric, elevating "rights" over "righteousness" as the supreme civic virtue. (In 1973, for example, the NCC's international relief agency, Church World Service, adopted a new policy embracing "liberation and justice"—rather than the biblical mandate to help the poor and hungry—as its guiding mission. When its longtime director,

James MacCracken, objected to the change, he was summarily fired.) Progressive evangelicals, by contrast, refused to give up their unabashedly biblical language. To do so, they believed, would be to squelch the unique prophetic voice that had provided moral authority to their chosen causes since the days of abolition. Not surprisingly, the bland, secular-sounding mainliners became the preferred partners of the political left while evangelicals were relegated to the margins— or were entirely ignored.

The Republican Party of the late 1970s, in danger of becoming a permanent minority in American politics, was more than happy to step into the void as a willing political partner for evangelicals. The idea of organizing evangelicals into a conservative political force was the brainchild of a group of mostly secular New Right activists who saw conservative Christians as "the greatest tract of virgin timber on the political landscape." Mobilizing dormant evangelicals into a cohesive voting bloc, the activists believed, offered the best hope of forging an enduring Republican majority. In May 1979, four New Right leaders—Paul Weyrich, founder of the conservative Heritage Foundation, Howard Phillips of the Conservative Caucus, Religious Roundtable founder Ed McAteer, and Robert Billings, a Christian educator—ventured to Lynchburg, Virginia, to recruit Jerry Falwell to their cause.

Falwell had recently undergone a personal political awakening. Like many fundamentalist ministers, he had preached for years against clergy involvement in politics. But Supreme Court rulings legalizing abortion and banning school prayer had changed his mind. In the late 1970s, he began using his *Old-Time Gospel Hour* broadcast to inveigh against abortion, calling it "America's national sin" and comparing it to the Holocaust. He soon realized, however, that preaching alone was not enough. Along with abortion, he would write in his 1987 autobiography, there were "other crises facing the nation that required immediate political action from men and women of Christian faith."

The four New Right leaders had no trouble convincing Falwell that the time to act had arrived. Out of the Lynchburg meeting came the Moral Majority—a grassroots organization headed by Falwell to register, inform, and mobilize conservative Christians precinct by precinct throughout the country. Billing the new organization as "pro-life, pro-family, pro-moral, and pro-American," Falwell raised more than $2 million in the first year. Within two years he claimed to have 4 million members, a $10 million budget, and a chapter in every state. With Falwell as its spokesman, the Moral Majority quickly emerged in media accounts as the voice of an awakened giant—a new "religious right" that would energize the Republican Party and help put Ronald Reagan in the White House.

Courting the religious right became a top priority for the Reagan campaign in 1980. To unseat the incumbent president, Reagan advisers believed he would have to reach into Carter's base of white evangelical voters, especially in the South. That the former California governor was not much of a churchgoer, was divorced and remarried, and had achieved his fame in Hollywood might have posed a problem for them. But those potential shortcomings were more than offset in the eyes of many evangelicals by his unflinching conservatism and his professed dedication to "traditional Judeo-Christian values."

The Great Communicator knew how to speak the evangelicals' language, even if it wasn't his native tongue, and he used it to good effect. Addressing a gathering of TV preachers and other religious right leaders in Dallas a few months before the election, Reagan hit all the right notes. He complained that the Supreme Court's school-prayer decision had "expelled God from the classroom." He reiterated his oft-made observation that everybody in favor of abortion had already been born. He spoke admiringly of the Bible, explaining that "all the complex questions facing us at home and abroad have their answer in that single book." And if there were any holdouts left among the assembled clergy, he melted their hearts by declaring, "I know you can't endorse me . . . but I want you to know that I endorse you."

The preachers were elated. They went home energized, and in

November, Reagan swept the evangelical vote by a nearly two-to-one margin, winning the election in a landslide.

The Moral Majority and the rest of the religious right had played a role by helping to register and mobilize conservative Christians—although subsequent analysis would show that Reagan would probably have won the presidency even without evangelical support. (He carried forty-four states and won 91 percent of the electoral college vote.) But that did not stop Falwell from accepting much of the credit. Looking back later, he would declare the 1980 election "my finest hour."

More important, the 1980 election had forged a strong and enduring bond between right-leaning Christians and the Republican Party. From the 1990s onward, evangelicals would become a key Republican constituency, accounting for more than a third of the total GOP vote in presidential elections. Conservative broadcasters such as Falwell, Christian Coalition founder Pat Robertson, and Focus on the Family's James Dobson would gain increasing recognition in the media and in Washington as the dominant political voice of American evangelicalism and as fierce Republican partisans.

Yet the evangelical movement was not nearly as monolithic as it was widely perceived to be. John Green, director of the Ray C. Bliss Institute of Applied Politics at the University of Akron in Ohio, estimated years later that roughly 25 percent of evangelicals—some 15 million in all—continued to lean toward Democratic candidates and policies. Many others were swing voters who tended to be critical of traditional Republican policies on poverty, the economy, and the environment. Were it not for such issues as abortion and same-sex marriage, which tended to galvanize conservative Christians, said Green, evangelicals "would not be a strong constituency of the Republican Party. There'd be many more Democrats among them." But as a new century began, those left-leaning evangelicals would largely be left to their own devices, struggling to be heard over the broadcast megaphones of the religious right.

\*    \*    \*

It becomes easier to understand how liberals could so quickly forget their own history, and the important role religion had played in the civil rights movement and Progressive Era reforms, once the religious right began to emerge. Suddenly evangelicals seemed to be everywhere. The media infrastructure they had amassed during their years in fundamentalist exile—the radio stations and then the television broadcasts financed by audience donations—enabled them to attain national visibility without going through the mainstream media. By the early 1970s, evangelical radio and TV broadcasts boasted a combined audience of tens of millions of listeners and viewers a week. Between 1970 and 1980, expenditures on programming for televangelists like Pat Robertson, Oral Roberts, and Jerry Falwell rose from $50 million to more than $600 million annually.

Soon enough evangelicals were also grabbing the additional free exposure of national news coverage. Mainstream journalists were captivated by this fascinating movement led by bombastic preachers with bad haircuts and funny accents who had a knack for quips and controversy. These journalists had also largely succumbed to the popular elite belief that religious fervor was largely a thing of the past, an element of conservative traditional communities but not progressive ones. And this affected the way they framed religious stories. The growing visibility and influence of evangelical leaders in the 1980s became self-perpetuating as journalists increasingly turned to religious conservatives for political comment and gradually forgot about the religious left altogether. When journalists did include a viewpoint from the left, it was often from a spokesperson from the ACLU or Americans United for the Separation of Church and State, leaving the impression that the right was religious and the left wanted religion scrubbed from the public square. By 2007, a study by the left-leaning think tank Media Matters found that conservative religious leaders were quoted or interviewed on television nearly four times as often as their progressive religious counterparts.

It would take religious liberals a long while to adjust to—or even recognize—this new reality. In the fall of 1980, as fundamentalists were still emerging from their self-imposed exile and reshaping American politics, talk-show host Phil Donahue invited William Sloane Coffin and Jerry Falwell to face off on his program. At the time, *The Phil Donahue Show* was one of the highest-rated programs on daytime television, with millions of American viewers. The matchup of Falwell, the fundamentalist preacher and founder of the nascent Moral Majority, against Coffin, one of the lions of the religious left, promised to be must-see TV.

And yet Coffin was strangely ineffectual. The senior minister of mainline Protestantism's flagship pulpit—Riverside Church in Manhattan—had been the chaplain at Yale during the 1960s and early '70s. His fiery sermons on campus inspired thousands of students to head South in support of the civil rights movement and to take to the streets in opposition to the Vietnam War. But on this morning, settled into his armchair on the *Donahue* set, Coffin was distant, seemingly disinterested. He halfheartedly jousted with the country preacher, but mostly addressed himself to the host, saying disdainfully of Falwell, "I think deep down, he is shallow. His biblical positions are not sound biblical study. Anybody who has done any real Bible study knows you can't come up with those conclusions from the Bible." His judgment rendered, Coffin didn't feel the need to explain himself further.

The feisty Falwell, by contrast, landed jab after jab, challenging liberal theology and the politics of Protestants like Coffin. But he couldn't get Coffin to fight back. Midway through the program, Falwell was running away with the show. During a commercial break, Donahue pulled Coffin aside to inquire if anything was wrong. Not particularly, replied Coffin. He was merely bored with the subject and didn't feel the need to defend his tradition to the likes of Falwell. Donahue couldn't believe his ears. Millions of Americans had tuned in hoping to hear Coffin present a vigorous case for liberal religion at a time when Falwell's followers were gathering momentum. If that wasn't enough to get the minister's blood flowing, Donahue demanded, "What the fuck would it take?"

Coffin's nonchalance about the nascent religious right movement was matched by a collective shrug of the shoulders on the political left at the defection of evangelicals to the GOP. The reaction undoubtedly betrayed a certain "good riddance" attitude among those who believed the Democratic Party was too progressive and tolerant for evangelical voters. It was also based on the confident assumption that the party could afford to lose evangelicals because Catholics still remained solid members of the electoral coalition that had supported Democrats since the New Deal. But that bond, as well, was beginning to break.

CHAPTER 3

# "KEEP YOUR ROSARIES
OFF MY OVARIES"

## HOW DEMOCRATS LOST CATHOLICS

The shuffleboard- and mah-jongg-playing retirees of Miami Beach
barely knew what hit them when the Democratic National Convention careened into town in July of 1972. The violent clashes that had
racked Chicago four years earlier were mercifully absent. But the
convention was nonetheless raucous. Wild-card candidate George
Wallace was on hand, just eight weeks after surviving an assassination
attempt that left him paralyzed from the waist down and in a wheel-
chair. A last-minute, unsuccessful "Stop McGovern" coalition was led
by Arkansas congressman Wilbur Mills, although his fifteen minutes of fame would be eclipsed two years later when he was caught in
Washington, D.C., with a stripper who ran out of his car and into the
Tidal Basin. Befuddled Miami Beach leaders met with a group of Yip-
pie delegates to hand over a key to the city, while Allen Ginsberg led
demonstrators outside the Miami Beach Convention Center in a
mass chant of "Ohm."

Inside the center—the site of Cassius Clay's defeat of Sonny Liston
for the world heavyweight championship in 1964—thousands of
first-time delegates filled the green folding chairs on the floor, eager to
put their newfound power to use. The appetite for debate was insa-
tiable. Sessions began early in the morning and ran long after mid-

night. The process of nominating a vice president took so long on the final night of the convention that George McGovern delivered his acceptance speech at three in the morning, not exactly prime time for television.

But the most contentious part of the convention was over the seating of delegates—and it would have serious consequences for the role of Catholics in the new Democratic Party.

The controversial outcome in Chicago—in which Vice President Hubert Humphrey, who had not competed in a single primary, was selected by party leaders as the Democratic nominee—had spurred a majority of delegates to vote for changes in the nomination system. The result was the McGovern Commission, named for the senator from South Dakota who served as chair of the twenty-eight-member group. With a mandate to open up the process and shift power away from party bosses, the commission instituted a number of reforms, many of which helped the commission chair become the Democratic nominee in 1972. Party leaders could no longer compel state delegations to vote as a bloc. The selection of delegates through state caucuses and conventions was largely replaced with the modern primary system. And state parties were required to choose women, minorities, and young people as presidential delegates in "reasonable relationship" to their numbers in the state population.

Some party bosses, however, weren't willing to cede their influence so easily. Foremost among them was Richard Daley, the powerful mayor of Chicago, who simply disregarded the new requirements and arrived in Miami with his slate of fifty-eight handpicked delegates. When a young African-American leader from Chicago named Jesse Jackson led a charge to contest Daley's slate, the mayor wasn't fazed. The upstarts were just a temporary irritation, no match for the Daley machine. He imperiously rejected a solution offered by McGovern aides that would have split the Cook County delegates evenly between Daley's men and the Jackson faction. The only "compromise" he would consider, declared Daley, would be to tack on the Jackson delegates to some other state's delegation. With Daley's all-or-nothing challenge hanging in the air, delegates gathered for an all-night hearing of the credentials committee to determine the fate of the Illinois delegation. The decision came down at 4:45 a.m. on the morning of July 18: the mayor and his delegates had violated the new rules. They were out of the convention.

The victory for the Jackson slate was a step forward for Democratic politics and a rebuke to the machine party bosses of old. The Miami convention did truly look like a whole new party—a party that was less white, less old, less male. In 1968, just 13 percent of the delegates had been women, and only 4 percent were under the age of thirty. Those numbers rose in 1972 to 40 percent and 21 percent, respectively, with some delegates as young as eighteen years old, thanks to the recent passage of the Twenty-sixth Amendment lowering the voting age.

The changes didn't come without a price, though. Thousands of new delegates meant thousands of traditional Democratic delegates had been displaced. As with the Chicago delegation, the reforms fell disproportionately on white ethnic Catholics who had been part of urban political machines. Men with surnames like Sydlowski and O'Malley came from neighborhoods like Jefferson Park and South Boston that had delivered votes for Democrats since the beginning of the New Deal. They admired the Daley machine—it had, after all, carried Illinois by the slimmest of margins (8,858 votes) in 1960 to make John F. Kennedy the first Catholic president.

While the unseating of the Daley slate was of marginal practical consequence—McGovern had more than enough votes to win the nomination—the symbolic message was clear to Catholics across the country: they had been kicked out of the Democratic convention. The insult was compounded by the fact that the slate that replaced the Daley group included delegates such as Jackson who had not been elected to the post by a single voter but were hand-selected by a small group of Chicago reformers who contested the Daley delegates.

It was not the first, nor would it be the last, rupture in the once-rosy alliance between Catholics and Democrats. Catholics had voted for Democrats in most of the century's presidential elections, starting with Al Smith's failed 1928 bid for the White House. Their loyalty was cemented by Franklin D. Roosevelt and his early New Deal programs. (It didn't hurt that FDR also quoted from Pope Pius XI's 1931 encyclical on the economy, *Quadragesimo anno,* at a Detroit campaign rally in 1932.) In 1960, Kennedy's run for the White House was dogged by charges that a Catholic president would take orders directly from the pope. But his victory—based on the support of more than three out of every four Catholics—dealt a blow to anti-Catholicism while also highlighting the importance of Catholics as a decisive voting bloc. By 1968, the stigma attached to Catholic candidates seemed to have vanished: two of the three major Democratic primary candidates were Catholics.

By the end of the 1960s, however, cultural and political changes on the left were starting to cause discomfort for traditional Catholics. The rise of a liberalism that focused on individual rights was at odds with the Catholic principle of solidarity and a communitarian approach to economic and social policy. Nor did many Catholics welcome the cultural revolution, with the new sexual and moral norms it ushered in. In the Democratic Party, activists celebrated these developments as long-overdue progress. But a few strategists wondered about the long-term implications for the party's appeal. "McGovern has got a great issue with alienation, but I wonder if he knows the cause," mused Democratic pollster Don Muchmore after the 1972 convention. "The people who are alienated are the ones who don't want pot, who don't want abortion, who don't want to pay one more cent in taxes."

The *Roe v. Wade* decision that came down soon after the 1972 election, and the sudden elevation of abortion as a national political issue, blasted the emerging rift between Catholics and Democrats wide open. The political motto of the era—embraced first by the women's movement—was "The personal is the political." While Catholics wouldn't use those words to describe their efforts, over the next few decades, the personal became political for them as well. And by the end of the 1980s, it would result in a dramatic political realignment.

Democrats—having lost 40 percent of their Catholic voters by that point—would no longer be the Catholic party.

The popular narrative about Catholic involvement in American politics holds that it was the *Roe* decision that woke Catholics from a complacent slumber, shocking them to the core and propelling them overnight into the world of politics. And it's true that the ruling took many Catholics by surprise. The legalistic, cold approach to an issue they considered deeply moral shook their belief that Catholic values and American values were one and the same.

But that simple explanation is only part of the story. In fact, the political awakening of the American Catholic Church had been set in motion a decade before *Roe*. In one of those uncanny alignments of the planets, the abortion issue came along just as the Church embraced a new philosophical and institutional willingness to engage political questions. The American Church in the 1970s was spreading its wings after years of shying away from involvement in political affairs and was about to crash up against the Democratic Party's steady embrace of social liberalism.

For most of the nineteenth and twentieth centuries, the Catholic Church had mainly operated as an immigrant church in the United States, helping its members assimilate, setting up institutions to serve the urban Catholic ghettos, and only intermittently entering into the political realm to secure aid for parochial schools and protect Church institutions from unwanted interference. Remaining on the periphery was a new experience for Church leaders in Rome. Historically, they had thrown their weight around, at the very least making gentlemen's agreements with European monarchs who treated them with respect. The challenge of a democratic country in which Catholics were the outsiders, the newcomers, was unfamiliar for the Church.

The relatively low profile and low importance of American bishops made things even more difficult. The First Vatican Council in the nineteenth century had firmly located the ecclesiastical balance of power in the hands of the papacy, reducing bishops everywhere to minor figures who were expected to focus their attention on local concerns. The closest thing the American hierarchy had to a national presence was the National Catholic Welfare Conference (NCWC), established in 1919, a relatively small, underfinanced, and under-staffed body located in Washington, D.C. The NCWC lobbied for measures to protect parochial schools and supported anticommunism in the 1950s. But to the extent that any real action took place, it was at the local level. Clustered in cities across the Northeast and Midwest, Catholics in the first half of the twentieth century relied on their neighborhood priests and bishops—as well as organizations such as Catholic Charities and St. Vincent de Paul—to help immigrant families settle and to provide a safety net. If they needed outside help, the priests turned to local politicians, many of whom ran their cities through disciplined party machines. Few national politicians knew the names of archbishops, and the ignorance was mutual.

As late as 1960, when Kennedy made a run for the White House, anti-Catholicism simmered close enough to the surface that Church leaders—and other prominent Catholics—had to fend off charges that they were more loyal to the Vatican than to their own country. In response, they hewed to a pragmatic strategy of keeping their heads down and piping up every so often with a "God bless America!" Until 1968, for instance, the American Catholic Church officially supported every war the United States entered—even the Spanish-American War, in which other Catholics were the opponents. For American Catholics, it was not yet the time for making waves.

That would all change with the Second Vatican Council, which turned the American Catholic world upside down. The First Council had addressed issues that affected the universal Church—establishing, most famously, the doctrine of papal infallibility—but its changes were felt most deeply in Europe. With a new vocabulary for religious political involvement and permission to become involved in political life, European Catholics were free to organize and to join Christian socialist movements that were gaining strength across the Continent. The effect of Vatican I was less obvious for their American counterparts, who were focused more on assimilating to their new country than agitating. In the century that followed the Council, however, the swirling political and economic changes that accompanied the democratization of Europe and the rise of the industrial revolution only accelerated. And so, not long after his election in 1958, Pope John XXIII announced that he would call the bishops of the Church back to Rome for a second gathering to determine how to respond—and, if need be, adapt—to the rapidly changing world around them.

The most visible of the Vatican II reforms were those that immediately impacted the worship experience and daily practice of everyday Catholics. Meat could now be consumed on Friday. Priests would no longer say the mass with their backs to the pews, but would face the congregation. To the relief of schoolchildren everywhere, services would no longer be performed in Latin, but in the local vernacular.

As radical as these internal changes were, however, it was a reconsideration of the Church's relationship to the external world that really set off shock waves. The Second Vatican Council was not overtly political, but was convened in part to address the appropriate place of the Church in society, which led directly to discussions about the Catholic role in politics. On this question, the Council reached a firm conclusion. "The Church should have true freedom . . . to pass moral judgments even in matters relating to politics," read *Gaudium et Spes,* one of the most significant documents to emerge from the Council, "wherever the fundamental rights of man or the salvation of souls requires it."

Those words represented a major shift in the development of Catholic social doctrine. By expanding the Church's mission beyond "the salvation of souls" to protecting "the fundamental rights of man," the Council was staking its authority over the behavior of individuals *and* of states, adding to the moral obligations of individual Catholics. It wasn't enough to just refrain from personal immorality or say the requisite number of Hail Marys as penance. Preaching the gospel also meant acting to correct injustice and alleviate global problems. There was a new kind of sin to supplement the concept of individual sin that had previously consumed the attention of the Church. "People are being kept poor," declared the bishops in their 1971 statement *Justice in the World,* "because the system is a social sin."

This new way of thinking about the responsibilities of Catholics broke down a psychological barrier between a sequestered, inward-looking Church and the world outside. The effect was revolutionary. Calling the new Church documents "blueprints for action," one American bishop told political scientist Mary Hanna in 1973 that they represented a dramatic change in Catholic thought. "Twenty or thirty years ago," he explained, "the Catholic people had no concept of acting on issues like welfare rights, war action. It just wasn't the kind of thing they did." Of course, papal encyclicals had often addressed questions of social and economic justice—such as the rights of workers to organize—but they were pitched as theological treatises for experts and scholars, not the masses. Vatican II redefined the Church as the priesthood *and* the laity, for the first time making clear that individual Catholics were part of the living Church body. "The Council addressed itself to everyone, the whole Church," another American Catholic official told Hanna. "It opened doors for normal Christians to become involved."

Yet if all Vatican II had done was allow ordinary Christians to get involved with the affairs of the world, giving them permission slips to go on political excursions, it would not have had such a dramatic impact on American political life. The Council didn't just encourage political involvement; it mandated such activity. It didn't just suggest that Church teaching was relevant to the moral questions of the day; it insisted that Catholic thought provided standards that should govern individual and collective action.

Pope Paul VI, who oversaw the second half of the Council after John XXIII died in 1963, outlined his thoughts on the duty of Catholics to apply their teaching to real problems in his encyclical *Octogesima Adveniens.* "It is up to the Christian communities to analyze with objectivity the situation which is proper to their own country," wrote Paul, "to shed on it the light of the Gospel's unalterable words and to draw principles of reflection, norms of judgments and directives for action from the social teaching of the Church." *Directives for action.* That phrase shot adrenaline into the previously quiescent American Catholic institution. The mandate catapulted Catholics into the midst of ongoing contentious debates in American politics and introduced an influential new political player (Catholics represented one-quarter of the American electorate) virtually overnight. Both the Democratic and Republican parties scrambled to adjust to the altered political landscape.

The bishops emerged from the Council with more power and discretion, thanks to institutional changes that strengthened their role and emphasized their teaching authority. Vatican II called for the establishment of national bishops' councils, which were given significant leeway to choose the political issues on which they would speak out and the form of their political involvement. In the United States, the National Conference of Catholic Bishops (NCCB) replaced the anemic NCWC in 1966 and became the institutional framework by which bishops engaged the political world. While the NCWC had focused on internal concerns such as parochial education and immigration, the NCCB's focus was outward: the bishops quickly set up divisions such as the Campaign for Human Development (an antipoverty program), the Division of Peace and Justice, and the Department of Social Development.

A Vatican decree also created the U.S. Catholic Conference (USCC), a policy shop of legislative and theological experts, to assist the bishops with the development of policy statements. Together, the NCCB and USCC provided an organizational network for the bishops, as well as a national stage from which to address social concerns. It didn't take long for the USCC to develop a formidable lobbying wing and to issue pronouncements that landed with considerable weight in Washington, D.C. Entering the decade of the 1970s in the wake of Vatican II, the Catholic Church in the United States was barely recognizable as the former immigrant church that had shied away from political disputes. The Council had declared that the Church's mission was to speak to "the whole of humanity," and thus unloosed, the American bishops wasted no time.

In January of 1973, when the *Roe* decision came down, it would have been difficult to find an issue on which Catholics were more united than abortion. The unanimity of Catholic opposition to abortion was more solid than opinion about any other matter—more than war, more than civil rights, even more than the death penalty. That isn't to say that all Catholics placed it at the top of their list of priorities. But there was no question regarding Church teaching: abortion was always wrong.

Ecclesiastical opposition to abortion dates as far back as the *Didache* in the first century. Theological development ever since has laid the groundwork for a doctrine of respecting the dignity of life at all stages. Abortion was not an issue on which individual episcopal conferences had leeway to apply Church doctrine as they saw fit. Still, even some abortion rights opponents were surprised at the forcefulness of the U.S. bishops' first statement about the issue in 1970. "Our defense of human life is rooted in the biblical prohibition, 'Thou shall not kill,'" the bishops wrote. "The life of the unborn child is a human life. The destruction of any human life is not a private matter, but the concern of every responsible citizen."

That last line took on unexpected resonance after 1973, when the U.S. Supreme Court grounded the legalization of abortion in a "right to privacy." To many Catholics, the decision to end a life—no matter how early in development—impacted the whole community. There was nothing private about it. With this latest decision, Catholics started to seriously worry that the Constitution didn't sufficiently reflect their values. A few years earlier in 1968, in *Board of Education v. Allen,* the Court had limited support for parochial schools, a majority of which were Catholic, by ruling that public schools could not lend them used books. And in 1971, the justices curtailed government aid to religious schools as well in *Lemon v. Kurtzman.* The majority opinion in *Lemon* noted the "hazards of religion's intruding into the political arena," and a concurring opinion from Justice Douglas was even more hostile, referring to a 1962 anti-Catholic tract that complained about the Church's "indoctrination" and "propaganda."

For American Catholics who felt alienated by the cultural revolution sweeping through American society, who saw their institutions being attacked by the highest court in the land, and who had just been kicked out of the Democratic convention, the *Roe* decision was the last straw. As one priest who had previously urged the Church to stay out of political issues vowed after the decision, "We're not going to shut up on this issue, no matter what our critics say. . . . Aid to parochial schools was important, sure, but it's nowhere near the same thing as this." Armed not only with papal permission, but a mandate to intrude into the political arena—no matter what a majority of Supreme Court justices said—the U.S. Catholic Church took on abortion as its first real political test.

Cardinal John Krol of Philadelphia immediately condemned the *Roe* decision as "bad logic and bad law" and proclaimed it "an unspeakable tragedy for the nation." Within days, a Catholic congressman—Lawrence Hogan from Maryland—had introduced a constitutional amendment to overturn the ruling, attracting widespread support from fellow Catholics and, eventually, the official support of his church. In November, the NCCB issued a statement giving notice "beyond a doubt to our fellow citizens that we consider the passage of a pro-life constitutional amendment a priority of the highest order."

In quick succession, the NCCB established the National Committee for a Human Life Amendment and sent four cardinals up to Capitol Hill to testify before a Senate subcommittee on the issue of constitutional amendments. And one year before the presidential election, in November of 1975, the bishops' conference released the *Pastoral Plan for Pro-Life Activities,* characterized by Catholic scholar Mary Segers as "the most detailed and explicit proposal for political action ever to emanate from the offices of the American Catholic hierarchy."

Among other actions, the plan specifically called for the establishment of pro-life "units" around the country. These grassroots advocacy groups were not to be divided up by diocese or parish. Instead, if the bishops' ambitious proposal was realized, each of the country's 435 congressional districts would have a pro-life organization. This was, above all, a political battle plan:

> Accomplishment of this [legal/public-policy effort] will undoubtedly require well-planned and coordinated political action by citizens at the nation, state, and local levels. This activity is not simply the responsibility of all Catholics, nor should it be limited to Catholic groups or agencies. It calls for widespread cooperation and collaboration. As citizens of this democracy, we encourage the appropriate political action to achieve these legislative goals. As leaders of a religious institution in this society, we see a moral imperative for such political activity.

Despite the fervent wishes of the American bishops, opposition to abortion rights was largely limited to Catholics in the years immediately following *Roe*, with the consequence that abortion was thought of as primarily a "Catholic issue." Most pro-life organizations were founded and run by Catholics, and even those that were not officially Catholic in origin—such as the National Right to Life Committee—were overwhelmingly Catholic in their membership. Given the enthusiasm with which evangelicals would later embrace the abortion issue, some of this early isolation of Catholics was undoubtedly due to a still-lingering anti-Catholicism among both mainline and evangelical Protestants. But the main reason why the Catholic Church had a hard time finding allies for its pro-life activities is that it had already given up a large portion of its credibility by opposing the use of contraception, a far less controversial practice.

In the first half of the twentieth century, the Catholic Church had placed the practice of birth control high on its list of moral evils—always mentioning it in the same breath as abortion, euthanasia, and eugenics. In his 1930 encyclical *Casti connubii,* Pope Pius XI described the use of contraceptives as "vicious" and "intrinsically against nature."

And throughout the 1950s and '60s, Catholics were at the front lines of fights in Massachusetts and Connecticut to defend nineteenth-century laws that prevented even married couples from purchasing contraceptives.

In making the case that Mr. and Mrs. Smith should bear seven or eight children instead of just using condoms, the Catholic Church found itself alone. Protestant theologians such as Reinhold Niebuhr respectfully disagreed with the Church's position, and ordinary Americans, particularly non-Catholics, saw it as an attempt to impose a specific religious teaching on the way they lived their own lives. What's more, many Catholics depended on birth control to limit their family's size—as early as the 1940s, one-third of all married Catholics admitted using contraception. The use of contraception only became more popular in the 1960s with the introduction of the Pill.

The issue came to a head in 1966, when a papal commission established to study questions of birth control and population growth issued a report stating that artificial contraception was not intrinsically evil and that Catholic couples should be allowed to decide for themselves whether they wanted to use birth control methods. In 1968, however, Pope Paul VI rejected the commission's recommendation and issued *Humanae Vitae,* which reiterated official Church opposition to birth control. The reaction in Catholic circles was swift and outraged. Within two days of the encyclical's release, a counterstatement was released by a group of dissident theologians who insisted that individual Catholic consciences—and not Church teaching—should carry the most weight in such a private decision. Over time, this dissident position became the majority opinion, particularly in the United States, where by 2003 fully 94 percent of adults in a *Washington Post* poll agreed that birth control was "morally acceptable."

The whole affair seemed to be a strategic setback for the Church. And to the extent that the continued opposition to birth control led people to think of Catholics as stubborn and backward-looking, it did make it harder for the Church to get a fair hearing when the debate moved on to abortion. But the real strategic mistake turned out to be the lessons liberal Democrats drew from the skirmish. To them, it appeared that the Church was fractured, led by an out-of-touch hierarchy that willfully ignored the advice of its own theologians and alienated its more progressive members.

Abortion rights supporters assumed that ordinary Catholics would reject the Church's teaching on abortion the same way they had with contraception. They had as little patience for those who expressed concerns about abortion as they had with those who questioned the morality of birth control. When the American Civil Liberties Union (ACLU) came out in support of legalized abortion in the late 1960s, an ACLU member—and Notre Dame law professor—who complained was told that the organization equated "antiabortion positions with anti-birth-control ones, and the defenders [of abortion restrictions] with an effort to enact theological positions into law." But Catholic laypeople didn't just think of abortion as another form of birth control. And that meant the Democratic Party would have to come to terms with the multitudes of pro-life Catholics within its ranks or risk losing them.

On the last day of August in 1976, Democratic presidential nominee Jimmy Carter sat in a suite at the five-star Mayflower Hotel, just a few blocks north of the White House, the only evangelical in a room full of Catholic bishops. A delegation from the National Conference of Catholic Bishops (NCCB) had summoned Carter to grill him on his policy positions. They were led by Joseph Bernardin, then archbishop of Cincinnati and NCCB president; a decade later, Bernardin would be the most vocal Catholic leader pressing the Church to focus on a broad pro-life agenda that wove issues from capital punishment and economic justice to support for disarmament and immigration reform into what he called the "seamless garment of life." But on that muggy, late-summer day, the bishops wanted to talk to Carter about just one issue: abortion.

Heading into the 1976 presidential campaign season, it wasn't obvious which political party would be more receptive to the Catholic

Church's new activism on abortion. In the previous election, Nixon had captured almost 60 percent of the Catholic vote—but that unusual result was more a function of the Democratic Party's off-putting cultural liberalism and the indirect appeal Nixon's Southern Strategy had for urban Catholics on the front lines of racial tensions than it was a reflection of a permanent Catholic shift in political allegiance. The heavily Catholic AFL-CIO chose not to endorse the Democratic ticket in 1972 for the first time in its history, an expression of its disgust with a party famously derided that year as standing for "acid, amnesty, and abortion." Democrats, meanwhile, seemed unable to grasp what had gone wrong. "Our main problem is the blue-collar Catholic worker," George McGovern told journalist Teddy White during the campaign. "You just don't know what would reach them."

After Nixon's resignation, however, it seemed that the reins of power in the GOP might be taken over by Rockefeller Republicans— socially liberal, economically conservative politicians who represented the country-club set. In the Northeast, Democratic politicians— many of whom came from socially conservative, blue-collar Catholic locales—were more likely to be pro-life than their Republican counterparts. The new president, Gerald Ford, seemed to be of that liberal Republican mold. While Ford halfheartedly deflected charges that he was of the pro-choice persuasion, his wife, Betty, was outspoken about her support for abortion rights, celebrating the Supreme Court's judgment in *Roe* as "a great, great decision." In 1975, Ford even approved a federal policy to limit population growth, a move that outraged pro-life activists.

For his part, Carter benefited in the early Democratic primaries from his image as a born-again Christian. While Democratic primary voters are now assumed to be more culturally liberal than the average voter, traditional Catholics were still a powerful voting bloc in the crucial Iowa caucuses in the 1970s. Carter successfully persuaded them that he had taken the strongest stance against abortion of any Democrat in the race, no mean feat given that Sargent Shriver, a pro-life Catholic, was one of his opponents.

But as evangelicals discovered that year as well, Carter's intention to run as a socially conservative candidate hit a wall after he clinched the nomination and Democratic Party leaders stepped in to take charge. Carter worried that traditional tensions between evangelical Protestants and Northern ethnic Catholics would create what he referred to as a "Catholic problem" for his campaign, and he turned to such figures as Notre Dame president Theodore Hesburgh for advice on how to tackle the abortion question. But national Democrats, in a break from the tradition of running to the center during a general election, demanded Carter prove his liberal bona fides *after* he became the nominee. When Bernardin met with Carter aides prior to the Democratic convention, he knew that the party wouldn't be willing to support a constitutional amendment to overturn *Roe v. Wade*. After their talk, however, the archbishop was hopeful that the Democratic Party platform would be neutral and simply avoid the topic of abortion altogether.

He was wrong. The platform—while giving a nod to the existence of "religious and ethical" concerns about abortion—expressed strong opposition to all efforts to "overturn the Supreme Court decision in this area." Bernardin felt betrayed and blamed the inserted language on "intense reaction among pro-abortion lobbying groups." His dismay was echoed by his colleague, the Reverend Robert Deming of the Cathedral of the Immaculate Conception in Kansas City, who had been asked to give the closing benediction for the convention in Madison Square Garden. After considering the invitation, Deming decided he just couldn't do it. Not, he told convention organizers, when he found himself in such opposition to the party's position on abortion.

Republicans did not hesitate to take advantage of the situation. Despite his personal ambivalence about abortion, Ford's advisers convinced him that the only chance he had of beating Carter—who would undoubtedly win a good portion of the South—was to move right on social issues and pick up support from white Catholics. After the Democratic convention, one White House aide wrote a memo urging Ford to take a more aggressive stand on abortion, "now that the Democrats have absolutely rejected and insulted the pro-lifers." Another campaign memo identified as a "target constituency" suburban blue-collar and white-collar workers, "many of whom are Catholics." Soon, Ford was making conspicuous campaign appearances at Catholic events. In August, the president drew a standing ovation from a crowd of one hundred thousand at a Catholic Eucharistic Congress in Philadelphia by declaring his concern about an increasing "irreverence for life" in American society. The Republican candidate also promoted new tax breaks for parents who sent their children to parochial schools, a perennial concern in the Catholic community.

In the third week of September, Ford closed the deal by inviting Bernardin and five other members of the NCCB's executive committee to the White House for a seventy-two-minute meeting. The president, as Carter had, assured the bishops that he shared their moral opposition to abortion. But unlike the Democratic nominee, Ford could point to a plank in the GOP platform that supported the reversal of *Roe* and turned responsibility for abortion back to the states. A few days later, the White House announced that Ford had ordered a study to determine ways to cut the number of federally funded abortions.

Having met with both candidates, the American bishops—who had little more than a decade earlier gone out of their way during JFK's campaign to assure the country they had no interest in impacting national politics—rendered their judgment. After his meeting at the White House, Bernardin declared himself "disappointed" by Carter and "encouraged" by Ford. The NCCB immediately tried to back away from placing weight on those characterizations, but their first lesson of big-time politics was that once spoken, words are no longer your own. *Time* magazine told the country that "the bishops' statement was a clear signal of support for Ford."

During the last weeks of the campaign, Carter faced pro-life protesters everywhere he turned. In Scranton, Pennsylvania, he emerged from a car to greet what he thought was a crowd of supporters only to be swarmed by pro-lifers chanting, "Life! Life! Life!" His closest aides, fearing that the campaign had drifted too far to the left, tried to pull it back to the center and focus on themes like fiscal responsibility and accountable government. In the end, Carter may have been saved by a verbal gaffe from his opponent—in one of their televised debates, Ford declared that Poland was not under Soviet domination. To the many Catholics of Eastern European descent, anticommunism was on a par with opposition to abortion, and Ford sounded insufficiently concerned about the Soviet threat. Carter won the election two weeks later, with 57 percent of the Catholic vote. Republican pollster Robert Teeter concluded that the defection of Catholics of Eastern European descent cost Ford the White House.

The Democratic victory was short-lived. Six months later, giving a commencement speech at Notre Dame, Carter repeated Ford's mistake. The country was now "free of that inordinate fear of communism," he told the audience, implying that human rights had replaced the Cold War as America's top foreign-policy concern. The economy continued to struggle, hitting especially hard in Rust Belt states with high concentrations of Catholic blue-collar workers. By the time of the 1980 election, unemployment had risen to 25 percent in Flint, Michigan—and other industrial cities weren't far behind. The Republicans had a candidate with a solid Irish name whose tough-on-communism stance appealed to disgruntled ethnic Catholics. When the two candidates appeared on the same stage at the Al Smith dinner—an annual fund-raiser hosted by the archbishop of New York to benefit Catholic Charities—just before the election, the crowd embraced Reagan with warm applause. Carter was booed.

Four years later, just a few short weeks before the 1984 presidential election, Reagan appeared at the Al Smith dinner alone. Tensions between the Catholic Church and the Democratic Party had become so strained by that point that Democratic nominee Walter Mondale simply passed up the dinner. With Reagan holding court on the dais by himself, the traditionally bipartisan event took on the feel of a campaign rally. On Election Day, Reagan captured 61 percent of Catholic votes, the largest share that any Republican presidential candidate had ever earned (nor has any GOP candidate matched it since). Surprisingly, it happened in large part because of an attempt on the part of Democrats to appeal to Catholic voters.

After the American bishops' first unsteady foray into presidential politics, they had largely stayed in the background during the 1980 election. They held no meetings with candidates, and in fact the NCCB issued a statement warning against single-issue voting that appeared to downplay the importance Catholic voters should place on a candidate's abortion position.

But that changed in 1984 when Mondale, the former vice president and senator from Minnesota, won the Democratic nomination. The son of a Methodist minister, Mondale was an unreconstructed social-gospel liberal. He was determined to make a statement with his selection of a running mate and was also very conscious that Democrats had lost fifteen points among Catholic voters between 1976 and 1980. So four days before the Democratic National Convention opened in San Francisco, Mondale announced that he had chosen New York congresswoman Geraldine Ferraro, a pro-choice Catholic, to be his vice-presidential candidate.

An ongoing debate had already been brewing within the bishops' conference regarding how much importance should be placed on abortion relative to other political issues. At the same time, the political discussion in Congress had shifted. While many pro-life politicians still wanted to see *Roe v. Wade* overturned, they had largely stopped advocating a constitutional amendment to outlaw abortion—a pragmatic move with which the Church reluctantly agreed—to focus on a more immediate concern: government funding of abortion. The new contours of the debate made life much more difficult for Catholic Democrats, changing the question from whether abortion should be legal to whether taxpayers should pay for procedures they considered immoral and evil. At that moment, the elevation of a pro-choice Catholic Democrat—and a woman, at that—was bound to become a lightning rod.

Sure enough, Ferraro's own archbishop of New York, John O'Connor, immediately went after her. O'Connor had been appointed to his position in January of 1984, one of a new generation of socially conservative Church leaders promoted by Pope John Paul II, for whom abortion was the ultimate moral issue. When it came to the Catholic Church's teaching against abortion, the archbishop stated firmly, "There is no variance, there is no flexibility, there is no leeway." In June 1984, O'Connor made his first foray into the campaign, telling a television interviewer that he did not understand how a Catholic could in good conscience support abortion rights. And then he upped the ante. Asked during the interview if the Church should apply the most extreme punishment and excommunicate pro-choice Catholic politicians, the archbishop refused to rule it out.

The statement sent an electric jolt throughout the Catholic Democratic community. "I did not anticipate," Ferraro later wrote, "that the Archbishop of New York would step out of his spiritual pulpit into the partisan political ring." After all, the last time a Catholic politician's faith had been an issue in a national campaign, it was Protestants raising concerns that John F. Kennedy would be too beholden to the Catholic Church. Now the archbishop was saying a politician might be kicked out of the Church for not advocating Catholic teaching in her public role.

For Mario Cuomo, this was a step too far. The Democratic governor of New York and pro-choice Catholic had been invited by the theology department at the University of Notre Dame to give a lecture on September 13 on the impact of religious faith on individual public officials. Cuomo decided to use the opportunity to push back against O'Connor. In the address, covered by national television networks, Cuomo applied his usual eloquence and thoughtfulness to the question of whether his duties as a Catholic superseded his responsibilities as a public official. Seeking to set himself in the tradition of Kennedy—who declared in his 1960 speech to the Houston Ministerial Association, "I do not speak for my Church in public matters and the Church does not speak for me"—Cuomo declared that he personally considered abortion to be "sinful" and would never encourage his wife or daughters to have one, but that this was his "private" view. As governor, he insisted, he was not obligated to promote laws that reflected Catholic teaching. In fact, Cuomo argued, if he did work to enact Catholic doctrine into law, he would be inappropriately mixing church and state.

The overflow crowd of mostly liberal Catholics at Notre Dame gave Cuomo a standing ovation. The speech was subsequently reprinted in elite publications such as the *New York Review of Books*. And it became the seminal point of reference for liberal Catholics who sought to defend both their religious and political convictions. These Catholics, along with many professional Democrats, considered JFK's Houston speech a foundational text that drew clear lines between a politician's "private" faith and "public" duties. In their minds, Cuomo's speech was a logical expansion of the Kennedy formulation: *My Catholicism doesn't affect my political views, and even if it did, my role as a public official in a democracy prevents me from making decisions based on my religious beliefs.* But JFK's point was precisely the opposite. What Kennedy told the assembly of Protestants ministers was that his Catholicism meant so much to him that if his presidential duties came into conflict with Church teachings, he would resign his position rather than set aside his religious beliefs.

Critics of Cuomo pointed out that he displayed no hesitancy applying his faith to the issue of capital punishment—over his three terms as governor, he vetoed bills that would have brought back New York's death penalty on seven different occasions. In addition, critics charged that Cuomo was trying to turn back the clock for American Catholicism, advocating a return to the quietism that had characterized the Church's immigrant years. Catholics had not come this far simply to be told by one of their own to stay out of politics. Still others were disturbed that Cuomo's well-reasoned defense seemed in the end to dissolve into a throwing up of his hands. "The hard truth," Cuomo had said, "is that abortion is not a failure of government. No agency forces women to have abortions, but abortions go on."

The high-profile shot from Cuomo predictably set off O'Connor, who responded by telling reporters he didn't see how a Catholic could vote for a candidate who favored abortion. When Cuomo asked whether that statement was directed at him or Ferraro, the cardinal somewhat unconvincingly demurred that he hadn't intended to tell voters whether to support or reject any specific candidate.

By the end of September, *Time* magazine noted that "the continuing debate over the proper role of religious leaders in trying to influence public policy and the conflicting pressures on elected officials who hold strong religious beliefs distracted Mondale and Ferraro from their planned campaign strategies." The spat between one of the country's most powerful archbishops and two leaders of the Democratic Party came to define what was already an uphill battle for the Democratic ticket. In late September, O'Connor once again targeted Ferraro when he addressed a pro-life convention in Pennsylvania, telling reporters that the vice-presidential candidate had "said some things about abortion relative to Catholic teaching which are not true." Incensed, Ferraro reached him by phone from Indianapolis to demand O'Connor identify what she had said to upset him. When he admitted that the reference was to a letter Ferraro had sent to other Catholic members of the House two years earlier, in which she had pointed out that Catholic public opinion on abortion was mixed, she accused him of timing his comments to hurt the Democratic campaign.

That same week in September, Ferraro made a campaign stop in Scranton, the same heavily Catholic Pennsylvania town where Jimmy Carter had run into protesters eight years earlier. This time, the local police were so worried about potential violence that they substituted plainclothes officers for volunteer drivers in Ferraro's motorcade and used a state police helicopter to monitor the route to her speech site. Her car moved swiftly past locals carrying angry slogans—FERRARO— A CATHOLIC JUDAS read one; I'M GLAD FERRARO WASN'T MY MOTHER said another, held by a young boy. Ferraro took the issue head-on in her talk, repeating Cuomo's argument that Catholic politicians could not impose their religious views on others. Within an hour of the event, the local bishop held a press conference denouncing Ferraro's attempt to separate her public duties from her religious views as "absolutely ridiculous." A few weeks later, Ferraro had to pull out of the annual Philadelphia Columbus Day parade when Cardinal Krol threatened to withdraw all the marching bands and children from Catholic schools from the celebration.

The *New York Times* ran an editorial coming to Ferraro's defense: "It must be said bluntly. The . . . effort to impose a religious test on the performance of Catholic politicians threatens the hard-won understanding that finally brought America to elect a Catholic politician a generation ago." But what neither the nation's leading newspaper nor the Democratic Party seemed to understand was that seismic political, cultural, and religious changes had taken place between 1960 and 1984. The Kennedy "religion is private" formulation was no longer operative. Abortion, an issue JFK never had to address, had become a legitimate national political concern. American voters were interested not just in candidates' positions on foreign and economic policies, but on moral questions as well. And the Catholic Church was not satisfied to sit quietly in the shadows just to help a Catholic candidate attain national office.

The defeat of Mondale and Ferraro was hardly a shock. Prior to the election, former president Richard Nixon wrote a memo noting of the predicted outcome: "You cannot beat an incumbent President in peacetime if the nation is prosperous." But the scope of the landslide was embarrassing—Mondale won only the District of Columbia and eked out a three-thousand-vote victory in his home state of Minnesota. And the election created a new voter, the "Reagan Democrat," out of the ranks of formerly Democratic Catholics.

Social scientists first identified this new species of voter in Macomb County, Michigan, a collection of Detroit suburbs home to blue-collar, socially conservative, anticommunist Catholic autoworkers. While Reagan won 61 percent of Catholic votes nationally, he picked up a full two-thirds of their support in Macomb County, where just a bare majority of Catholics had supported GOP candidates in the previous two presidential elections (51.2 percent in 1976 and 51.9 percent in 1980). The shift in support was staggering and, if permanent, sounded a death knell for national Democrats.

The outcome emboldened the American bishops in two different ways. First, it provided ammunition for an ongoing internal debate over what the Church's policy priorities should be. And second, it proved the value of targeting high-profile politicians who strayed from Church teaching. One of the unforeseen consequences of Vatican II reforms had been a weakening of the hierarchy's authority over average Catholics, making it harder to enforce Catholic doctrine. The prospect of targeting and making examples of high-profile dissenting Catholics appealed to some bishops in the conference.

Not everyone agreed that abortion should be singled out as the most important focus of the Church or that Catholic politicians should be denounced for their position on abortion but not capital punishment or disarmament or poverty. The tug-of-war between the abortion-first side and those in favor of a broad agenda extended back to the Church's political awakening in the early 1970s, when some nuns and priests grumbled that the energy put into antiabortion efforts was missing on other issues. "There are other issues which need the impetus of the Church, of individual Catholics," one Michigan bishop told political scientist Mary Hanna in 1973. "Prison reform, for example, war, poverty." Indeed, the reason Catholic abortion opponents chose the label *pro-life* and not *antiabortion* for their political movement was to call attention to all of the political concerns related to life.

Cardinal Joseph Bernardin became the Catholic leader most closely associated with this comprehensive approach. Although to his embarrassment he was remembered for his statements during the 1976 presidential election that passed judgment on Carter and Ford solely on the basis of their abortion positions, by the early 1980s Bernardin was the public face of a group of theologians and policy experts who advocated a concept he famously dubbed "a consistent ethic of life." In a 1983 address at Fordham University that made front-page news across the country, Bernardin laid out the contours of the idea, calling on all Catholics to focus on a cluster of issues related to the "sanctity of life," among them disarmament, abortion, and capital punishment. "We intend our opposition to abortion and our opposition to nuclear war to be seen as specific applications of this broader attitude," Bernardin declared. Like-minded intellectuals such as Father J. Bryan Hehir at the NCCB authored a series of influential pastoral letters on economic justice and just war that sought to expand the national Catholic conversation. (In political turnabout, the letters were welcomed by political liberals and fiercely attacked by conservative critics.) At the grass roots, some Catholics were active in the disarmament movement and opposed U.S. involvement in Central America.

But by the end of the 1980s, the debate was over—Bernardin and his compatriots had lost, in part due to the new pope, John Paul II, elected in 1978. The Holy Father issued frequent condemnations of both contraception and abortion, refused to appoint as bishop any priest not willing to defend *Humanae Vitae* and its denunciation of contraception, and spoke vividly later in his papacy of the choice between a "culture of life" and a "culture of death." Abortion also become the main focus of the American Church almost by default as other issues resolved themselves over the decade. The end of the Cold War took away the urgency of the disarmament struggle. Democratically elected governments in Central America diffused the peace movement that had protested Reagan-era involvement in that region. Even on the economic front—perhaps the most consistent subject of Church statements in the nineteenth and twentieth centuries— Catholic intellectual thought was taken over by neoconservatives such as Michael Novak and George Weigel, who argued that capitalism and Catholicism could go hand in hand.

The abortion debate was also effectively over in the Democratic Party by the end of the decade. Liberals had weathered the initial outcry over *Roe v. Wade* and emerged with a majority of the country supporting the legalization of abortion. But they were swiftly losing the public fight over how unfettered access to abortion should be and who should pay for it. By the late 1980s, 62 percent of voters opposed government financing of abortions, with the result that two-thirds of the states had already passed bans or sharp restrictions on abortion funding. One-third of the sixteen states that did subsidize abortions did so only because their state constitutions mandated it. Taxpayer funding of abortion was not a popular stand, but Democrats—having framed the issue as a matter of equity—held to it firmly.

Beleaguered and exhausted from state-by-state battles, Democrats found it hard enough to hold the line against outside attacks without also enduring criticism from within the party. The language of the 1976 platform that acknowledged the "religious and ethical" concerns that led many to oppose abortion had given way to a "you're either with us or against us" mind-set. There was no middle ground. And a growing number of party donors—led by organizations such as EMILY's List, which was established in 1985 with a mission to support pro-choice candidates—were not shy about making it clear that abortion was their litmus test.

The pressure on Democratic politicians went back to 1972, when Michigan Senate candidate Frank Kelly found himself buffeted on one side by Catholics eager to have him declare his opposition to abortion and on the other by women's groups who warned him that if he did so, he would be denounced by Democratic women all over the state. By the 1988 primaries, almost all of the Democratic candidates were men who had renounced pro-life positions. Al Gore and Joe Biden both adopted pro-choice rhetoric for the first time upon deciding to run for president. Jesse Jackson, who used to compare abortion to slavery and denounced those "who argue that the right to privacy is of a higher order than the right to life," converted for his first presidential run in 1984.

Dick Gephardt had perhaps the most dramatic change of heart. A strong abortion opponent when he first entered the House in 1976, Gephardt had written as recently as 1984 that the *Roe* "ruling was unjust, and it is incumbent on the Congress to correct the injustice. I have always been supportive of pro-life legislation. I intend to remain

steadfast on this issue. . . . I believe that the life of the unborn should
be protected at all costs." That steadfastness, however, ran into the reality of Democratic politics. When Gephardt decided in 1986 to run in
the next presidential election, he consulted with some liberal activists—
particularly in the women's community—about how his pro-life
stance might affect his chances. They told him bluntly that a pro-life
Democrat had little chance of capturing the party's nomination.
Shortly after, Gephardt met with the Missouri Citizens for Life and
broke the news to them: he had changed his views and was no longer
pro-life. "When the meeting was over," remembered Loretto Wagner,
the group's president, "there was nothing more to talk about with him.
Ever again."

With abortion firmly established as the number one issue by which
a Catholic public official's performance would be judged—and the
number one issue by which Democratic nominees would be
screened—some Church leaders used their authority to exert pressure
on pro-choice politicians in their jurisdictions. In 1990, Archbishop
Apuron of Guam threatened to excommunicate any Catholic senator
who voted against legislation that would have prohibited abortion
except when the life of the mother was threatened—the most restrictive abortion legislation in any U.S. state or territory. In the same year,
Bishop Reiss of Trenton announced that pro-choice Catholic politicians would be barred from speaking at church-sponsored events, and
Cardinal O'Connor wrote in diocesan newspapers that these same
politicians "must be warned that they are at risk of excommunication."
Mincing no words, Bishop Austin Vaughan of New York piled on,
informing Governor Cuomo that he was "in danger of going to hell if
he dies tonight"—unless, of course, Cuomo changed his stance on
abortion.

Many Catholic politicians tried to avoid becoming targets by maintaining a low profile on abortion. It didn't help that for a number of
years the Washington publication *Congressional Quarterly* singled out
Catholic legislators by placing asterisks next to their names when
recording votes on abortion-related bills. The practice was not used to

identify how Jewish representatives voted on aid to Israel or how African-Americans came down on affirmative action legislation. But it served to solidify the impression that Catholic politicians had a special responsibility when it came to abortion policy.

The Catholic campaign against pro-choice politicians continued throughout the 1990s. In 1996, the retired archbishop of the New Orleans diocese announced that a vote for the Democratic candidate for Senate—the Catholic, pro-choice Mary Landrieu—would be considered a sin. Two years later, Bishop Trautman declared that Catholic politicians who supported abortion rights were unwelcome at church events in his diocese, even denying Republican Pennsylvania governor Tom Ridge access to his church (a rare instance in which a member of the GOP was the target of such pressure).

That same year, the NCCB issued a document called *Living the Gospel of Life,* which explicitly encouraged bishops and priests to take action to sanction pro-choice Catholic politicians. "Catholic public officials who disregard church teaching on the inviolability of the human person indirectly collude in the taking of innocent life," wrote the bishops. "We urge those Catholic officials . . . to consider the consequences for their own spiritual well being, as well as the scandal they risk by leading others into serious sin." *Consider the consequences.* As the *Washington Post* noted at the time, "The bishops' resolution could be construed as an attempt to intimidate those who don't follow the church's teachings."

Even decades after her first run-in with a bishop as a newly elected congresswoman from Connecticut, Rosa DeLauro's eyes well up with tears as she recounts it. For a number of years before running for Congress in 1990, DeLauro served as a trustee for the Catholic high school she had attended as a girl, the Academy of Our Lady of Mercy in Milford. She recalled her experience at the academy as "one of the best times of my life" and was thrilled to have a way to give back to the school. Then DeLauro, a pro-choice Democrat, decided to pursue a congressional seat. "I was told," she remembers, "that my continued presence on the board of trustees would prompt the archbishop to decertify the institution as a Catholic institution."

DeLauro was distraught. For at least part of her tenure as a trustee, she had worked as executive director of the pro-choice fund-raising organization EMILY's List. That had not posed a problem, but her position as a public official apparently did. She went to see the archbishop to plead her case. The school, she argued, trained young women to be leaders, to accomplish great things. Why would the archbishop want to send the message that there were limits to those possibilities? "Let me be perfectly clear," he told DeLauro. "You, Kennedy, Dodd, Moynihan—you are not welcome in the Church."

Unwilling to put her alma mater in jeopardy, DeLauro stepped down from the board. But it was, she soon learned, just the beginning. "All of us deal with this," she says, referring to her Catholic colleagues in Congress. "We get invited by the nuns, the teachers, to give speeches at graduations." But once word about their scheduled appearances reaches Catholic leaders higher up in the hierarchy, those nuns and teachers are often instructed to rescind their invitations. "And then you wait, because the call will come within a day or two of the event to say, 'So sorry, but you can't come.'" DeLauro shakes her head. "You can't come."

When the disinvitations and subtle (or, in some cases, direct) threats started coming their way, some Catholic Democrats fought back, speaking out as Cuomo and Ferraro had. DeLauro's colleague Representative David Obey from Wisconsin recalled "a big shouting match with the good monsignor," a prelate in Madison who "tried to roast me alive because I had the temerity to refuse to vote for legislation that outlawed family planning." But many decided that the best way to survive was to lie low, doing their best not to court conflict with the Church. In some ways, that came naturally. While many Protestants, particularly evangelicals, grow up learning to speak freely about their personal relationship with God, that kind of verbal reflection is just not part of the Catholic tradition. The negative attention that now followed any public discussion of their Catholicism reinforced the instincts of many Catholic Democrats to avoid talking openly about their faith. As a preservation technique, the strategy made sense. But it was a problem for a party that was already largely seen as secular when the elected officials who made up its largest religious bloc stopped talking about religion.

It also made it more difficult for the people who ran the Democratic Party to remember that Catholics were still a key constituency in their electoral coalition, even after the defections in 1984. With Catholicism so universally associated with opposition to abortion, many liberal activists stopped thinking of Catholics as potential political partners, even though they still shared positions on a wide array of domestic and foreign issues such as strong welfare programs and liberal immigration laws. The goodwill that had greeted the bishops' pastoral letters on behalf of economic justice and peace in the early 1980s had vanished by the end of the decade. The Catholic Church was easily caricatured as a bullying institution run by celibate, single men who wanted to impose their moral views on women's reproductive decisions. This belief that Catholicism posed a challenge to women's rights was summed up in the phrase "Keep your rosaries off my ovaries," a popular bumper sticker and chant at pro-choice rallies.

If 1972 holds significance in the collective Catholic memory as the year that Democrats pushed them out of the convention, 1992 is the year that the party refused to let them speak. That year, then Pennsylvania governor—and pro-life Catholic—Bob Casey wrote a letter to the chair of the Democratic National Committee, asking for a chance to address delegates. Casey was a true-blue liberal who lobbied for universal health care in his state and created model child-care programs. The year before, he helped raise $1 million to help Harris Wofford defeat President Bush's attorney general in a special election for the U.S. Senate. Democratic strategist Paul Begala said at the time, "Save for Bob Casey, Harris Wofford would have lost."

But Casey didn't want to talk about health policy or labor issues at the Democratic convention. He wanted, the letter said, to let Americans know that "Democrats do not support abortion on demand and believe that the number of abortions should be reduced."

The theme of the convention that year was "unity and inclusion," but that openness didn't extend to abortion opponents. Casey's letter went unanswered, and the Pennsylvania delegation—one of the party's largest and most important—was seated as far away from the podium as you could possibly get in Madison Square Garden. Compounding the snub, one of Casey's political opponents was brought onstage and honored as a "Republican for choice" during a prime-time segment organized by the National Abortion Rights Action League (NARAL). The clear message to viewers at home was that the Democratic Party prized fealty to the pro-choice position over even party affiliation. And Casey wasn't the only pro-life Democrat conspicuously absent from the festivities. Kansas governor Joan Finney was the first woman to defeat an incumbent governor and won her 1990 campaign despite being outspent $2 million to $300,000. She was, however, also pro-life, and so Finney was excluded from the convention's "Year of the Woman" celebration that highlighted the record number of women holding and running for office in the Democratic Party that year.

Later that fall, Governor Casey was invited by the *Village Voice* to speak at Cooper Union in New York City on the topic "Can a liberal be pro-life?" The newspaper's publisher sponsored the lecture because he said he was "annoyed" by the Democrats' treatment of Casey and thought "it was great for a newspaper that doesn't agree with him . . . to let him give the speech." The topic for the evening of October 2 was apparently a rhetorical question for many of the audience members, however. More than one hundred protesters in the crowd greeted Casey with the chant "Racist, sexist, antigay! Governor Casey, go away!" Eventually, after sitting through thirty-five minutes of full-throated screaming and yelling, Casey relented, and the lecture was canceled.

Democratic leaders defended the decision to deny Casey a speaking slot at the convention by arguing that he hadn't yet endorsed the Clinton/Gore ticket. That was true—but neither had then California governor Jerry Brown, who was nonetheless allowed to address the assembly in Madison Square Garden. Regardless of whether the decision was justified, it was a startlingly stupid public relations move. Vice-presidential candidate Al Gore tried to limit the damage, calling Casey with an abject apology on behalf of the campaign when he learned of the additional insult the Pennsylvania delegation endured. But the damage had been done. As far as pro-life voters, and particularly Catholics, were concerned, the convention had unveiled the true colors of the Democratic Party. The snub soon achieved canonical status in the pro-life community, deepening the perception that Democrats were out of touch, pro-abortion, and intolerant of dissent.

Against this backdrop, Bill Clinton entered the national political stage. Defying conventional wisdom about secular Democrats, the Bible-quoting, Catholic-educated Southern Baptist sought to win back evangelical and Catholic voters who felt alienated by the Democratic Party. But he would face an even greater challenge: convincing his fellow Democrats to take religion seriously.

# CHAPTER 4

# ISAIAH 40:31

## BILL CLINTON'S FAITHFUL PRESIDENCY

All those who have been on the receiving end of the famous Bill Clinton temper know it's an experience they'd rather not repeat. And on the morning of August 30, 1993, Clinton was irate. Downstairs in the East Room of the White House, several hundred religious leaders from across the country were gathering for a breakfast that the president's staff had organized while he was away on vacation on Martha's Vineyard. Gripped in one presidential hand was the text one of his speechwriters had drafted for the occasion. In the other was a list of the morning's attendees. The more Clinton looked at each sheet of paper, the angrier he got. It was wrong. All wrong.

Unlike many of his colleagues in the Democratic Party, Clinton wasn't unnerved by the prospect of addressing a roomful of clerics. Barely six months into his first term, the Southern Baptist had already made religion a prominent part of his political and personal life. He had chosen the label "The New Covenant"—a richly significant biblical phrase—for his 1992 campaign platform. Just a few weeks after moving into the White House, he had hosted a private dinner for Billy Graham, whose preaching he credited for the "come to Jesus" moment he had experienced as a young boy in Arkansas. When it came to religion, Clinton could go toe-to-toe with anyone—whether over Scripture quotations, Catholic doctrine, or Jewish teaching.

The crowd waiting for him, however, was not just anyone. It was a carefully culled group of 250 "safe" religious leaders chosen without his consultation by White House aides, who narrowly defined Democratic religious supporters as mainline Protestants, black pastors, and Jewish leaders. Precious few were representatives of Clinton's own evangelical tradition or from the Catholic Church. Clinton understood that the previous three Democratic nominees had failed to win the presidency in part because the party had simply stopped trying to reach out to those two major religious communities. He also knew that critics would seize on the unrepresentative guest list as proof that the Clinton White House was just Democratic politics as usual: religious moderates and conservatives not welcome.

Religion was too important an issue to screw up or treat cavalierly, and now Clinton wanted to know who was to blame for assembling this particular group. Ironically, it was the first lady who had inadvertently gotten the ball rolling before they left for vacation with an off-hand comment about how they should include more religious leaders at White House events. Thinking it would be a nice surprise, eager-to-please aides had put together a faith breakfast for the Clintons' first day back at the White House without "bothering" either of them. Not until approximately 6 a.m. on the morning of the gathering did the president see the final list of invitees, and when he did, he went ballistic. Bypassing the White House operator, Clinton picked up the phone himself and placed a call to a friend he thought might have been consulted on the planning. "I'm looking at this list," he yelled at her, "and I see a lot of missing names. Where is everyone? Who put this together?" A few minutes later, her phone rang again. "The president just called me," said White House chief of staff Mack McLarty, adding in his typically dry manner, "It wasn't the list he had in mind, shall we say."

Nor was the text the White House speechwriting shop had prepared for him what the president wanted to read. Pacing the second-floor residence, Clinton flipped through the sheets of feel-good pabulum about how much religious communities have enriched society, blah, blah, blah, and exploded again. "This is ridiculous!" he sputtered, tossing the speech aside. At the other end of the hall, the first lady huddled with a senior adviser, trying to get her own answers about what had gone wrong. Before they crowded into the elevator to descend to the East Room, Clinton grabbed a copy of *The Culture of Disbelief*, a book by Yale law professor Stephen Carter that he had picked up at a bookstore on Martha's Vineyard and devoured soon after. "I know what I'm going to talk about," he announced to no one in particular.

Downstairs, the president cleaned his plate of scrambled eggs and calmed down a bit over chitchat with his table companions, including Joan Brown Campbell, general secretary of the National Council of Churches. Then he rose to address the group of religious leaders and denominational representatives. He began by praising Carter's book, a volume that had attracted middling attention up to that point (thereafter it became a best seller on the strength of that coveted White House endorsement) for the controversial argument that liberalism had an "intolerant" secular mind-set. Referring to his job as a "ministry," Clinton reminded those in the room that freedom of religion "doesn't mean that those of us who have faith should not frankly admit that we are animated by that faith, that we try to live by it, and that it does affect what we feel, what we think." Sounding much like a Republican president would eight years later, Clinton added that some policy problems could not be solved by secular solutions alone: "You cannot change somebody's life from the outside in unless there is also some change from the inside out."

The idea that religion could be a force for good in individuals' lives—and perhaps even provide a salve for some social ills—was not new to Clinton. But he was becoming keenly aware that this understanding that he had always taken for fact might be a radical thought to many within his party and perhaps even to members of his own staff. "Sometimes," he mused aloud to the audience, "I think the environment in which we operate is entirely too secular." *Damn it,* Clinton seemed to be thinking, *apparently if I want this done right, I'm going to have to do it myself.* After the event, the president made plans to set up two additional meetings that fall—the first with a handful of leaders from his own conservative Southern Baptist denomination, and the other with more moderate evangelicals, a constituency most Democrats had forgotten ever existed.

The event—and Clinton's off-the-cuff talk—was basically well received by the national media. On September 5, the editors of the *Los Angeles Times* wrote an editorial giving the Clintons "credit . . . for diving into the fray," noting that "through their interest in the tricky confluence of private beliefs and public actions, they in effect have begun to challenge the idea that discussion of values has to be ceded as the exclusive province of the so-called religious right." But as Clinton had anticipated, skeptics seized on the fact that the audience was predominantly drawn from the ranks of religious liberals. "Judging from the invitation and attendance lists at the President's interfaith breakfast," the conservative Catholic scholar George Weigel wrote elsewhere in the *Los Angeles Times,* "the Clinton White House seems blissfully unaware that the religious left is a dried-up husk and that the growing sectors of religion in this country are evangelical Protestantism and Roman Catholicism."

Seven years later, Bill Clinton would leave the White House as the most overtly religious president the country had ever seen, a man who could quote biblical passages chapter and verse, and who insisted his staff work with religious communities across the ideological and theological spectra. His aides would put together a religious outreach operation that surpassed even Republican efforts in its sophistication and breadth. The policies of the Clinton administration would have a greater impact on religious freedom and liberty than any of his predecessors' going back to James Madison. And yet for all these achievements, the president could never convince his party to take religion—and religious voters—seriously. When he left office, Clinton's approach to religion left with him.

Democrats weren't used to having a president who got mad because his aides didn't take religion seriously enough. Then again, Democrats weren't used to having a president of their own, period. Nothing focuses the mind of a party like three consecutive losing presidential campaigns, and after 1988, Democrats were willing to take a chance on a Bible-quoting, saxophone-playing centrist over a slew of more traditionally liberal candidates.

Democrats hadn't yet reached that point following Reagan's reelection in 1984. They were depressed, not desperate, and despite the landslide defeat, the party was not prepared to change course. That isn't to say that some leaders in the party didn't try. Soon after the election, the Democratic National Committee commissioned a nationwide survey of five thousand Americans, as well as a series of focus groups, to determine why the party had lost its appeal. The results were not surprising, but they were controversial. According to a report prepared for the DNC, the greatest loss of support came from middle-class whites in the South and ethnic Catholics in the North who no longer felt the Democratic Party represented their economic interests or social values. On the economic front, it seemed, Democrats had erred by not changing their policies even as their core voters moved up the income ladder. The ideas and arguments of the War on Poverty continued to dominate Democratic rhetoric and left voters skeptical about the party's ability to represent the economic interests of the middle class. But on social issues, Democrats had changed too much, assuming a combative stance in favor of abortion and gay rights that was not always shared by these same traditional voters. "The white ethnic voter is accurate," read the report, "when he says that the Democratic party left him." As far as the focus group participants were concerned, the Democratic Party of their past had been taken hostage by liberal extremists and special interest groups.

None of this was news to anyone who had read the election results. But for Democratic leaders who had to work with those "liberal extremists" and special interest groups, the conclusions were too sensitive to release. The DNC officials who read the report decided to suppress it, destroying all but a few bootleg copies and withholding its findings even from other DNC members.

The underlying challenges for the party, however, weren't going to go away without some attention. And since every problem needs a commission or a committee, in 1985 DNC chair Paul Kirk established the Democratic Policy Commission. The group of one hundred elected officials from all levels of government was charged with reviewing Democratic issue positions and then developing a midterm policy platform for the party, preferably one that wouldn't scare away potential voters. Over the next two years, the commission convened five meetings around the country to consider different policy areas. The most controversial was a gathering in Salt Lake City in the spring of 1986 on the subject of family and community issues. There the commission heard from an expert on the problems of the Democratic Party—William Galston, the former issues director for the Mondale campaign. Galston, who was also a political scientist, argued that family issues had become a liability for Democrats. "We are not seen as responsive to the needs of the family," he told the commissioners. "We are seen as the party of individual rights, but not the party of individual responsibility. We are seen as the party of self-expression, but not the party of self-discipline." Among Galston's recommendations was for Democrats to express respect for religion and for stay-at-home mothers.

Over the previous two decades, liberals had taken extremely worthy positions—equal rights and opportunities for women (including reproductive freedom), civil rights for racial minorities, acceptance of homosexuality, and a willingness to acknowledge that the model of a nuclear family no longer described many American households—and raised them to the level of doctrinal fetishes. Support of equal rights for women quickly morphed into a pro-choice litmus test for presidential nominees. Celebration of civil rights for minorities somehow resulted in opposition to any attempts at reforming the welfare system. Instead of developing a political philosophy that balanced individual rights against the common good, liberal Democrats had replaced communitarianism with individualism, at least in the social sphere. They believed that people had economic responsibilities to each other that required them to support a minimum wage, welfare programs, and efforts to hold corporations accountable. But liberals drew the line at acknowledging the effect personal actions had on the community. Choices, they insisted, were private and sacrosanct. The days of William Jennings Bryan, when progressive populists believed in economic *and* social communitarianism, were long gone.

Liberals' defense of hard-earned individual rights often prevented them from confronting—or even acknowledging—other social problems. The social turbulence of the 1960s and '70s had resulted in positive changes for many Americans, but had also given rise to a number of troubling developments. By the late 1980s, divorce rates had soared, teen pregnancies had increased, and family stability was at an all-time low. Without public policy changes to accompany the growth in two-parent working families, more children were unsupervised for more hours of the day. And a general coarsening of popular culture—another unanticipated consequence of relaxed social norms—meant that those children were exposed to higher levels of profanity, sex, and violence on television and in movies. Conservatives jumped at the chance to blame these trends on liberals, and were particularly eager to lay every negative social indicator at the feet of the women's movement.

But as liberals rightly rejected those charges, they too often went in the opposite direction and denied that there was a problem at all. Tipper Gore learned this lesson in 1985 when she took on the music industry, calling for voluntary labels on albums that had "explicit lyrics or content." It was a sensible request for busy parents who didn't have time to prescreen every track in their kids' music libraries. But even as polls showed that a majority of Americans shared Gore's concerns about the messages in rock music and supported the idea of labeling albums, she was accused of advocating censorship and widely ridiculed for her "prudish" sensibilities. Musician Frank Zappa derided Gore's campaign as an "ill-conceived housewife hobby project," while Dave Barry joked that "the obvious solution, of course, would be to make it illegal for Tipper" to purchase "record albums without a federal guidance counselor." Gore's efforts were even immortalized in song, albeit with lyrics that required one of her labels. On his 1989 album *Free of Speech,* Ice-T rapped, "Yo Tip, what's the matter? You ain't gettin' no dick? You're bitchin' about rock 'n' roll, that's censorship, dumb bitch."

The criticism didn't stop Gore from founding the Parents Music Resource Center and eventually extracting cooperation from the recording industry. But it did prompt her husband to make a pilgrimage to Hollywood in a wink-wink-it's-just-my-wife gesture before he launched his 1988 bid for the White House.

When it came time for Democrats to select a nominee to go up against George H. W. Bush, they went with the proudest liberal in the bunch. Michael Dukakis had supported abortion rights since he first took public office in the 1960s and was a thoroughly modern secular Democrat. Although culturally Greek Orthodox, Dukakis married outside the Church and did not raise his children in a religious tradition. "None of us is very religious," his wife, Kitty, explained to a reporter in 1987, an admission that struck her and most everyone else in the Dukakis camp as unremarkable. Indeed, when asked which book most influenced him, Dukakis usually mentioned Henry Steele Commager's *The American Mind,* which argued that religion was fundamentally irrational and that real Americans were pragmatic and secular.

Dukakis's secularism made it painfully difficult for him to connect with religious audiences. Vernon Jordan once told journalist Marjorie Williams about a speech the Dukakis campaign asked him to review before the governor spoke to the National Baptist Convention, the nation's oldest and largest African-American religious delegation. "And so I get it," Jordan told her, "and I read it and I call them back and they say, 'What do you think?' and I say, 'You all ever heard of *Jesus?*' They say, 'What do you mean?' . . . I said, 'This speech quotes John Winthrop five times. John Winthrop doesn't mean *anything* to forty thousand black Baptists.'"

But at least Dukakis tried to talk to black Baptists. In 1988, the Dukakis campaign became the first in Democratic history to turn down all invitations to appear at Catholic universities. With the dust-ups of 1984 fresh in their minds, Dukakis advisers feared that abortion protesters would disrupt the events and that attempts to reach out to Catholics would backfire. What they didn't notice was that Catholic leaders had far less interest in targeting a Greek Orthodox than one of their own coreligionists. Nor did anyone on his campaign realize that Dukakis's opposition to capital punishment and support for social welfare programs actually held appeal for Catholic audiences. In 1972, McGovern and his allies hadn't known what to say to Catholic voters. By 1988, Democrats had just stopped talking to them.

Republicans could not have been more thrilled. Bush was an old-school New England preppy, an Episcopalian who had to swallow hard to tell South Carolinians that "Jesus Christ is my personal savior" to beat back the surging primary campaign of televangelist Pat Robertson. Bush was famously unable to estimate the price of milk and set eyes rolling when he marveled over the UPC scanner gizmo at a supermarket—the vice president had clearly not done his own shopping for years. Any reasonably populist Democrat would have posed a serious challenge to the vice president. But in choosing the wooden, secular, technocratic Dukakis, Democrats had found that rare politician who actually made Bush seem in touch with average Americans.

As a result, the Bush campaign not only neutralized the cultural liabilities of its own candidate, but created serious problems for the Democrats. In their hands, Dukakis's veto of a bill requiring public-school children to recite the Pledge of Allegiance and his membership in the American Civil Liberties Union became evidence of sinister secular plots, largely because the legalistic, detached way in which the governor spoke about them made such accusations plausible. If anything, Dukakis seemed befuddled that his connection to the ACLU was a campaign issue at all. Evangelicals, however, had not forgotten that organization's role in bringing the Scopes case to trial, and the Bush campaign exploited that bitter memory. In November, more than three-quarters of evangelical voters cast their ballots for Bush, putting him over the top and keeping the White House in Republican hands.

Three years later, Bill Clinton stormed onto the national political scene, knocking askew assumptions about the political parties and religion. A big Labrador of a politician, Clinton had an innate feel for the culture and faith of Middle America that put both Dukakis *and* Bush to shame. Clinton sought out the Catholic audiences Dukakis had avoided. He ad-libbed his speeches to religious crowds, drawing on a deep familiarity with the Bible. If Dukakis and Bush were model Northeastern secularists, Clinton was a genuine Southern evangelical.

The young governor had been raised in Arkansas by a mother who only occasionally attended church herself. Every Sunday morning as a boy, Clinton would get dressed up and walk down the street to Park Place Baptist in Hot Springs on his own. After a youth minister took a group to hear Billy Graham preach, Clinton started sending part of his allowance to the Billy Graham Crusade, sometimes sneaking around the block to mail the envelope because he didn't think his stepfather would approve. For college, Clinton attended Georgetown University, a Catholic school that nurtured his fascination with a broad range of religious traditions. Clinton so immersed himself in the study of Catholic theology that one of his philosophy professors, Father Otto Hentz, asked whether he had considered becoming a Jesuit. (The future president admitted he might have a problem with the whole celibacy requirement.) And Clinton would always tell friends that his favorite undergraduate course was Religions of the World.

As the attorney general—and later governor—of Arkansas, Clinton got to know the Pentecostals who gathered every summer in the northwest corner of the state and attended each of their annual camp meetings from 1977 until he ran for president. (For the church service that precedes each presidential inauguration, Clinton selected the Scripture passages and hymns himself and brought some of his Pentecostal friends to Washington to sing.) In Little Rock, Clinton worshipped at the theologically conservative Immanuel Baptist rather

90

than the town's progressive Baptist church. Although educated at Oxford and Yale, Clinton remained thoroughly Southern in his approach to religion, a man who unashamedly described himself to ABC News in the second year of his presidency as "a person who has sinned, as a child of God, who has sought forgiveness, searched for redemption, and is struggling to grow and struggling to find the guidance of God in this job."

Democrats had seen religious candidates before. Gary Hart, the senator from Colorado, and Al Gore, then a senator from Tennessee, ran for the Democratic nomination in 1988; both were personally religious and had studied at divinity school. But both were creatures of Washington and had been socialized into politics at a time when Democrats just didn't talk about religion. Jimmy Carter was a Southern Baptist and an outsider like Clinton, but even he wasn't as effortlessly open about his faith. Nor was Carter able to maintain his cultural conservatism under pressure from the liberal party apparatus. Clinton, by contrast, thought he had discovered a way to talk about Middle American values without abandoning Democratic core principles.

In 1989, a San Diego bishop barred Lucy Killea, a California state assemblywoman, from taking Communion because she supported abortion rights. In a letter to Killea, the bishop told her that her views amounted to "a grave scandal against the Church." A local ruckus ensued as Killea fought back. In the midst of it all, Sam Popkin, a political scientist at the University of California–San Diego, contacted Killea with a suggestion for how she could frame her position on abortion to reflect the fact that she didn't celebrate abortion for its own sake. Up until that point, abortion rights supporters had always described their goal as keeping abortion "safe and legal." What if, Popkin said, Killea instead declared that she wanted abortion to be "legal, safe, and rare"?

Killea used the line in her reelection campaign in 1990, and it worked. So the next fall, Popkin sent a note to Hillary Clinton, whose husband had just announced he was running for president. Before long, Popkin received a response from Mrs. Clinton, who thanked him and said that they were already using the line, with one small modification: she had switched the order to "safe, legal, and rare." Bill Clinton rolled out the slogan at the Florida straw poll in December 1991, where he came under attack from women's groups because of a parental notification law that he had signed as governor. "Safe, legal, and rare" hardly eased their concerns, nor did it satisfy pro-life activists who noted that the governor had backed away from his earlier antiabortion views. But the line did describe the position most Americans held about abortion—they didn't like it, but they didn't want to outlaw it. Making abortion rare seemed like a good goal to them.

Clinton won the straw poll. And in an odd twist of fate, he managed to avoid the kind of further scrutiny of his abortion position that might have hamstrung his campaign when the media—and the rest of the country—became distracted by stories about Gennifer Flowers, possible draft-dodging, and the crucial question of whether he'd ever inhaled marijuana. By the time Clinton emerged, bruised and battered but with the nomination in hand, the new approach to abortion was part of his platform. The Clinton strategy didn't change the Democratic Party's general discomfort with pro-life views. The decision by organizers of the 1992 Democratic National Convention to deny pro-life Pennsylvania governor Bob Casey a speaking spot was evidence of that. But Clinton used his podium to set a different tone. "I am not pro-abortion," the nominee told the crowd in Madison Square Garden and a national television audience in his acceptance speech. "I am pro-choice."

At a breakfast meeting the next morning, a brigade of prominent women leaders went after his top advisers, including Mandy Grunwald, Dee Dee Myers, Stanley Greenberg, and George Stephanopoulos. The women were outraged over Clinton's speech and what they heard as an insufficient commitment to abortion rights. They demanded that the campaign dial back the "safe, legal, and rare" rhetoric. Finally, an African-American woman in the back spoke up. "I don't know what the women you represent are into," she said, addressing her fellow activists, "but in my community, they're a lot more pro-life. And they're a lot more concerned about other issues. They don't wake up in the morning and say, 'My goodness, there's a threat to my right to have an abortion.' They wake up saying, 'My kid's going to get shot or I need a job or I need health care.'"

The operating assumption of the Clinton campaign was that there were more voters like the ones the woman at the breakfast had described, and that Democrats hadn't been connecting with them. By implying that abortion should be less prevalent, Clinton signaled that those who didn't want to outlaw abortion could have moral qualms about it. This created an opening for Catholics and evangelicals who supported Democratic policies on the economy or education or health care, but who weren't comfortable with a party they saw as aggressively pro-choice. While the Dukakis campaign had turned down invitations to appear at Catholic schools because they knew that many Catholics were upset with his position on abortion, Clinton's approach gave him a starting point for talking to these voters. And when the University of Notre Dame invited him to speak on campus in the last month of the campaign, Clinton eagerly accepted.

On September 11, nearly eight years to the day from Mario Cuomo's historic address, Clinton gave a speech at Notre Dame's Stepan Center that the New York Times described as "at times confessional and at times like a homily to the converted." Clinton stressed his ties to Catholicism—"I felt completely at home in the Catholic tradition of Georgetown"—and staked a claim for Democratic "family values," a phrase much beloved by GOP politicians. "I want an America that does more than talk about family values," declared Clinton. "I want an America that values families" by supporting family-leave legislation, creating jobs, and establishing a living wage. Events elevated the importance of the speech—that same day, President George H. W. Bush addressed the Christian Coalition, and just a few weeks earlier, the Republican National Convention had featured speakers who all but declared a holy war against Democrats and liberals. The Clinton campaign hoped to appeal to religious moderates who were turned off by the angry rhetoric coming out of the GOP.

In late October, after a campaign stop in Saginaw, Michigan, Clinton returned to the subject of his faith in an expansive interview with Patricia Zapor, a reporter from Catholic News Service, the official media arm of the U.S. Catholic Conference. As the two of them talked in a corner of the Tri-City Airport, famished campaign aides chowed down on sandwiches and waited for yet another flight to yet another small town. No one paid attention to the candidate, who, as it happened, was musing aloud about the dual influence of his Baptist heritage and Catholic schooling.

"From my Southern Baptist heritage," Clinton began, "I have a deep belief that the First Amendment separation between church and state is what guarantees the religious freedom of all people. That's something that's really deeply ingrained in the history of the Baptist Church in America, going back to its founding." Catholics, as Clinton knew, have a much more complicated approach to the church/state relationship. So, warming to the topic, he shrewdly pivoted to draw a distinction that favored Catholics. The experience of studying at Georgetown, Clinton told Zapor, taught him "that we are morally obliged to try to live out our religious convictions in the world, that our obligation to social mission is connected to religious life. . . . That I got out of my Catholic training more than from the Baptist Church, which is much more rooted in the notion that salvation is a matter of personal relationship between an individual and God and carries with it no necessary burden to go out into the world and do things." Clinton's comfort in both evangelical and Catholic milieus was so apparent from the interview that conservatives complained its publication had unfairly made the Democrat "palatable" for Catholics.

On Election Day, Clinton captured a plurality of Catholics, making him the first Democrat since Jimmy Carter in 1976 to win the Catholic vote. Evangelicals also migrated away from the GOP; Bush lost twenty points among evangelical voters between 1988 and 1992. In the end, it was unclear whether a Democratic ticket of two Southern Baptists who believed abortion should be more rare had neutralized dire warnings about a cultural Armageddon—or whether a failing economy, basement-level approval ratings, and a crazy Texas third-party candidate—had doomed Bush's reelection hopes. The result was the same: Democrats were back in the White House for the first time in twelve years.

In case anyone missed the signs during the campaign, Clinton made it immediately clear after the election that he was a different sort of Democrat. Although he'd earned just 28 percent of the evangelical vote, the president-elect wasted no time going after that constituency. In January 1993, before the first family even moved to Washington, a group of about ten evangelical leaders—including nationally known figures such as Max Lucado and Adrian Rogers—arrived at the Governor's Mansion in Little Rock for a luncheon with the president-elect. In Arkansas, evangelicals voted for Democrats all the time—heck, most Democrats *were* evangelicals. But that clearly wasn't the case at the national level, and Clinton wanted to rehabilitate the relationship. "I thought it would be helpful to have an informal discussion with them," he wrote in his memoir, "so that at least I'd have some lines of communication into the evangelical community." Clinton was particularly impressed by a young minister from outside Chicago named Bill Hybels, who had founded one of the first megachurches in the country, Willow Creek Community Church. The two held conflicting positions on sensitive issues such as abortion and gay rights, but discovered that their areas of agreement—from antipoverty programs to fixing welfare to reducing partisanship—were far more numerous. They agreed to keep in touch.

That pastoral relationship would be more important than Clinton had anticipated once he and his family relocated to the nation's capital. Not long after arriving, he told friends that it was the most secular city he'd ever lived in. In that first difficult year, the Clintons needed more than just secular comfort. Aside from the political troubles— botched cabinet nominations, a contentious policy regarding gays in the military—that consumed the first few months of Clinton's term, the first family had a personally wrenching year. Within just a few months, Mrs. Clinton's father died, the couple's close personal friend and counselor Vince Foster committed suicide, and Clinton's mother had a relapse of the cancer that would kill her in early 1994. On April 6, 1993, the day before her father passed away, Mrs. Clinton gave a speech in which she grappled with the spiritual vacuum of modern life and called for a "politics of meaning." The remarks earned her ridicule in the press, most notably in a *New York Times Magazine* cover story that depicted "Saint Hillary" as a moralizing shrew.

Far from their church communities in Little Rock, the Clintons needed to create new networks of spiritual support. They found a welcoming congregation at Foundry Methodist Church, a mile north of the White House on Sixteenth Street—Chelsea Clinton soon became a fixture at youth-group meetings and choir practices, and the whole family slipped in during the first hymn on most Sundays. Every Saturday night, Clinton spoke and prayed by phone with Rex Horne, his pastor back in Little Rock. Along with Tipper Gore, Mrs. Clinton attended a women's prayer luncheon hosted by Doug Coe, a well-connected evangelical known as the "stealth Billy Graham," who organized the annual National Prayer Breakfast. Some of the women there invited the first lady to join their bipartisan prayer group of a dozen women, including Susan Baker, the wife of former Reagan chief of staff James Baker. One of the members faxed daily Scripture readings to Mrs. Clinton throughout the eight years that she was in the White House.

As for the president, his new friend Bill Hybels had been having trouble getting through the White House gatekeepers, who weren't sure that a phone call from a pastor in Illinois merited presidential attention. Hybels managed to get access to Clinton when the president passed through Chicago in the spring of 1993 and gave him some intelligence from the evangelical world: James Dobson, the head of Focus on the Family and a religious right heavyweight who was already no fan of Clinton's, was upset. A White House aide had blown off a request from his wife's National Day of Prayer organization. "You need someone who knows these people and can be your eyes and ears with them," Hybels told him. Clinton knew just the person.

Linda Lader met the Clintons in the early 1980s at Renaissance Weekend, an invitation-only retreat held over New Year's that she and her husband had founded and ran. With an impeccable evangelical pedigree—her father was editor of the popular Christian magazine *Guideposts,* her stepmother authored the best-selling Christian novel *Christie,* and Lader herself spent years working on the National Prayer Breakfast—she had exactly the contacts that Clinton needed. When Clinton approached Lader in the late spring of 1993, however, she responded with two requests of her own. The first was that she did not want to be an official part of the White House staff; she would help Clinton, but only as an informal liaison to the evangelical world. And in a display of her political savvy, Lader also demanded access to Clinton through his personal assistant, Nancy Hernreich, bypassing the legions of junior aides who would shuffle religion-related requests to the bottom of the pile. Clinton agreed and gave Lader her first task: getting a monthly meeting with Hybels on Clinton's schedule.

Six months later, the faith-breakfast debacle his aides organized was a wake-up call for Clinton, convincing him that religious outreach might require more than his own personal relationships with pastors and a deputized friend. Because Lader wasn't part of the White House staff, it hadn't occurred to other aides to run religious issues by her. Lader was out of the loop on the breakfast planning, learning of the event just in time to add a handful of names to the guest list.

In the fall of 1993, Clinton and Lader worked to minimize fallout in the evangelical community by setting up two separate meetings. The first, on September 16, was a tense gathering with heavyweights from the Southern Baptist Convention. Vice President Gore, a Southern Baptist as well, joined the meeting, at which most of the SBC leaders insisted on talking only about abortion and gay rights. To their surprise, they found that Clinton could quote all of the relevant Bible verses on the two topics, even though the conclusions he reached were not the same as theirs. More than a few left with grudging respect for his religious knowledge.

A few weeks later, Clinton held a sprawling breakfast discussion with a dozen figures from the world of moderate evangelicalism—holdovers from the old neo-evangelical days. David Neff, editor of the center-right magazine *Christianity Today,* suggested names for the gathering, which included Fuller Theological Seminary president Richard Mouw, popular evangelical speaker Tony Campolo, and Philip Yancey, the best-selling author of *Disappointment with God* and other Christian books. Clinton aides were startled to hear Wheaton College professor Mark Noll tell the president that his daughter led the Young Democrats chapter at Wheaton. She regularly defended Clinton to her classmates, Noll said, arguing that his policies regarding health care, budget priorities, and foreign policy were "pro-life." They were also pleasantly surprised by the remarks of pro-life, anti-gay-rights pastor Jack Hayford of the Church of the Way, whose inclusion in the breakfast group had initially worried them. As journalist Fred Barnes later reported, Hayford shared a revelation when it was his turn to talk, telling the others that the morning after Clinton was elected, "God flooded his heart with love for [the president]."

When Clinton bade farewell to the group, he told Campolo to call when he was in Washington. The evangelical took the remark to be a passing nicety, only to receive a disappointed phone call from the White House the next time he was in the nation's capital: "I thought you were going to let me know when you were in town!" The seriousness of Clinton's request properly impressed upon him, Campolo became another spiritual mentor to the president, making regular sojourns to the White House to pray with him.

At times, it was hard to remember who was the minister and who was the president. Shortly after Thanksgiving, Clinton convened yet another breakfast with religious leaders to discuss how their communities were responding to the HIV/AIDS crisis. At the end of the conversation, a pastor from Grand Rapids named Ed Dobson asked if the president would close the meeting with a prayer. During the 1980s, Dobson had served as a deputy to the Moral Majority's Jerry Falwell. If he had expected Clinton to hesitate at the request, he was mistaken. Without delay, the president clasped the hands of the leaders on either side of him in his meaty grip and bowed his head. "Heavenly Father," began Clinton, with all the ease of a Baptist who has led prayers for most of his life.

By the end of the year, Clinton asked his head of public liaison, Alexis Herman, to establish a religious liaison division within her office to complement the work of Linda Lader. The request represented a first for Democratic politics. While both the Reagan and Bush White Houses included operations to maintain relationships with faith communities, the Democratic Party had never had any institutionalized way to reach out to religious leaders. Starting from scratch, Herman brought in Flo McAfee, a longtime public relations expert and devout Episcopalian, to set up and run the first Democratic religious outreach effort. McAfee did her homework, studying how Republican liaison offices had worked, making notes on successful strategies and suggesting tweaks where she deemed them necessary. She decided that a Democratic White House could not get away with publicizing its religious events as much as Republicans had without risking accusations that it was trying to leverage religion for political gain. In addition, just as Clinton aides had erred by largely limiting the first faith breakfast to religious liberals, McAfee learned that the invitation lists from Reagan and Bush were heavily tilted toward religious conservatives. She decided that the Clinton White House would be open to all religious comers. If Ralph Reed and his compatriots at the Christian Coalition didn't want to show up to their events, that was fine—but they were on the list.

Above all, the religion outreach strategy was to engage and, by engaging, to neutralize some of the knee-jerk opposition to Democrats from more conservative religious communities. "There is always some issue we can come together on" was Clinton's mantra, repeated often to aides. The president's optimistic attitude was due in part to his famous need to be liked and his confidence that if he could just get people to sit down in the same room with him, he could win them over. But it was also based on his experience of knowing there usually *was* something to agree on. The tough part was getting people to talk to you in the first place.

Melanne Verveer, the first lady's chief of staff and an old college friend of Clinton's who often acted as his go-between with the Catholic community, remembers the president putting his strategy to use in a meeting with the Catholic bishops at the White House. "Obviously, there was disagreement on an issue," she admits, referring to abortion. "But Clinton said, 'Hey, I agree with these guys most of the time.' And sure enough, when they sat down and had a conversation, they were completely taken aback." The discussion wended its way through areas of Catholic social teaching, philosophical understandings, and Church doctrine, and though White House aides pointedly looked at their watches, hoping to get Clinton to wrap it up, he stayed put. "We ought to do this more often," he told the bishops when the meeting did finally draw to a close. "They probably surprised themselves," Verveer says, "by saying, 'Yeah, we're enjoying it, too.' They had no idea the depth of his convictions."

Catholics were at the policy table in the Clinton White House, giving aides their input on issues ranging from immigration to welfare reform to health care (all those Catholic hospitals were teeming with useful insights). Sometimes the mutual respect that had formed allowed the two sides to quickly resolve tensions that might otherwise have festered. As Mrs. Clinton prepared to represent the United States at the United Nations Conference on Women in 1995, Verveer heard rumblings that the Catholic Conference might condemn the first lady's trip because of her support for reproductive rights. So Verveer preempted the criticism. "A group of us went over to the Catholic Conference offices and said, 'Wait a minute,'" she remembers. "'There may be disagreement over this one issue, but what about everything else the conference is going to address—from poverty alleviation to economic opportunity to education? Why would you just blast everything?'" At the conference in Beijing, Mrs. Clinton's speech was a hit. The hall erupted in cheers and she got a standing ovation. That included the delegates from the Vatican, one of whom approached the first lady to say, "Mrs. Clinton, that could have been our speech."

The Clinton administration also worked to establish strong ties with evangelical leaders, bringing in board members from the National Association of Evangelicals (NAE) for briefings with National Security Adviser Sandy Berger on the administration's efforts to prevent religious persecution overseas, and inviting prominent evangelicals to state dinners. After the first faith breakfast, Clinton reviewed every guest list and often penciled in the names of specific religious leaders who needed to be included. National Association of Evangelicals vice president Richard Cizik recalls one day in 1996 when he and a colleague stopped by the White House to drop off a copy of their organization's soon-to-be-released policy statement, "just to give them a heads-up." On their way out of the White House, Cizik says Herman came running after them. "The next thing I knew, someone was straightening my tie, and we were in the Oval Office. I've never even been invited to the Bush White House."

Evangelicals such as Cizik also found the Clinton White House more committed to working on issues of religious freedom and liberty than any previous administration. Clinton's Baptist identity played a major role in those efforts—Baptists place special importance on protecting religious liberty (the Baptist Joint Committee for Religious Liberty and the Ethics & Religious Liberty Commission are two of the most active religious organizations in Washington). Clinton was a strong supporter of the Religious Freedom Restoration Act—intended to protect individuals from laws that would interfere with the free exercise of their religion—which he signed in a Rose Garden ceremony in the fall of 1993. Two years later, he directed Secretary of Education Richard Riley to prepare detailed guidelines and explanations about the range of religious expression that was allowed in public schools. "There was a lot of controversy about how much religious expression could be allowed in public schools," Clinton remembered in his memoir. "Some school officials and teachers believed that the Constitution prohibited any of it. That was incorrect."

The so-called Riley Rules gave teachers and principals ways to determine, for example, whether a teenage Sikh boy could carry his traditional kirpan, a small knife, without being suspended for bringing a weapon to school. And they highlighted the distinction between teaching about Christianity or Judaism and the legally inappropriate terrain of conducting devotional courses in either faith. The rules were the first of their kind and resulted in a lowering of tension and lawsuits around the country. Decades earlier, the political mobilization of evangelicals came about partly in response to the sense that liberals were driving religion out of schools. Now a Democratic president was reopening the doors.

International religious freedom was another area in which some evangelical leaders found the Clinton White House to be a sympathetic ally. After years of isolationism, evangelical churches had begun to recognize that the U.S. government could play a role in preventing religious persecution overseas—an issue that directly affected the missionaries they supported. When Republican politicians responded to these concerns by writing legislation to create an office for International Religious Freedom (IRF) at the State Department, however, they found themselves butting heads with a White House that thought the efforts didn't go far enough. Clinton advisers were concerned that the office's proposed focus was too narrow, limited primarily to combating religious persecution instead of embracing a broader mandate to encourage religious freedom globally. They also worried that the creation of a special office would allow the State Department to ghettoize religious concerns and avoid integrating those issues into the general work of the agency. (Both criticisms are now widely echoed by conservatives, ten years after the establishment of the IRF office.)

The Republican approach eventually won out, and Clinton named Robert Seiple, head of the Christian relief organization World Vision, as the first ambassador for international religious freedom. In his second term, the president also appointed Brady Anderson, a boyhood friend from Arkansas, to run the U.S. Agency for International Development (USAID). An evangelical, Anderson worked to ensure that

USAID had close relationships with faith-based organizations that served needy countries. And when the president and the first lady visited China in 1998, they took with them a trio of religious leaders to press the Chinese on religious freedom. Although mainline Protestants pressured Clinton to designate one of their own to accompany him, he chose instead to bring Rabbi Arthur Schneier of New York City's Park East Synagogue, Washington cardinal Theodore McCarrick, and an evangelical friend—Don Argue, president of the National Association of Evangelicals.

One theme comes up over and over in the stories former Clinton aides tell about their boss and religion. The president is on his way to address a religious audience, he looks over the remarks drafted for him by his speechwriters, and he discards them as insufficient for the occasion, relying instead on his ability to speak extemporaneously on matters of faith. George Stephanopoulos remembers watching Clinton just before he took the stage in November 1991 to address the annual Church of God in Christ convention in Memphis. "He was staring straight ahead, almost in a trance, oblivious to the crowd," Stephanopoulos writes in his memoir. "I would soon learn the meaning of that look: Clinton was composing his speech." Easing into the rhythms of an old-fashioned sermon, Clinton began with a deceptively slow and low-energy delivery. But like any good preacher, he built momentum, drawing *Amens* from the crowd as he told them about "the new covenant, a solemn agreement which we must not break." Knowing the resonance of "covenant" language with that audience, Clinton explained that government was charged with providing opportunity, but people had to take responsibility. "If you can go to work, you ought to go to work."

One story in particular is still repeated by Democrats in awed tones. On April 3, 1996, a plane carrying Commerce Secretary Ron Brown and thirty-three others crashed in Croatia, killing all aboard. Soon after the news reached the White House, Clinton decided to head over to the Commerce Department to eulogize his friend and address the agency's employees. His speechwriters had half an hour to quickly type up some remarks. One of them called Alexis Herman, who had been a protégé of Brown's at the DNC, to ask if Brown had a favorite Bible verse. Still somewhat distraught, Herman rattled off a few sentences, which the aide scribbled down before Herman hung up the phone. But there was a problem. None of them knew the citation for the verse, so they couldn't get the exact wording. In a panic, the speechwriting staff thumbed through Bibles, contacted ministers, and used online Bible search engines, looking for the right passage. Unable to find it, they used Herman's paraphrase and rushed a copy over to Clinton, who was about to start speaking.

Communications Director Don Baer slipped Clinton the speech, apologizing that they couldn't locate the correct line of Scripture. Scanning the text, the president stopped him, saying, "Oh, Isaiah 40:31. This is the New English translation. I prefer the King James version myself. That's the one I'll use." And then he stepped to the podium to remember Ron Brown's life. Clinton bade him farewell with Brown's favorite verse, quoted from memory: "They who wait upon the Lord shall have their strength renewed. They shall mount up with wings as eagles. They will run and not grow weary. They will walk and faint not."

Clinton's personal religiosity and openness go a long way toward explaining why his administration worked more closely than that of other Democrats—or most Republicans—ever had with religious communities and to highlight issues like religious liberty. The president set the tone and made it clear that religious communities should be thought of as allies, not opponents. But Clinton also benefited from an unusual cast of advisers. Unlike Jimmy Carter, who worked amid a sea of secular Democrats in his administration, Clinton was surrounded by senior aides who were, as a group, more religious than the average professional Democrat. There was George Stephanopoulos, whose father was a priest in the Greek Orthodox Church, and who had studied theology as a Rhodes Scholar at Oxford; Rahm Emanuel, an observant Jew who met weekly with his rabbi; Mike McCurry, an active Methodist who served as Sunday school superintendent at his local church in Maryland; Paul Begala, a devout, pro-life Catholic who named his first son John Paul.

There was no grand plan to hire or nominate Democrats who were personally religious. Good political advisers are valuable, no matter what their beliefs. But the fact that so many of the men and women who filled key roles in the Clinton White House had a keen respect for faith themselves meant that no one avoided religious issues or saw them as political obstacles. The embrace of "safe, legal, and rare" as an abortion position, for instance, would have been hotly debated in most Democratic campaigns, but was largely uncontroversial in the Clinton camp. There were no grumblings that Clinton's work on behalf of religious freedom violated the separation of church and state. No one pushed back at the idea of Clinton taping an interview for the VISN Christian cable network, or sitting down for a few hours with a *Christianity Today* writer, or giving time to the Catholic News Service. For eight years, the Clinton White House reversed what had become the Democratic flight-or-fight instinctive reaction to all things religious.

To the everlasting frustration of Clinton and his top advisers, it didn't matter how many Bible verses he could quote from memory or how often he reached out to work with conservative evangelicals or which Christian television programs he appeared on. He and the first lady couldn't shake the "secular liberal" tag that was automatically pinned on elected Democrats by voters and pundits alike. Oh, sure, he could talk it up in front of religious audiences, aping the cadences of a preacher. But that was just Clinton the politician, they'd say, trying to be everything to everyone. It didn't mean he actually believed any of it. Some conservatives even went so far as to argue that Clinton's regular church attendance was proof that he was not really religious. After George W. Bush took over the White House, Michael Cromartie of the conservative Ethics and Public Policy Center compared him to Clinton, noting approvingly, "This president has not made an issue of where he goes to church. I find it refreshing that we don't have a president coming out of church with a large Bible under his arm."

It wasn't hard to see why conservatives would think Clinton was faking his religiosity. They were deeply skeptical about every aspect of the Clintons' personal and professional lives, alternately awed and repulsed by the smooth charm of the man they called Slick Willy. For liberals, the matter was trickier. They were largely unaware of the Clinton administration's efforts to protect religious liberty and wouldn't necessarily have trumpeted those accomplishments if they'd known. But to the extent that they heard him use religious rhetoric and speak about his own faith, it was simply incongruent with what they "knew" about who was religious and who wasn't.

If liberals believed that religion and reason were inherently in conflict and that it was therefore impossible to be religious and an intellectual, and if they also believed that religion automatically swung in a conservative direction, then no amount of evidence to the contrary could convince them that Clinton was sincerely a man of faith. No one disputed that Clinton was brilliant, a policy wonk who could absorb information like a sponge. The obvious conclusion for liberals, then, was that his frequent religious references and centrist social positions were simply political pandering. Political observer Larry Sabato reflected this cynical outlook when he told a reporter that Clinton's religious outreach was backed up by "bones and thin gruel," instead of substance. "He must be really chuckling over this," scoffed Sabato.

Two major issues that arose during Clinton's time in the White House seemed to confirm the charges of his skeptics. The first was abortion. Although "safe, legal, and rare" was a compelling line that appealed to that majority of Americans who want abortion to be neither outlawed nor unrestricted, voters soon began to question whether it was anything more than just a clever turn of phrase.

Upon moving into the Oval Office, Clinton quickly issued a series of executive orders. One overturned the so-called Mexico City policy, ending the restriction on federal funding to nongovernment organizations (NGOs) that provide abortions. A second order removed restrictions on Title X money that funds family-planning services, and a third reversed a federal ban on fetal tissue research. Any Democratic president would have taken these reasonable actions after twelve years of Republican rule. But the timing suggested a payback to the abortion rights groups that had supported his candidacy. And it left pro-life voters wondering about the commitment to making abortion rare.

Clinton pursued a number of policies—including increased funding for programs that supported pregnant women and efforts to make contraceptives more affordable and available—that actually lowered abortion rates by more than 18 percent over his eight years in office. That accomplishment was never trumpeted by Democrats, though, in part because the party wasn't on board with the rhetoric of reducing abortions. Virtually no one in the Democratic leadership or pro-choice community disputed the goal, but many believed that stating it out loud implied that abortion was bad and played directly into the hands of Republicans.

The reluctance to suggest that fewer abortions was a good thing made Democrats particularly vulnerable when Republicans opened up a new front in the abortion war in the mid-1990s. Having won the fight over federal abortion funding, but having so far failed to convince a majority of Americans that abortion should be outlawed, pro-life forces cooked up an ingenious new way to sway public opinion to their side: they would focus on the specific procedures used to perform abortions, starting with one they vividly called "partial-birth" abortion. If Americans dislike talking about abortion as an issue, they are even less eager to think about what happens during an abortion. Republicans exploited this squeamishness, waging a public relations war that relied on illustrations depicting an intact dilation-and-extraction procedure—in which a fetus's skull is collapsed before the body is removed from the mother's body. The tactic worked: by January 1998, a CNN poll found that almost three-quarters (74 percent) of Americans thought the procedure should be illegal.

Yet when Congress passed a ban and sent it to the White House in

April 1996, the president—who was moved by stories of women who had undergone the procedure because delivery of their severely abnormal babies would have put their health at serious risk—vetoed the legislation. Among those who were upset by his decision were the liberal Catholics who had been close Democratic allies on most other issues. Columnist Mary McGrory was at a party for the liberal Catholic magazine *Commonweal* on the night of the veto and reported the reaction of supporters, who felt betrayed. "When he said that abortion should be 'safe, legal, and rare,' we all believed him," railed the magazine's editor, Margaret Steinfels. Another guest thought Clinton had missed "a chance to draw the line, to lead and say, 'We go this far and no farther.' He blew it."

Some of the president's advisers also thought he had made a mistake. Paul Begala begged Clinton not to veto the bill. "There wasn't a single restriction on abortion that we supported," he says. As a result, the phrase "safe, legal, and rare" was heard less and less around the White House. "I think that's part of why we moved away from it," argues Begala, "because the record no longer matched up and people were cynical about it."

Above all, Clinton's veto of the partial-birth ban made his pro-life supporters wonder if they'd been duped. If his veto had followed visible efforts to reduce abortion rates, to focus on the "rare" part of his famous formulation, it would still have disturbed them, but it might have been somewhat more palatable. But after the Democratic convention's snub of Governor Casey (an event that had already been awarded canonical status in pro-life lore), the early pro-abortion-rights executive orders, and the absence of a policy campaign to lower abortion rates, the veto was the last straw. Critics concluded that, like Carter before him, Clinton was captive to a Democratic Party that would brook no dissent on abortion. At the 1996 Democratic convention in Chicago, Clinton aides tried to atone for the Casey fiasco by inviting Ohio congressman Tony Hall to give a short statement about being a pro-life Democrat. Before Hall took to the stage, however, convention organizers scrambled to send one instruction throughout the arena to delegates in the audience: please don't boo him.

The discrediting of Clinton's signature cultural centrist phrase dealt a blow to his religious reputation. Nothing, however, undermined it so much as his own actions with a young intern who became known forever after simply as Monica. An extramarital affair with a twenty-four-year-old intern in the Oval Office wouldn't burnish the moral credentials of any president. And, indeed, the vast majority of Americans said they thought Clinton's relationship with Lewinsky was morally wrong. Nor did it help that the president lied to his family, his colleagues, and the country, denying the affair for eight months in 1998.

Clinton's moral failure became the proof many skeptics needed to expose what they had always believed to be the insincerity of his religious convictions. They had never quite been able to square the idea that a Democratic politician could truly be devout and knowledgeable about religion. Now they could rest easy, trusting once again the instincts that had told them it was all an act.

Privately, both Clintons turned to the ministers in their lives to work through their anger and guilt. Mrs. Clinton relied on Donald Jones, who had been her youth minister when she was a teenager at First United Methodist Church in Park Ridge, Illinois. He prayed with the first lady, reminding her that sin and grace coexist—each is necessary for the other. The president asked three pastors—Phil Wogaman, the senior minister at Foundry Methodist; Campolo; and Gordon MacDonald from Lexington, Massachusetts—to help restore his "spiritual health." At least once a month, the men came to the White House to pray, read Scripture, and force Clinton the man to answer some tough questions. For their efforts, the men of faith bore the brunt of outrage from their colleagues. "Don't you understand that this man does not deserve grace?" one pastor wrote to Campolo.

Conservative Christians, who hold as a key theological doctrine that man is inherently sinful ("For all have sinned and fallen short of the glory of God"), were hardest on Clinton. When the president reacted as most Christians are taught—by confessing his sin, asking for forgiveness, and expressing his desire to repent—they savaged him for exploiting religion.

Some of the harshest criticism followed the annual White House breakfast for religious leaders in September of 1998, at which Clinton asked the assembled clergy for their forgiveness. "I have been on quite a journey these last few weeks to get to the end of this, to the rock-bottom truth of where I am and where we all are," he told the crowd. "I don't think there is a fancy way to say that I have sinned." A few months later, in December, more than two hundred theologians and religious leaders signed a "Declaration Concerning Religion, Ethics, and the Crisis in the Clinton Presidency," expressing their concern over the role religion played in the president's public statements of contrition.

Richard Jewett, a professor at Garrett-Evangelical Theological Seminary, proclaimed Clinton insufficiently shamed, complaining that the president's statement at the faith breakfast "evokes religious sentiments but admits not a single sinful act." Another theologian, Stephen Pope from Boston College, charged, "The president has tried to use Christian ministers and the Christian churches as a way to gain cheap forgiveness." Still others took issue with the fact that Clinton attended church every week with a Bible under his arm (most Baptists bring their Bibles with them to church services). "It's a message sent to us that he is a believing Christian and truly repentant," said Gabriel Fackre, a professor at Andover Newton Theological School and one of the drafters of the declaration.

Clinton couldn't possibly be repentant, Fackre appeared to be saying, because he was Clinton. As a Democrat, the president was presumed to be a secularist at heart; if he embraced religion, it could only be for false reasons. But this view stands in stark contrast to assumptions about conservative politicians and faith. Republicans often benefit from having a narrative of moral failure followed by repentance—it is seen as proof that their personal faith is sincere and that they recognize that all humans are fallible. Almost nine years after Clinton's confession, Newt Gingrich would appear on the radio show hosted by conservative Christian leader James Dobson to declare that he, too, had been cheating on his wife with a political aide at the same time that he was leading the charge for Clinton's impeachment. Gingrich's announcement was not condemned as exploitation of religion; it was a necessary prelude for a potential presidential campaign, providing evidence of his humble faith. "Conservatives," says Flo McAfee, Clinton's religious liaison, "can say, 'I have fallen and I have sinned,' and then they can rise again. And again and again."

In the 2000 presidential election, George W. Bush used this religion double standard to full advantage. The former first son boasted a blockbuster conversion story—a drunk, irresponsible husband and father who hit bottom and found Jesus, with Billy Graham in a supporting role. He sought to make right-wing politics palatable to suburban moms and other swing voters by repackaging it as "compassionate conservatism." In the tradition of Jimmy Carter and Bill Clinton, Bush did not hesitate to talk about his faith, even bringing it up unexpectedly in traditional campaign venues. Many political observers were startled during a December 1999 GOP debate when Bush named Jesus Christ as his favorite political philosopher, explaining that it was because Christ had "changed my heart."

Pundits guffawed, but voters heard a man who sounded authentic. The answer also went a long way toward winning over influential social conservatives who had previously settled on John Ashcroft as their chosen candidate. Senator Ashcroft was a Pentecostal from Missouri and a reliable conservative, but he was also flatlining in the polls, never breaking into double digits. Religious right leaders largely remembered Bush as the hotheaded young man they'd met during his father's 1988 run for the White House, a campaign in which the younger Bush held the odd designation of point man for conservative religious organizations. That in the interim Bush had found Jesus made it easier for them to accept him as a candidate worthy of their support.

Given the incredible economic boom that had taken place on Clinton's watch, as well as the relative peace that prevailed on the international stage, Bush's best chance of winning the presidential election rested on his ability to make the campaign about character and values. To that end, the Lewinsky scandal, which still hung like a specter over the Democratic White House, was a godsend. The most reliable applause line in Bush's stump speech was a barely veiled jab at Clinton—a promise to "restore honor and dignity to the White House." As Carter had nearly twenty-five years earlier in the wake of Watergate, Bush staked his campaign on the hope that Americans were primed for a candidate whose religiosity and upright character were central to his political persona.

That kind of strategy struck Democrats as irrelevant and unlikely to succeed. As far as they were concerned, the 1998 midterm election results had repudiated the idea that Americans were concerned about Clinton's moral lapse. That year, Democrats gained seats in both the House and the Senate; it was the first time since 1822 that a president's party had not lost ground in the sixth year of his administration. However, while Americans were indeed tired of the impeachment proceedings and held Republicans responsible for turning the affair into a show trial, they were not—as Democrats assumed—untroubled by President Clinton's having had a sexual relationship with an intern in the Oval Office.

Vice President Al Gore, the Democratic nominee, was the walking embodiment of his party's preoccupation with issues over values. A born technocrat, Gore was most comfortable dissecting policy details, not making emotional appeals. If voters associated Clinton with his oft-repeated phrase "I feel your pain," they knew Gore by his references to a "Social Security lockbox." Gore was a Southern Baptist just like Clinton and had studied theology at Vanderbilt Divinity School; he was simply much more private about his faith. Behind closed doors, Gore often referenced biblical passages in conversation with his campaign manager, Donna Brazile, a devout Catholic. When the candidate decided to shake up his campaign in September 1999 and relocate the whole operation to Nashville, he explained the move to Brazile by quoting from the Old Testament story of Gideon: "The Lord said unto Gideon, the people that are with thee are too many for me to give the Midianites into their hands." In her memoir, Brazile wrote that the political translation of this verse was clear: "[The] campaign is too big, too bloated, too busy hurting each other to defeat Bill Bradley and take on George W. Bush."

In public, Gore was reticent. After he was roundly mocked by political pundits for telling the *Washington Post*'s Sally Quinn in July 1999 that he often asked himself, "What would Jesus do?" Gore largely stayed away from discussions of his faith on the campaign trail. But Gore's difficulty connecting with religious voters stemmed from more than his inability to communicate his faith. His campaign lacked a religious outreach effort of any kind, as did the Democratic National Committee. The relationships that the Clinton White House had nurtured over eight years had not been tended by others in the party leadership. And the new approach to religion that Clinton had brought to the Democratic Party never made it past the edge of the South Lawn of the White House. Believing that their religion problems had been solved by the charismatic Clinton, party leaders had not created a religious liaison position in the national party, they had created no databases of faith leaders, and they had no advisers capable of putting together an invitation list for a faith breakfast. As for the Gore campaign, it reverted to the traditional party approach to religion: focus on black churches, ignore everyone else.

Democrats also made a key tactical error in not rebutting Bush's attacks on Clinton as a secular liberal who was hostile to religious communities. In the Texas governor's first campaign speech in Indianapolis on July 22, 1999, he said that a Bush administration would "rally the armies of compassion," which had, he declared, been discriminated against and unfairly denied federal funds. In response, Democrats did not point out that Gore himself had endorsed the funding of faith-based organizations in February 1999. They did not mention that many of Clinton's cabinet secretaries had worked closely with religious nonprofits through their agencies. Or that the capstone of Bush's faith-based plan—the expansion of tax incentives to encourage charitable giving—had been promoted by Hillary Clinton that same year in a White House conference on philanthropy.

Instead, Democrats took the bait and attacked Bush for inappropriately mixing religion and politics. Gore's advisers also convinced him to back away from promoting faith-based partnerships and prevailed upon vice-presidential nominee Joseph Lieberman to turn down a chance to speak about faith and public life at the University of Notre Dame in October of 2000 (Lieberman gave the speech anyway). They liked the idea of a Democratic president who kept religious groups away from government funding more than one who encouraged cooperation with faith-based organizations. Just as they preferred the Clinton who defended an unpopular abortion procedure to the one who talked about how there should be fewer abortions. And they certainly liked the idea of a Democrat who was attacked by religious conservatives more than one who worked with those same leaders.

When Bush won a narrow and contested election in the fall of 2000, Democrats lost the White House. But they also lost the party's best religion liaison, as Bill Clinton moved on to building his presidential library, writing his memoir, and pursuing various philanthropic ventures. The party would spend the next four years sneering at the latest evangelical to occupy the Oval Office and forgetting the lessons of the Clinton White House's religious outreach effort.

# CHAPTER 5

# "WE DON'T DO WHITE CHURCHES"

## JOHN KERRY'S RELIGION DISASTER

On a clear April morning in 2004, as a few determined cherry blossoms still clung to the trees ringing the Tidal Basin in Washington, D.C., Mara Vanderslice walked into the Kerry campaign headquarters at the corner of Fifteenth and I streets. She was ready to praise the Lord and kick some GOP ass. Although still a campaign neophyte—she'd logged her first months of campaign experience just a few months earlier on Howard Dean's Iowa staff—the petite twenty-eight-year-old had just been hired to oversee religious outreach for Senator John Kerry's presidential campaign.

Vanderslice arrived for her first day armed with memos, statistics, and plans for helping the campaign connect with religious voters. In many ways, she had been preparing for the job her whole life. A native of Colorado, Vanderslice was raised as a Unitarian in Boulder, just outside the shadow of the conservative Christian empire in Colorado Springs. She had never met an evangelical who wasn't also a Republican until she went off to college at Earlham, a Quaker school in the Midwest, where Vanderslice became involved with Christian student groups and was eventually baptized as an evangelical Christian. After graduation, she worked for a series of social justice nonprofits and progressive religious organizations before landing in Iowa in the months leading up to the 2004 caucuses.

Surveying her new professional digs, Vanderslice saw a mix of overstuffed leather chairs and gleaming tables with whiteboards and wall-mounted televisions permanently tuned to CNN. It formed an aesthetic of shabby campaign chic. In general, though, the operation bore closer resemblance to an incumbent campaign than a scrappy opposition effort. Clinton-era cabinet secretaries strode through the halls while former State Department officials conferred during smoking breaks on benches across the street in McPherson Square. Vanderslice would work out of the campaign's constituency section, a wide-open space packed with desks manned by twentysomethings who were each in charge of a special interest group.

The Democratic Party has spent decades compiling lists of veterans' groups and leaders in the Asian-American community. They know when each labor union holds its annual conference and which issues mobilize activists for the disabled. All around Vanderslice, her new colleagues were hard at work updating preexisting databases of leaders and activists for every conceivable constituency. Ready to jump into the action, she asked where her preexisting databases were. The answer: nowhere. They didn't exist.

Across town, Vanderslice's GOP counterparts had already put in place a religious outreach operation that was humming along at full speed. Martin Gillespie, brother of Republican National Committee chair Ed Gillespie, headed up the party's Catholic operation. Under his direction, the RNC enlisted fifty thousand Catholic team leaders—volunteers who called into local talk radio programs, coordinated strategy via conference calls, and recruited fellow parishioners—and hired between seventy-five and one hundred Catholic field coordinators who would spend four months in targeted swing states. On the evangelical side, the Bush/Cheney campaign had hired former Christian Coalition executive director Ralph Reed to oversee outreach. One of the first things Reed did was appoint chairpersons in each of eighteen battleground states. In Florida alone, the campaign employed a state chairwoman for evangelical outreach who brought on board outreach chairs in each of Florida's sixty-seven counties. Every county chair, in turn, recruited between thirty and fifty volunteers to contact and register their evangelical neighbors.

The matchup between the two parties in pursuit of religious voters wasn't just David versus Goliath. It was David versus Goliath and the Philistines and the Assyrians and the Egyptians, with a few plagues thrown in for good measure. By Election Day, the Kerry campaign would become a case study in how to mishandle religion during a political race.

Despite what happened later, however, John Kerry's presidential campaign started out strong. By early March 2004, the Democratic contest was essentially over. Kerry had endured the Howard Dean antiwar boomlet that dominated political coverage throughout the fall and heading into the Iowa caucus. He overpowered Democratic perma-candidates such as Dick Gephardt and Al Sharpton and even outmuscled the other war hero in the race, retired general Wesley Clark. Kerry clinched the nomination when Democratic primary voters decided they were more worried about the party's ability to compete in foreign policy than its economic platform, and John Edwards's populist appeal began to wither.

The Brahmin Kerry didn't set anyone's heart aflutter, but he did set Democratic minds at ease. With gravitas, intellectual heft, a staff of political veterans, and a wife worth hundreds of millions, Kerry was a substantial candidate. He would not put the party through any embarrassing Gennifer Flowers revelations. And if, as so often happened in campaigns, the Republican National Committee pumped a last-minute infusion of cash into the race, Kerry would be able to neutralize the GOP advantage by reaching into his own pocket. He even seemed to have figured out a way to address religious questions that avoided the pitfalls that traditionally bedeviled Democrats, a particular accomplishment for the first Catholic presidential nominee since John F. Kennedy.

The various discomforts and insecurities Democrats have about religion had been on display throughout the 2004 primary season. Gephardt, although a Southern Baptist, grew up in a German-American community outside St. Louis among Catholics and Lutherans who considered public discussion of religion prideful. His sole reference to religion in the campaign was a single-phrase allusion, tucked at the end of his announcement speech, to the church scholarship he used to attend college. Edwards, who was raised Southern Baptist, calculated that talking about religion would only hurt his standing with Democratic primary voters. But that left him befuddled when at a Democratic gathering in Iowa he was asked about his faith. "I haven't talked about it [my faith] because I only usually talk about it when asked," Edwards responded in an impressively inarticulate nonstatement of belief. When the religion and spirituality Web site Beliefnet attempted to interview each of the Democratic presidential candidates about his faith, the inquiries were met with puzzlement more than anything else. Bob Graham's press secretary summed up the reaction best with an e-mail intended for colleagues that was inadvertently sent back to Beliefnet: "Geez not high priority . . . I mean is Graham prepared to talk about his spirituality/religion?"

The most proudly secular of the bunch was Dean, who told audiences in several appearances throughout the South that voters in that region needed to stop basing their votes on "God, guns, and gays." When Vanderslice, who had joined the Dean campaign because of his staunch opposition to the Iraq War, tried to reach out to her Lutheran and Catholic contacts in Iowa, she found that they had concerns about her new boss. Dean's story about leaving his Episcopal church in Vermont because of a dispute over a bike path just didn't ring true to many clergy and activists, who thought it sounded more like an excuse for why Dean didn't attend church. But they were more concerned about the former governor's dismissal of abortion as "an issue about nothing . . . an issue about extremism."

That these Democratic activists found Dean's comments off-putting made Vanderslice worry that the candidate was hurting her efforts to reach out to religious communities. But when she raised the issue with the campaign's political and communications directors, her concerns fell on deaf ears. "That's why primary voters like us," they told her. "It's because we're against the religious right." Vanderslice tried to explain that what seemed like a distinction to them—bad religion versus everyone else—came across as a broad attack on religion in general. But what she quickly learned was that the people who ran the Dean campaign—like most Democratic operatives—thought religion irrelevant to their world and their voters.

Vanderslice wasn't the only one who noticed the Dean campaign's secular attitude. One Washington, D.C.–based Democrat who was courted to join Dean's policy operation explained politely that he couldn't meet with advisers on Sunday morning because he taught a Rite 13 confirmation class at his Episcopal church. He might as well have said he spent Sunday mornings going on buggy rides. "How quaint," replied his Dean contact. A senior Dean adviser from Vermont was more blunt when he visited Iowa and was introduced to Vanderslice. Told that her role in the campaign was to handle religious outreach, the political veteran turned to her in bewilderment and asked, "How the fuck did *you* get hired?"

With that sort of welcome to Democratic politics, Vanderslice was relieved to join the Kerry campaign after the Massachusetts senator secured his party's nomination. Mary Beth Cahill, the campaign manager, had served as director of public liaison for Bill Clinton's second term and saw firsthand the success of religion liaisons Flo McAfee and Maureen Shea in building relationships with diverse religious communities. If it worked in the White House, Cahill reasoned, there was no reason a campaign couldn't do the same thing. When Shea recommended Vanderslice as a possible religious outreach director, Cahill's deputy brought her aboard without interviewing anyone else for the job.

By the time Vanderslice arrived in April, the senator had given a handful of speeches to black congregations, including the twenty-five-hundred-member Greater Bethlehem Temple Apostolic Faith Church in Jackson, Mississippi. Speaking at the church in early March, Kerry went on the offensive, charging that Bush had failed to practice the "compassionate conservatism" he so often preached. "What good is it, my brothers," Kerry quoted from James 2:14, "if a man claims to have faith but has no deeds?" The attack was classic Karl Rove jujitsu, taking Bush's perceived strength—his oft-professed religious faith—and using it against him.

In addition, *Time* magazine had published a story about Kerry's faith in early April. The article raised the question of whether Kerry would face criticism from the Catholic Church over his pro-choice views, but the text was less important than the prominent photo that accompanied it: an image of Kerry coming out of church on Ash Wednesday with the sign of the cross on his forehead. The campaign had already hired staff to oversee outreach to black churches and to Jewish groups. Vanderslice's mandate was to handle everything else in the religion portfolio.

No one yet knew what it would mean for the campaign that Kerry was the first Catholic to be nominated by a major party in forty-four years. But at a minimum, Vanderslice wanted to be prepared for any challenges or criticisms that might come at Kerry from the Catholic Church. She had already developed strategies that might allow the campaign to soften the public perception of Democrats as godless, but as an evangelical, Vanderslice felt ill-equipped to handle the Catholic questions on her own. The campaign's religious adviser needed advisers of her own. And so, every Tuesday evening, a collection of religious leaders, social justice activists, and the odd political operative gathered in a conference room overlooking McPherson Square to plot strategy.

It didn't take long for them to get results. Within a month of her arrival, Vanderslice convinced Kerry's senior advisers that the phrase "separation of church and state" should be stricken from the candidate's vocabulary. It is vitally important to ensure that neither church nor state exert influence over the other. But, she explained, Democratic politicians have for years misused the words, trotting them out when they would prefer not to talk about their personal faith—"I'd love to get into that, but we do have separation of church and state in this country." What was once a resonant phrase that described a valuable principle had become a dodge, at least to the ears of voters. That had impaired Democrats' ability to weigh in when real separation issues did actually arise. They had to regain their credibility so as to engage in fair fights over the establishment and free-exercise clauses. When Kerry spoke instead about not wanting to "impose [his] articles of faith," the formulation assured listeners that he respected church/state separation, without triggering the radar of skeptics.

By the end of May 2004, a *Washington Post* poll showed Kerry leading Bush 49 to 47 percent when registered voters were asked whom they would support in the election. Bush's poll numbers were plummeting as the situation in Iraq worsened, the Abu Ghraib prison scandal came to light, and Americans lost their confidence in his ability to manage the economy as well.

Democrats were riding high as summer arrived and a muggy blanket settled on the nation's capital. But the Kerry campaign already had serious troubles. The conventional wisdom about 2004 is that things didn't go south for Kerry until after the Democratic National Convention, when the Swift Boat attacks—and Kerry's refusal to respond to them—sealed his fate. The allegations that Kerry's acts of valor during the Vietnam War were overblown and that his reputation as a military hero was undeserved were indeed damaging. But before there was Swift Boat, there was "Wafer Watch." Months before the problems became obvious, the Kerry operation set the course of the campaign with a similar nonresponse to a damaging charge.

Throughout the spring, a handful of conservative Catholic leaders—led by newly appointed archbishop Raymond Burke in St. Louis—revived their decades-long tactic of singling out Democratic pro-choice politicians for criticism. John Kerry, they declared, could not present himself to receive the Eucharist because he did not vote for legislation that would restrict abortion. Politically, it wasn't much different from the criticism Cardinal John O'Connor had lodged at Geraldine Ferraro twenty years earlier when she was the Democrats' vice-presidential nominee. If anything, the fact that Kerry's own bishop and cardinal did not support denying pro-choice politicians Communion made the story less compelling than Ferraro's struggle with her own archbishop. But for the press, it was an irresistible tale of conflict.

The traveling press corps that accompanied Kerry everywhere became obsessed with what one reporter termed the Wafer Watch. They trailed Kerry to mass every Sunday hoping for the money shot—an image of the senator dutifully proceeding up the aisle for Communion, only to be denied the body and blood when he arrived at the altar. When Kerry attended Protestant churches, reporters wrote that he was avoiding his own church. When he went to mass instead, they asserted that he was courting a showdown with the Catholic leadership. "Kerry Takes Communion on Mother's Day" ran a typical Monday-morning headline above an Associated Press story that began, "Democrat John Kerry attended Mother's Day Mass on Sunday and took Communion although some Roman Catholic leaders say he should not receive it because his abortion-rights stance violates church teachings."

The narrative of the world's most powerful religious institution taking on a presidential candidate was so enticing that only a handful of journalists bothered to place the story in any sort of meaningful context. Only rarely, for instance, did anyone note that a majority of Catholics agreed with Kerry that abortion should not be used as a litmus test for judging whether a politician was sufficiently Catholic—or that a majority of American Catholics were pro-choice. Left unreported was the fact that Pope John Paul II had given Communion to the outspoken pro-choice former mayor of Rome just a few years earlier. If the Holy Father himself had no problem with a pro-choice politician receiving Communion, someone might have asked, why were some American bishops making an issue of it during an election? When a right-wing cardinal from Africa who was positioning himself to be the next pope spoke out against pro-choice politicians, the news was breathlessly reported as the "Vatican" weighing in on the issue, even though the cardinal's remarks were immediately challenged by the incoming archbishop of Dublin, who argued, "The Eucharist must not become a political battleground."

But it wasn't just the thrill of a Catholic brawl that drew journalists to the Wafer Watch. There was also the satisfaction of unmasking Kerry as a fake Catholic, to prove that his religiosity was insincere. Conservatives complain about liberal media bias, but when it comes to religion, journalistic assumptions actually work in their favor. Republicans, for instance, are always assumed to be religious unless they can prove otherwise. Even when pundits mock their religious beliefs and practices, it at least confirms that Republicans are indeed religious. It's understood, however, that Democrats are not religious. If they do talk about religion, journalists jump into "gotcha" mode to prove that the rhetoric is just a ploy to pander to voters. That's a problem for Democrats in a country where 87 percent of the people say religion is an important part of their lives and 70 percent want their president to be a person of faith.

By early summer, the charge that Kerry was a dissenting Catholic at odds with his church had already begun to stick. Al Gore had barely edged George W. Bush to win the Catholic vote in 2000 (by a margin of 50 to 47 percent), and the GOP had spent the previous four years engaged in an intensive campaigned to pick up support from moderate and conservative Catholics. If he wanted to win, Kerry would have to maintain Gore's advantage or improve upon it. Being publicly labeled a "bad Catholic" wasn't exactly a boon to that cause. Nor did it improve the default perception of Democrats as irreligious. When Kerry spoke about religion or quoted from the Bible, it was only to critique Bush's faith, not to define his own. Now voters were hearing that he wasn't even in line with his own church's teachings. It didn't come as a surprise when a *Time* magazine poll in June 2004 reported that only 7 percent of Americans thought Kerry was a "religious" man.

\*　　\*　　\*

The media frenzy around the Wafer Watch metastasized, with journalists doing everything but checking Kerry's molars for evidence that he had indeed been given Communion. The candidate's senior advisers huddled to discuss strategy. Amazingly, none of them had seen this coming. The campaign appeared to still be operating on the John F. Kennedy model, not realizing that the situation had changed in forty-four years from one in which Kennedy had to prove he wasn't really Catholic to one in which Kerry had to prove he was Catholic enough. Catholic Democrats from Tom Daschle to Gray Davis to David Obey had endured the same threats from Church leaders in previous years. And Archbishop Burke had issued his first warning to Kerry in early January of 2004. Yet no one—not Kerry, not his friends, not his campaign staff—had anticipated the criticism or the attention it would provoke. "It never crossed our minds that this could happen," recalls Cahill's deputy Christine Stanek. So there was no plan in place for a next step.

Kerry and his advisers struggled to reach a decision, and when they did, it was underwhelming: ignore the story and hope it goes away. At most, a few select surrogates could defend Kerry in the press, people such as former congressman Father Robert Drinan or Illinois senator Dick Durbin. But the campaign itself would maintain radio silence. The campaign followed the same strategy a few months later when the Swift Boat attacks began. The flaw in this approach, of course, was that ignoring the situation didn't mean the stories went away. It just ensured that the Kerry campaign forfeited any ability to influence the coverage. On one side of the rapidly accumulating media accounts were a handful of unusually conservative bishops whose presence suddenly loomed much larger when left unchallenged. On the other? "The Kerry campaign did not return calls for comment."

The instinct to ignore the Communion stories came from Kerry himself. Northeastern Catholics aren't used to talking openly about their faith, particularly those raised in the pre–Vatican II era. They are especially loath to take on Church leaders directly, and certainly not in public. As far as Kerry was concerned, the matter was private, between him and the Church. "We weren't looking for a fight," he said in an interview three years later. Furthermore, Kerry knew that he was safe on technical grounds—"Nothing in canon law condones using the Eucharist as a retaliatory tool or weapon"—and that most bishops recognized that. "There was a sense that it was being handled," remembered Kerry. "There was nothing to be served by having a big, open fight."

Kerry's reluctance to publicly defend himself was understandable, but it made Mara Vanderslice beat her head against her desk. While her superiors on the campaign huddled to figure out a response to the Catholic charges, Vanderslice sought the advice of her informal religion squad. They wrote talking points that went on the offensive, promoting Kerry's commitment to his Catholic faith. They developed a media strategy to counteract the attacks. They sought out Catholic supporters around the country who were willing to write op-eds on Kerry's behalf. Vanderslice packaged all of the suggestions and delivered them to the senior advisers running the campaign. And what she heard in response was, "Thanks, but we have it all under control."

Vanderslice retreated to her desk in the constituency zone and watched in despair as the hits kept coming. She knew what Kerry's top aides failed to grasp: the ongoing questions and criticism about the senator's faith posed a larger image problem. Their candidate was running against a president presenting himself as the only option for religious voters. In such a race, standing silently by as your candidate's faith was impugned played right into the other side's hand. And it raised the question for voters of whether the allegations were true.

No one at the senior staff level, however, was wired to appreciate the situation, much less deal with it. The Catholics among them were largely divided into two groups: those who explicitly thought of themselves as ex-Catholics and took an angry "good riddance" posture, and those observant Catholics who shared Kerry's reticence. "Mary Beth was terrified of the politics of taking on the Church," says one close personal friend of the senator's. For their part, the non-Catholics on staff didn't see what the big deal was. They believed the whole brouhaha would only impact how conservative Catholics viewed Kerry. Since they had always thought Kerry should keep his faith private, the decision to keep quiet seemed sensible to them.

If Kerry's advisers hadn't been alternately spooked or bored by religion, they might have realized that between the candidate and his eventual running mate, North Carolina senator John Edwards, the Democrats had a ticket just as devout as Clinton/Gore. Or, for that matter, Bush/Cheney. While Bush only occasionally attended church and Cheney made no pretense of religiosity, Kerry could be found at mass at least once a week, election season or not. Ray Flynn, the former mayor of Boston, liked to tell people that Catholics of a certain age always knew where to find the last mass in any city. Even if he was occupied earlier in the day, Flynn explained, a good Catholic would want to observe the holy day of obligation. In Boston, the last mass is held at 7 p.m. on Sunday evening, at a small church in South Boston called Our Lady of Good Voyage. Flynn, a late-mass-goer himself, often saw Kerry there, not for the benefit of cameras or reporters, but because it was his Catholic duty.

In a similar practice of faith, Edwards carried with him *The Purpose-Driven Life,* a popular devotional book by the evangelical author and megachurch pastor Rick Warren. Though reticent to talk about his faith background, Edwards had been raised in the Southern Baptist Church and became an active member of Edenton Street United Methodist Church in Raleigh after his son Wade's death in 1996. His copy of *The Purpose-Driven Life* was leatherbound, with his name embossed on the cover, the hallmarks of an evangelical Bible. It was also worn from daily reading, a discipline he shared with the tens of millions of other Americans who had bought Warren's book.

Yet the Kerry campaign ran just one television commercial highlighting Kerry's faith, featuring footage of him exiting a church—and it was seen by few voters because it was in Spanish and aired exclusively on Spanish-language television stations. As for Edwards, voters never learned about his *Purpose-Driven* reading. A GOP strategist would have told any reporter who would listen about his candidate's devotional reading habits. Indeed, the White House had made it known earlier in Bush's term that he started each morning with a reading from *My Utmost for His Highest,* a collection of essays by the nineteenth-century Scottish minister Oswald Chambers that has gained popularity in evangelical circles. Most Democratic operatives, however, were oblivious to the existence of evangelical culture. The few who weren't would have been hard-pressed to identify the personalities within it. At one point during the summer of 2004, Terry McAuliffe was actually at the same event as Rick Warren and the two were introduced. With a good-natured smile but a blank stare, McAuliffe stuck out his hand. "Nice to meet you, Rick!" the Democratic National Committee chairman said. "And what do you do?"

One person on the Kerry campaign knew exactly who Rick Warren was, but by summer, Mara Vanderslice had been silenced. After a *USA Today* article identified her as Kerry's "director of religious outreach," calls started pouring into the campaign from reporters and average citizens around the country, intrigued by the idea that a Democratic campaign would have someone handling religion. Everyone, it seemed, wanted to talk to this young evangelical working for John Kerry.

But all the attention had also put Vanderslice on the radar screen of William Donahue, head of the conservative Catholic League. The blustery Donahue was best known for his furious press releases, which arrived on journalists' fax machines within minutes of any slight—real or imagined—against Catholicism. His targets ranged from Madonna to the cast of *The View* to Abercrombie & Fitch, and he was beloved by cable television bookers for his willingness to fulminate about any topic while working himself into a red-faced froth. Donahue's specialty was the empty threat; though quick to shout "Boycott!" he lacked the legitimacy in Catholic circles to command numbers. Donahue was undoubtedly a bully, but a fairly harmless one.

So when Vanderslice learned that Donahue had issued a press release blasting the Kerry campaign for hiring her, she laughed. The text of the release lived up to his usual overblown standards—Donahue attacked Vanderslice for coming late to evangelical Christianity, in college (an odd charge, given Bush's midlife conversion), and accused her of "tr[ying] to shut down Washington, D.C. in a protest against the IMF and the World Bank" (when she worked for the debt-relief organization Jubilee 2000). "Her résumé is that of a person looking for a job working for Fidel Castro, not John Kerry," Donahue concluded.

Unfortunately for Vanderslice, her bosses—constituency director Mona Pasquil and political director Steve Elmendorf—didn't find Donahue's broadside as ridiculous as she did. The story had already been picked up by Fox News and MSNBC, which sent it spinning irretrievably into the ether. The response within the campaign was swift. There would be no public reaction, no defense of Vanderslice. She would remain on staff, but would be quarantined to limit the damage. "You're never allowed to talk to reporters again, on the record or off," Pasquil informed Vanderslice. "And you should have let us know something like this was going to happen."

Because no one else on the campaign understood the world of religious organizations and personalities, Kerry's advisers mistakenly assumed that Donahue was an important Catholic voice, ascribing to him a level of influence that not even he thought he possessed. Having already decided to opt out of a fight over Kerry's Catholicism, the senior advisers didn't think they could take on more criticism from Catholic corners. That Donahue was widely considered a blowhard by other Catholics and that his statement about Vanderslice was absurd did not matter.

Emboldened, Donahue set his sights on another target a month later. In July, the DNC hired its first religious liaison, Brenda Peterson. A feisty, red-haired Disciples of Christ minister, Peterson had previously run a Washington-based organization called the Clergy Leadership Network. She had also, as a private individual, signed onto an amicus curiae brief on behalf of the effort to remove the words *under God* from the Pledge of Allegiance. For her heresy, Peterson found herself the subject of three blistering Donahue press releases that called the decision to hire her "political suicide." Within three days of the first release, Peterson agreed—under pressure within the DNC—to step down from her post. Donahue immediately issued a crowing statement taking credit for her departure.

With Peterson gone and Vanderslice muzzled, Democrats had no one who could speak knowledgeably about religious issues and communities. The communications operation had determined early on that religion press calls would be lumped in with "specialty press," a catchall category for niche publications—for example, Armenian community newspapers, gay and lesbian press, Irish-American publications. Communications assistant Jin Chon, a capable young man with no religious background, was overwhelmed by the sheer number of specialty areas. He was particularly ill-equipped to field calls from the religion reporter at the *New York Times* or Associated Press or NPR, much less prominent political writers working on stories with religious angles. His solution was to refer reporters to Vanderslice, knowing full well that she was under strict orders not to talk to the press. As a result, reporters who contacted the campaign for comment on religion stories were told that they would receive a call from Vanderslice that never came. Journalists know that it's never easy to get through to a presidential campaign, but after months of unreturned calls, irritation turned to bewilderment and finally anger, at Vanderslice and, by extension, Kerry.

While the Bush campaign was busy pursuing a sophisticated strategy of under-the-radar outreach to religious publications, the Kerry communications office labeled all religious media "unfriendly." Despite pleas from Vanderslice, Chon refused to talk with Catholic News Service, the evenhanded newswire that supplies copy to most diocesan newspapers. Former White House press secretary—and active member of St. Paul's United Methodist Church in Kensington, Maryland—Mike McCurry came aboard the campaign in September and assumed responsibility for religion press calls. But he admits it was almost too late by that point. "In a campaign, you have to be able to pick the phone up and churn the calls out. When it came to religion, there was no one who could do that."

One of the reasons Kerry's senior advisers didn't worry about the vacuum in their communications operation was their single-minded definition of "religion" as a constituency problem and not something that also factored into general strategy or communications. Under the metrics used by campaigns, a constituency "earns" a place in the candidate's message by demonstrating significant numbers and strength of support. Outreach directors prove that their constituency is worth serious attention by producing lists—of endorsements, of volunteers, of local leaders. That's a somewhat trickier task in religious circles. Clergy are under special restrictions, whether legal or self-imposed, that don't similarly bind the leaders of other constituencies.

Although some Catholic priests and bishops made what amounted to political statements during the 2004 race, strictly speaking a Catholic prelate cannot endorse a candidate. Ministers may come out in support of a particular candidate in their role as individual citizens, but they do so at the risk of upsetting their congregations. If a pastor appears to be leveraging his position for political influence, he can quickly find himself in hot water with parishioners. He might also be putting his church's tax-exempt status in jeopardy.

Despite these inherent challenges, and despite having started with no lists or resources, Vanderslice was subject to the same metrics as her colleagues in well-established constituency areas. "We didn't have networks, we didn't have lists," she says. "But all they wanted to know was 'How many ministers were going to sign up to support Kerry, what are your numbers?'" When Pasquil told Vanderslice she had to sign up 750 religion team leaders around the country and 50,000 names of supporters before the campaign would pay attention to religion, Vanderslice threatened to quit. Backing down, Pasquil allowed her to hire an intern to help with the task—but they would have to share the same phone.

The confining of religion to a constituency box treats it as a purely functional tool. And in 2004, with the GOP focused on Karl Rove's stated goal of registering 4 million new evangelical voters to increase the party's turnout, it wasn't hard to see why Democratic advisers might think that religion could be reduced to a numbers game. But that assumption missed a political fact that Republicans had figured out years earlier: millions of Americans look to the faith of their political candidates as a proxy for a general moral worldview. Many voters understand that it is possible to be a good and moral person without necessarily having religious faith. But in the fog of a campaign, it can be hard to develop a good sense for a candidate's moral foundation. Talking about faith—or, broadly, about the values that underlie issues— gives voters insight into what motivates the men and women who ask for their support. Democratic strategists like to assume that those values don't need to be articulated, that they go without saying. Why waste time talking about a moral responsibility to protect the environment when you could spend that time outlining the details of your gas-tax proposal or carbon-cap plan? Throughout the 2004 campaign, Kerry repeated the phrase "I have a plan" to explain what policies he would pursue as president. One year later, Democratic candidate Tim Kaine would win the Virginia governorship by relying on a more resonant phrase, "That's what I believe," to conclude each of his campaign commercials.

Of course, the right policy initiatives can also communicate a candidate's values or the sense that he understands the concerns of different constituencies. Liberal religious communities, for instance, are often mobilized by calls to end discrimination or pursue peace or eliminate poverty. Bush's faith-based initiative was intended to target some of those same groups, in addition to religious conservatives, by arguing that the federal government had unfairly prevented faith-based organizations from competing for grant money.

To the everlasting frustration of a handful of religious Democrats in the party, the failure of the Kerry campaign to grasp these nuances had become obvious by the summer of 2004. One longtime Capitol Hill aide, an evangelical from the South, decided he would weigh in with some discrete ideas that could help the Kerry campaign improve its image among religious communities without requiring the senator to flaunt his religiosity. None of his proposals would have changed the world, but together they would have been a gesture to religious communities, a signal that the campaign understood their specific needs. One initiative was to expand the tax deduction for a parsonage allowance to cover the growing number of individuals who were called upon to serve understaffed religious institutions, particularly in rural areas, but who did not qualify for the deduction because they lacked seminary degrees. Another would have created a division at the State Department to facilitate overseas mission work by nonprofessionals, a booming trend in evangelical circles, by simply sorting out visas and other logistical difficulties.

The Capital Hill aide's memo outlining a dozen of these policy proposals made it into the Kerry campaign. Not surprisingly, however, it was routed to the constituency division. The Hill veteran did score a phone conversation with Pasquil, who told him she would send the memo around and get back to him. When Pasquil never called back or returned messages, he reached out to a friend on the campaign who delivered the bad news. "They had a discussion about it and decided you're crazy," he remembers her telling him. "They're not interested."

The Kerry campaign's inability to think strategically about religion extended even to the Democratic convention. Compared to previous Democratic gatherings, the four days in Boston were awash in religious rhetoric. But that had more to do with the gifted instincts of individual speakers than a conscious effort by the party to communicate with religious voters and speak about values in addition to policy positions.

Former president Bill Clinton led off the first night, reprising a riff on Isaiah 6:8 that he had used throughout his presidency. The Old Testament verse reads, "Then I heard the voice of the Lord saying,

'Whom shall I send? And who will go for us?' And I said, 'Here am I. Send me!'" Clinton told the rapt crowd that Kerry had throughout his life answered calls to serve his country, whether in the military or in politics, with that same response—"Send me."

On the second night of the convention, a young state senator from Illinois named Barack Obama made himself a household name by giving a stirring keynote speech. He also displayed a gift for seamlessly weaving religious references into his language, a skill that rivaled both Clinton's and Bush's. Without quoting chapter and verse, Obama dropped scriptural phrases such as "I am my brother's keeper" and "belief in things not seen" into his address. But he really got the crowd going with the cry "We worship an *awesome* God in the blue states!" Most of the Democratic delegates on the floor of the Fleet Center wouldn't have identified the allusion to a popular evangelical praise song by Christian musician Rich Mullins ("Our God is an awesome God, He reigns from heaven above"). But they did recognize an audacious move to wrest religion away from the Republican Party and roared their approval.

The one victory Vanderslice and her religion squad claimed at the convention was the concluding passage of Kerry's acceptance speech. On the last night of the four-day event, John Kerry ascended to the podium to address a national audience. He spoke about his time in Vietnam, about the economy and health care, about the values of hard work and responsibility. And then Kerry spoke these words: "In this campaign, we welcome people of faith. America is not us and them." Going on, the Democratic nominee told the nation that he did not wear his faith on his sleeve, but that it had given him the values that shaped his life. Before closing, Kerry subtly jabbed Bush, using the tactic from those March speeches about "faith without works." The era of unquestioning, overconfident faith was over. "As Abraham Lincoln told us," Kerry declared, "I want to pray humbly that we are on God's side."

Vanderslice had thrown all of her energy into lobbying to keep that passage in the speech, and she had some outside help. Both speechwriter Bob Shrum and outside adviser Paul Begala had urged the campaign to make a statement welcoming people of faith.

Begala was one of the operatives from the 1992 Clinton campaign who bitterly regretted the way pro-life Pennsylvania governor Bob Casey had been treated when he'd asked to address the convention that year. He would have been chagrined to find out that twelve years later the party rejected another speaker for not sufficiently passing litmus tests on cultural issues. This time, the unlucky soul was Bill Hybels, the founding pastor of the Willow Creek megachurch and the religious adviser who met monthly with President Clinton throughout his presidency. Given the growing influence of megachurches within the evolving evangelical community, Vanderslice thought the selection of Hybels to fill the slot set aside for prime-time remarks by a religious leader would be symbolically powerful. A Democrat, Hybels had endured significant criticism for welcoming Clinton to Willow Creek following the Lewinsky scandal. He had also taken a lead role in encouraging evangelicals to pay attention to issues of poverty and hunger.

When Vanderslice submitted Hybels's name to convention planners in Boston, however, a quick Internet search told them that he failed two crucial Democratic tests: the megachurch pastor was opposed to abortion and to gay marriage. "Absolutely not" came the word back from Boston.

Hybels's socially conservative views were a problem, but so was something else that couldn't be mentioned: his race. No one likes to talk about it, but the Democratic Party has for decades ghettoized religion, outsourcing it to African-Americans within the party. Democrats who give high-minded explanations for why they consider it inappropriate to mix religion and politics and why they don't approve of wearing religion on their sleeve don't bat an eye at politicians visiting black churches. Religion in black churches, they seem to think, isn't really religion. It's an ethnic characteristic of an important voting bloc.

Until Kerry gave his acceptance speech at the convention, all of his religious references had been in speeches to African-American audiences. Although his advisers must have considered it good strategy to limit religious rhetoric to "safe" crowds, the decision was problematic in two ways. First, by speaking about religion only when it could be politically advantageous, Kerry seemed to confirm the criticism that he was pandering and insincere. If religion was really important to him, voters might think, he would talk about it in other settings. But it was also insulting to African-Americans, leaving the impression that white politicians were at best humoring their silly religion habit and at worst using them for cover.

That's certainly what it seemed like to Ari Lipman, an organizer with the Greater Boston Interfaith Organization, when a convention planner called him a week before the big event. As Lipman later wrote in an article for the *Boston Review,* the staffer wanted his help finding a religious leader to open a Sunday caucus meeting with prayer. When Lipman asked whether the organizers were looking for someone from a particular denomination, the caller answered, "We want a minister of color." Lipman explained that most ministers of color were likely to be in church on Sunday morning. Were they interested in a rabbi? "We really want a black minister," said the staffer.

Lipman suggested they contact Eddly Benoit, the senior elder of a twelve-hundred-member Haitian congregation in Dorchester and a Seventh-Day Adventist. Because Seventh-Day Adventists observe their Sabbath on Saturday, Benoit would likely be available on a Sunday morning. Lipman passed along the elder's information and hung up the phone.

On Friday evening, Lipman got another call, this time from a different, frantic convention staffer. They had forgotten to call the elder during the week and now they couldn't reach him. Lipman explained that because Benoit's Sabbath had already started, he wouldn't be answering the phone until Saturday evening. But Lipman did agree to show up at Benoit's church the next morning and assure the confused clergyman that the Democrats did indeed still want his services.

Benoit arrived at the Democratic meeting on Sunday morning with Lipman by his side, only to find that his name had been rendered

"Elder Erdy Dinot" on the caucus program. Although Lipman flagged down a convention staffer to point out the error, the emcee for the event mispronounced Benoit's name three times throughout the morning. To Lipman, there was no doubt why they were there: "Elder Benoit's role had been ornamental—a prayerful black face for a photo opportunity."

The convention planners never asked Benoit or James Forbes—the African-American senior minister of Riverside Church who was eventually given the prime-time religion slot—the same litmus questions that disqualified Hybels. It might have surprised the Democrats to learn that many African-American clergy are not just cuddly social justice mascots, but are in fact quite conservative on social issues such as abortion and gay marriage. Religion is not just a cultural attribute of black churches, but a biblically rooted theology that often leads to strict teaching on sexual morality and life issues. Republicans had already figured this out and were targeting socially conservative African-American voters with appeals focused on Bush's faith-based initiative and with gay marriage ballot initiatives around the country.

When Pasquil found out that Vanderslice had been lobbying for Hybels, she ordered the religious outreach director to stay away from convention planning and focus her efforts on more important matters.

The campaign wanted Vanderslice to organize a series of "People of Faith for Kerry" service projects around the country in the hopes of generating positive press coverage. "The idea," Vanderslice remembers, "was that volunteers would wear their 'People of Faith for Kerry' T-shirts, and we'd get press for doing good works in the community." The names on her volunteer lists were of religious activists who already spent a good portion of their time on service projects, but if it would help the campaign, they were willing to organize a few more. On one weekend in early September, fourteen service projects took place at the same time, everyone decked out in Kerry campaign swag while clearing public parks or erecting low-cost houses.

Just one thing was missing: not a single reporter or photographer showed up to cover the endeavors. Jin Chon in the Kerry communications office had insisted on controlling the press outreach, instructing Vanderslice not to allow her volunteers—many of whom had relationships with local publications—to contact the press themselves. But with too many issue areas on his plate, Chon had simply run out of time to publicize the service projects. The practical effect was to tie up hundreds of Kerry volunteers in make-work tasks with zero benefit to the campaign.

Vanderslice then found herself in hot water over the cost of the PR flop. She had shipped the PEOPLE OF FAITH FOR KERRY T-shirts overnight so they would arrive in time. But when the service projects failed to generate positive—or any—press coverage, Pasquil declared them a waste of time. Although the campaign would still have $15 million in its coffers on Election Day, Pasquil presented Vanderslice with a bill for $2,000 to cover the cost of the T-shirts and shipping.

On the third night of the GOP convention that September, a gauzy "W." video-mercial appeared on the JumboTron in the middle of Madison Square Garden. Images of Bush surrounded by people of color flashed across the screen, while in a voice-over the president reminded viewers, "I rallied the armies of compassion." More than with any other piece of his domestic agenda, Bush had linked himself personally to the faith-based initiative. During a campaign stop in March 2004, he told a crowd of religious social service providers that he—and he alone—was responsible for the changes that had taken place regarding funding for faith-based organizations. "Congress wouldn't act," Bush said, "so I signed an executive order—that means I did it on my own."

The Bush/Cheney campaign explicitly marketed the president as the savior of religious organizations, never missing an opportunity to assert that Bush had "leveled the playing field" and eliminated supposed government discrimination against religious organizations that wanted to apply for federal grants. The convention itself was like a four-day megachurch service, complete with performances by popular Christian artists such as Third Day and Michael W. Smith, and screenings of the documentary *The Faith of George W. Bush.*

In addition to using his own religiosity as a political asset, Bush was surrounded by advisers with sophisticated knowledge of religious communities. His chief speechwriter, Michael Gerson, was a graduate of the evangelical Wheaton College and had a special gift for weaving into speeches subtle religious phrases that slid under the radar of most liberals but that were immediately recognized by a target audience of evangelical Christians. When, for instance, Bush spoke of the "wonder-working power" of Americans in his 2003 State of the Union address, many television viewers may have considered it simply a nice rhetorical turn of phrase, an eloquent way of describing the potential social impact of volunteerism. Millions of evangelical listeners, however, knew better. They were already humming along to the rest of the chorus of an old gospel hymn that speaks of changing the world through divine, not human, intervention: "There is . . . wonder-working power in the blood of the lamb."

The Bush White House also took the religious liaison operation developed under the Clinton administration and launched it into hyperdrive—at least half a dozen senior Bush aides were involved in ongoing outreach efforts to religious constituencies. Evangelical leaders around the country were kept in the loop through weekly conference calls; conservative Catholic leaders had their own separate calls both with the White House and the Republican National Committee. The president hosted the first-ever White House Hanukkah party and was the first president to consistently use the phrase "church, synagogue, and mosque." (The first White House celebration of Eid, the feast marking the end of Ramadan, took place during the Clinton administration.)

Despite the aggressive effort to brand Bush as the Christian candidate, the president was vulnerable. While he had originally run in 2000 on a platform of "compassionate conservatism" as a way to win over suburban moms and more moderate evangelicals, the policies Bush pursued in office were conservatism-as-usual. Democrats charged that the faith-based initiative was being used as a slush fund for religious conservatives, but in fact the Bush administration had cut back social service grants. More religious organizations might have been applying for the funds, but less money was available for everyone. Bush's tax cuts made it more difficult to fund programs, including antipoverty efforts. The war in Iraq had been vigorously opposed by virtually every religious tradition outside the evangelical community, including the Catholic Church and Bush's own denomination, the United Methodist Church. After four years, compassionate conservatism had been unmasked as an empty slogan.

Fortunately for Bush, the Kerry campaign was too caught up in its own religion problems to go on the offensive. White House surrogates fanned out to question Kerry's faith, knowing that Bush would win reelection only if they could successfully paint the choice as Bush the pious versus Kerry the heathen. Meanwhile, the Massachusetts senator continued to struggle with whether to talk about religion at all.

Heading into the homestretch of the campaign in September, Kerry trailed Bush in the polls. The Swift Boat attacks of late summer had taken their toll on Kerry's credibility as a military hero, and the president benefited from a postconvention bump. Kerry's only hope of rebounding was to perform well in the three upcoming presidential debates. They would provide him with an opportunity to present himself to the country as a credible, capable leader. But they also posed a risk to the senator—he would not be able to escape questions about his faith on national television.

The Communion issue had continued to heat up over the summer, as several right-wing bishops took the matter a step further, declaring that any Catholic who even voted for a pro-choice politician was unfit to receive the Eucharist. It wasn't hard to guess that one of the moderators would ask Kerry about his faith. But how he should answer was the subject of tense discussion during the campaign's debate prep. It's already a stressful experience, requiring the candidate to study binders of suggested talking points on dozens of potential questions and then test out responses in front of a roomful of aides who are trained to identify and attack any weaknesses. Overlaying the dicey subject of religion—especially after the campaign had done everything possible to avoid it up to that point—only ratcheted up the tension in the room.

Kerry's faith, however, was more than just a political calculation. Ron Klain, a former chief of staff to Al Gore who helped lead Kerry's debate prep, remembers that the senator was extremely concerned about the possible ecclesiastical consequences of speaking too openly about his Catholicism. "He was constantly wrestling with the question of 'If I talk about it, am I antagonizing the Church? . . . If I stand up and say I'm a devout Catholic, is the cardinal going to push back and say, "No, you're not"?'" Klain says. Some of Kerry's senior advisers believed there might be a political benefit to standing up to the Catholic leadership, both in support from sympathetic Catholics who disagreed with the Church's political involvement and in the chance for Kerry to show passion about something. It made for some awkward conversations. "It's all well and good for me to sit there as a political strategist," Klain admits, "and say, 'Let me tell you how excommunication would affect your election. Five voters would like you more, four would like you less—see, we're up one voter by you being excommunicated!' In the end, it's *his* soul."

Archbishop Burke raised the stakes in October before the second debate, which would be held in St. Louis, his diocese. The prelate issued a statement reiterating his position that no one who cast a vote for a pro-choice politician should present themselves for Communion. The St. Louis debate was a town hall, with local voters asking their own questions, and the Kerry campaign was sure someone would reference the archbishop's letter. "Of the fifty debate answers we prepared for the three debates," Klain says, "there was no one answer we spent more time on than his answer to the question that never came, which is, 'What's your response to the letter?'" And more than any other answer, this was the one Kerry had to figure out for himself.

It was hard for anyone, even Kerry's closest advisers, to understand how alone he felt defending his personal convictions. He was far from the only Catholic who believed that Archbishop Burke and the handful of other conservative bishops had gone too far. In fact, many of the bishops' own colleagues felt the same way. But in the American Church, bishops operate independently, each within what some have called their own "fiefdom." The unspoken agreement to stay out of each other's business contributed to the horrific scale of the Church's sex-abuse problem. And in this political dispute, it meant that bishops who believed that Catholic politicians should be punished for their pro-choice views could dominate the discussion without being challenged by those who disagreed.

Deepening Kerry's isolation was the fact that many of his Catholic colleagues felt constrained from vocally defending him, in large part because they had similar struggles with their own bishops or cardinals. Congressman David Obey of Wisconsin had been denied Communion the year before, but refused to talk about it publicly. In South Dakota, Senate Democratic Leader Tom Daschle was in the fight of his political life amid criticism from a bishop who declared that the senator should no longer refer to himself as a Catholic in campaign literature. None of the Catholic Democrats wanted to make trouble for anyone else by making a scene. They were conditioned to deal with their individual disagreements discreetly, even if Church leaders chose to turn them into very public issues.

Knowing how painful the whole matter was for Kerry, his staff tried to protect him. They chose not to tell him, for example, that they had to call ahead to every Catholic church he planned to visit to guarantee that the local priest wouldn't deny the senator Communion that Sunday. A few outside Catholics—including Ted Kennedy's wife, Victoria, and Democratic fund-raiser Elizabeth Bagley—tried to impress upon him the seriousness of the situation and offer ways to deal with it. But in a presidential campaign, the candidate is usually far too busy to make even the big decisions, and this one was no exception. Kerry had to just hope that his aides had everything under control.

After all of the agonizing and preparation for questions about his Catholicism in the debates, Kerry's responses were smooth and clear. Asked about the position a few bishops had taken against giving Communion to pro-choice Catholics, Kerry answered briefly, then moved into an unprompted explanation of how his faith informed his politics: "I think that everything you do in public life has to be guided by your faith. That's why I fight against poverty. That's why I fight to clean up the environment and protect this earth. That's why I fight for equality and justice. All of those things come out of that fundamental teaching and belief of faith."

In contrast, when Bush was asked directly to explain the role his faith played in his policy decisions, he was tongue-tied. The president gave a rambling response about how often he prayed, how much it meant to him that other people prayed for him, how Christians and Jews and Muslims were all Americans. But he didn't answer the question. To most observers, Kerry seemed to have won all three debates handily.

And he would have if not for a singularly convoluted answer about abortion in the St. Louis town hall. Having caused an uproar among pro-choice supporters early in the campaign when he told an Iowa woman that he believed life begins at conception, Kerry knew his answer had to satisfy pro-choice supporters. But he needed to let Catholic voters know—in St. Louis, especially—that he was personally troubled by abortion. Kerry's response managed to convey support for public funding of abortion, which most Americans oppose, and hesitation about the legal right to an abortion, which most Americans support. He finished it off with a somewhat tortured version of the Mario Cuomo I'm-personally-opposed-but-can't-do-anything-about-it-as-an-elected-official formulation that didn't make anyone happy:

> I can't take what is an article of faith for me and legislate it for someone who doesn't share that article of faith, whether they be agnostic, atheist, Jew, Protestant, whatever. I can't do that. . . . Now, I believe that you can take that position and not be pro-abortion, but you have to afford people their constitutional rights. And that means being smart about allowing people to be fully educated, to know what their options are in life, and making certain that you

don't deny a poor person the right to be able to have whatever the Constitution affords them if they can't afford it otherwise.

Bush spoke for most home viewers with his immediate reply: "I'm trying to decipher that."

Kerry's failure to clearly articulate his stance was a particular problem given the "pro-abortion" image that continued to haunt Democrats. The party set the tone a year earlier when each of the primary candidates pledged his opposition to a ban on so-called partial-birth abortion at the annual NARAL dinner, a position favored by only 20 percent of Americans. In the spring of 2004, the March for Women's Lives in Washington, D.C., yielded unhelpful news coverage of speakers ranting about the "Cunstitution" and marchers carrying signs like KEEP YOUR GOD OFF MY BODY. While the Republican National Convention featured keynote speeches by pro-choice politicians on three out of the four nights, Democrats kept a pro-life minister off their platform. Most Democratic speakers at the convention felt the need to reiterate their commitment to a woman's right to choose—perhaps thinking voters might have forgotten where they stood on the issue— but uttered not a word about supporting policies that would prevent unwanted pregnancies in the first place.

The effect was to make crystal clear to pro-life Americans that the Democratic Party considered them, in the language of many a Democratic campaign, "right-wing ideologues." In most elections, between one-quarter and one-third of Democratic voters are pro-life. The party is happy to accept their votes—just so long as those voters keep quiet about their opposition to abortion. That leaves people like Pat and Kristin Headley in an uncomfortable position. The two are proud pro-life evangelical Democrats from Erie, Pennsylvania. Like many moderate Catholics and evangelicals, the Headleys disagree with the party on abortion, but nonetheless vote for Democratic candidates because of their positions on social, economic, and foreign policies. So when they heard back in May that Kerry was passing through Erie on a campaign tour, the Headleys were excited. They bundled their young son and daughter into the car for the drive out to the airport, where a small crowd planned to greet the candidate, bringing along some poster board and markers to make signs on the way.

The Headleys decided to write PRO-LIFE FOR KERRY on their sign, to show that it was possible for pro-life voters to support Democratic candidates. Kerry's event staff thought differently. Hurrying over as the message bobbed in the crowd, some Kerry campaign workers asked the Headleys to put down their poster. Only "sanctioned" signs, they said, were allowed at the rally.

Because the Headleys are almost too cheerful and understanding to be believed—the homegrown Midwesterners have holiday flags for every season to hang on their front porch and serve pumpkin-shaped cookies to guests—they didn't think of leaving the Democratic Party. They didn't even blame the Kerry campaign. The problem, the couple concluded, was that too many people equated religion with conservatism. If religious liberals and moderates did a better job of speaking up, maybe Democratic operatives wouldn't assume that it was impossible to be pro-life and a good Democrat.

Not long after the airport rally, Pat—who is a math professor at nearby Gannon University—appeared on a special $10 million superedition of *Who Wants to Be a Millionaire*. He hung out with Regis, made it all the way to the twelfth round, and walked away with $500,000. (Pat chose not to guess which Native American tribe shared the first Thanksgiving with Pilgrims.) Suddenly free to, as Pat puts it, "be a bit less concerned about ourselves and a bit more concerned about the world," the Headleys joined forces with Jim Wallis's Call to Renewal organization. The group had been placing ads with the tagline "God Is Not a Republican. Or a Democrat" in newspapers around the country. Pat and Kristin helped finance a full-page ad in *USA Today* during the week leading up to the election.

The ad campaign was just one piece of what turned out to be the religious left's most impressive year of political activism in decades. Religious liberals raised millions of dollars to place ads in more than five hundred newspapers and other media outlets throughout 2004. They launched voter registration drives that signed up more than one hundred thousand voters. Wallis led a cross-country bus tour that hit thirty cities on a crusade against poverty. They held rallies in Boston and New York during the conventions that produced standing-room-only crowds.

Even so, a showdown between the religious left and religious right was like a tricycle going up against a Mack truck. The Christian Coalition alone mailed out 30 million voter guides in 2004. The group Priests for Life spend $1 million in one month to advertise on television and buy ads in forty diocesan newspapers. Catholic Answers—a hard-right pro-life organization—distributed 5 million pamphlets to Catholic parishes highlighting the "non-negotiable" issues of abortion, gay marriage, and stem-cell research. Focus on the Family mailed "I Vote Values" kits with voter registration materials to twelve thousand churches across the country and distributed 8 million voter guides. All told, the religious right registered approximately 4 million new voters.

The disparity had a lot to do with the fact that religious conservatives had a three-decade head start and millions in funds at their disposal. It's nearly impossible to make up that kind of ground in one election cycle. But it also didn't help that Republicans had incredibly sophisticated methods of reaching religious voters, and they coordinated those efforts with the work of religious conservatives.

Republicans had perfected the art of microtargeting—that is, identifying not just Hispanics or Protestants but suburban middle-income dads who drive SUVs and could be reached by advertising on the Golf Channel. The strategy turned out to be especially effective for finding subgroups within religious constituencies. By contrast, according to several veteran Democratic operatives, the only method the party had for identifying Catholics was to guess based on surnames. Despite the preponderance of Irish, Italian, and Polish Catholics, it's safe to assume this was not the most effective way of targeting voters.

In addition, the scope of the GOP's institutionalized religious outreach operation was awe-inspiring. Starting in 1998, the Republican National Committee had launched a Catholic Task Force to generate support for Bush's presidential bid. The RNC initially concentrated its attention on Catholics in the Rust Belt, figuring their softest targets might be the old Reagan Democrats who could be lured back to the party. A Grassroots Development Team of twelve RNC staff members was created to focus on Catholics and Hispanics. In 2000, the party's Catholic outreach expanded into such states as Florida, New Jersey, and Louisiana, and the party hired Brian Tierney, an adviser to the archbishop of Philadelphia, to chair the task force. By the end of the election cycle the RNC had a list of 3 million church-attending Catholics who were the targets of a $2.5 million direct-mail and outreach effort. Each Catholic received a minimum of two phone calls and two direct-mail pieces highlighting GOP positions on such issues as abortion and same-sex marriage. One flyer featured a priest on the cover and the headline "American Catholics ask: Which presidential candidate represents our values?" Bush split the Catholic vote with Al Gore that year, the first time a Republican had managed that feat since Ronald Reagan.

Not yet satisfied, the RNC ramped up its efforts in 2002, hiring a prominent Catholic publisher as its national chairman for Catholic outreach. (By contrast, the Democratic National Committee would not hire anyone whose job was to work with Catholics until 2007.) By 2004, the operation reached its zenith with a massive voter registration project that relied on the highly questionable practice of collecting membership directories from thousands of evangelical and Catholic churches and funneling them to national headquarters. RNC employees checked the names listed in the directories against lists of registered voters to generate a database of targets. The names of those unregistered were then distributed to volunteers across the country who made personal contact and signed them up to vote.

Democrats had a somewhat different strategy. The common assumption among national Democrats in 2004 was that newly created 527 organizations such as America Coming Together (ACT) would blanket the country with canvassers and drive up voter turnout, making the difference on Election Day. But while ACT and others did demonstrate an impressive show of force, it wasn't enough. "[The RNC] created new Republican supporters in places that weren't on the GOTV [Get Out the Vote] maps," says Mike McCurry. "We got eight million more voters for John Kerry than the party got for Al Gore, but they got twelve million more votes for George Bush the second time around."

It certainly didn't help Democrats that the organizations of the religious left couldn't reach voters and deliver support the way the religious right did for Republicans. Despite a renewed sense of energy among religious liberals—motivated in part by frustration at how religion had been co-opted by the GOP—they continued to battle the same litany of problems that had hampered them for three decades. In June of 2004, former Clinton chief of staff John Podesta—now head of the liberal think tank Center for American Progress (CAP)—convened a meeting of the religious left heavyweights at a hotel on Capitol Hill. Although Podesta had a personal interest in religion and had established a research initiative at CAP on faith and progressive politics, he was really there because none of the old lions could stomach letting any one of them take charge over the rest.

On the agenda were two seemingly simple tasks: to isolate two or three common policy areas that the groups could focus on for the election season, and to develop a list of messaging phrases to describe their movement. True to form, everyone proposed his or her own organization's pet issues—hunger, poverty, peace, human rights, civil rights, minimum wage, the environment, religious liberty. . . . The list streamed down one easel pad and then another. After several hours, the group tentatively settled on four: war, poverty, inequality, and human dignity. Then they turned to messaging. The goal was to come up with some resonant phrase that would define them in the media, the way the religious right had latched onto *family values*. It was a political operative's nightmare. As Podesta fidgeted in his chair, tapping ever more fiercely on his BlackBerry, the former sixties liberals voted on such phrases as "beloved community" and "peace and equality" and "global citizenship for a just world." They disbanded without arriving at a consensus.

Without any institutional structure to coordinate their efforts—again, no one wanted to let anyone else take the lead—even the tentative agreement about election-year issues fell apart. Throughout the summer and the fall, the communities of the religious left organized around Darfur and torture and Iraq and poverty and hunger and the minimum wage. In a sad illustration of just how irrelevant the religious left had become, the press statement released on the day before the election by the National Council of Churches bore the headline "NCC Urges U.S. to Accept Responsibility for Uighur Chinese Refugees at Guantánamo."

While the granddaddy of the religious left was busy advocating for the rights of Chinese Muslim prisoners on the eve of the election, a series of new organizations were emerging on the left. Many of them were started by moderate and liberal Catholics who were disturbed by the political role their church had taken in the presidential election and by the implication that Catholics only cared about abortion. Three twentysomething friends created a Web site called the Catholic Voting Project that allowed visitors to take an online quiz to see how their positions matched up with those of the Church—and those of the presidential candidates. More than fifty thousand people took the quiz and learned that Kerry actually agreed with the U.S. Catholic Conference more than Bush did, a result that was confirmed by the conference itself when it sent questionnaires to the two campaigns.

Another organization—Catholics for Kerry—began as a Web site started by Eric McFadden, a ticked-off Catholic in Columbus, Ohio. It didn't take long for McFadden to connect with other angry Catholic Democrats, and to hear from Mara Vanderslice. She encouraged McFadden to get involved with the local campaign in Ohio, one of the most critical swing states for the election. But the Ohio Kerry campaign wasn't much interested in his help. Undeterred, McFadden spent much of the summer and fall sneaking CATHOLICS FOR KERRY signs into rallies and doing his own freelance outreach work.

In late October, McFadden decided it was time for a splash, so he organized a Catholics for Kerry rally in Columbus. Having lined up the Plumbers and Pipefitters Hall as a venue and talked to producers from *Nightline* who wanted to cover the event, McFadden once again approached the Ohio Kerry operation for support. When they declined, he pulled out a trump card, threatening to talk to the media about how the Kerry campaign wasn't interested in support from Catholics. That did the trick. Within twenty-four hours, Illinois senator Dick Durbin was lined up to speak, the campaign helped draft and distribute a media advisory, and John Kerry's priest from Boston, Father John Ardis, had a plane ticket to Columbus. The rally was a hit, but the Kerry campaign staff in Ohio weren't yet believers.

McFadden spent the last weeks of the election working with Alexia Kelley—a thirty-year-old Catholic who had replaced Brenda Peterson as the DNC's religious liaison—to canvass heavily Catholic counties in Ohio. Democratic volunteers in those areas had been barraged with questions about Kerry's faith, and they were desperate for materials that could provide a fuller picture of his Catholicism. Kelley and McFadden had flyers they wanted to deliver that highlighted Kerry's faith and the drop in abortion rates during the 1990s. But when they approached the Ohio field director for permission, explaining that they wanted to help organizers appeal to Catholic voters, she told them that the plan didn't fit into the orthodoxy of Democratic outreach: "We don't do white churches."

The Kerry campaign never did quite figure out what to do about its candidate's faith. All the way to Election Day, the need to connect with voters versus the instinct to keep religion private created tension. When Kerry did finally begin talking openly about his religious faith— first during the debates, then later in a major address about faith and values—it struck many as coming too late to be sincere. "Kerry . . . has been reticent about his faith but plans to talk of it more," reported the *Washington Post* in mid-October, giving the clear impression that the senator's new openness about his faith was carefully calculated.

Kerry may have become more vocal about his personal faith, and more willing to discuss its impact on his political views, but not all of his supporters had gotten the memo. In early October, National Public Radio religion reporter Barbara Bradley Hagerty was preparing a two-part series on the candidates and their faith. A longtime confidante of Kerry's gave her a transcript from a talk the senator gave at the National Prayer Breakfast in the early 1990s. In his remarks, Kerry spoke comfortably and without notes about the Holy Spirit, drawing on the story of Jesus and Nicodemus. Thinking it would be perfect for her segment—"It showed an intimacy with faith that he just had not expressed during the campaign," she says—Hagerty tried to track down an audiotape of the speech. She called everywhere—Kerry's office, the Senate Press Gallery, the National Press Club—and finally heard that Senator Bill Nelson might have a copy.

Less than twenty-four hours before Hagerty's piece was to air, she went to Nelson's office to get the tape. But the Florida senator told her he couldn't give her the tape because he was afraid it might be used to "damage" Kerry. Hagerty argued that, on the contrary, the recording might help personalize Kerry's faith for listeners, but Nelson wouldn't budge. Desperate, Hagerty asked him to call Mike McCurry, who was by then a senior adviser on the Kerry campaign. Nelson explained the situation to McCurry, saying he was not inclined to hand over the tape. McCurry asked to be put on speakerphone. Putting on his best diplomatic voice, McCurry thanked the senator for his concern and desire to protect Kerry, but said that he thought it might not be such a bad idea to give the tape to National Public Radio so they could play it for America. Please.

The radio piece ran the next morning, with audio of Kerry speaking about authentic faith: "Jesus tells us that the real spiritual renewal that we need requires a faith that goes beyond even accepting the truth of his message. It requires literally a movement toward the person of Jesus, an attachment that requires us to live our lives in a manner that reflects the fullness of our faith and that allows Jesus to become for us truly a lifesaving force." The tape was the best evidence yet that Kerry's faith was not an election-year conversion, but was instead a long-standing part of his life. Yet a misguided attempt to protect the senator almost prevented it from being made public.

Finally, nine days before the election, Kerry gave a landmark speech about faith and values. Terry Edmonds, a former Clinton speechwriter who was gifted at working with religious rhetoric and ideas, drafted the address. But Kerry himself worked extensively on it, wanting to get the tone and the concepts just right. The result was entirely unlike anything John Kerry had said throughout the campaign. He spoke about the faith that had sustained him in Vietnam. He talked about the Catholic concepts of "the common good" and "solidarity" and connected them to the political values he held. He quoted from Matthew, he quoted from James, he gave a shout-out to the "Creator."

"The Bible tells us that in others we encounter the face of God," Kerry told twenty-five hundred supporters. "I was hungry and you fed me, thirsty and you gave me a drink. I was a stranger, and you received me in your home, naked and you clothed me. . . . This is the final judgment of who we are, and what our life will mean."

The original venue for the speech—the product of careful negotiations by Vanderslice, Kelley, and outside advisers—was John Carroll University, a Jesuit school outside Cleveland. Although Catholic Democrats are often banned from speaking at Catholic institutions because of their support for abortion rights, the university was prepared to welcome Kerry to talk about his faith. In addition, the local bishop had agreed not only to allow the senator to speak, but to appear on the dais with him as well. While certainly not an endorsement, the symbolic image of the two would provide a powerful rebuke to the criticism Kerry had received from other bishops.

Once the details had been worked out, however, the campaign's senior advisers stepped in and vetoed the idea. They were concerned that protestors might disrupt the event or that someone might ask a question about the senator's position on abortion. Kerry gave the speech instead at a Jewish senior center in Broward County, Florida.

Just over a week later, Kerry lost the Catholic vote in Ohio by a margin of 44 to 55. It was a six-point drop from Al Gore's support among Catholics in that state four years earlier. Kerry lost Ohio by slightly more than 118,000 votes and, with it, the election.

# CHAPTER 6

# PRO-LIFE
# *AND* PRO-CHOICE

## A BREAKTHROUGH ON ABORTION

One week after John Kerry lost the race for the White House in 2004, evangelical preacher and activist Jim Wallis answered his telephone and heard the unmistakable voice of Ted Kennedy. "Vicki and I need you to come over to the house and talk," Kennedy said in his broad Boston accent. The Massachusetts senator had lived through his share of Democratic defeats, but the loss suffered by his fellow Catholic had struck him more deeply. "They're saying we're not religious," he told Wallis. "But we know that's not true." The two men had never met, and their conversation took place a few weeks before Wallis's book *God's Politics* hit bookstores, becoming a best seller and vaulting him to celebrity status. But Kennedy knew *Sojourners,* the magazine that Wallis had founded in the early 1970s, and he had a feeling that the preacher was a kindred spirit.

Many politically active religious leaders on the left—whether ministers of mainline Protestant churches, liberal Catholic priests, or rabbis in Reform Judaism—combine liberal politics with an equally liberal theology that elevates social justice principles above religious doctrine. But Wallis is both politically liberal and theologically orthodox, believing wholeheartedly in the immorality of poverty and the literal resurrection of Jesus. That has made him an unlikely confessor to

153

politicians such as Kennedy who are inextricably linked to the label *liberal,* but who struggle to reconcile their politics with traditional religious beliefs. Within days of the first phone conservation, Wallis and his wife, Joy, an Anglican minister who was the inspiration for the popular British television show *The Vicar of Dibley,* drove to the Kennedy home in Washington's Kalorama neighborhood to talk religion.

Wallis was particularly impressed with Victoria Kennedy, the senator's wife, whom he describes as a "serious Catholic." Throughout the campaign, she had been one of a handful of Catholics who tried to warn Kerry that he was mishandling questions about his faith. On that evening, seated around the dining room table, she and her husband held their own with the two ministers, quoting Scripture easily and accurately. "It was a serious conversation," Wallis recalled later. "We spent hours talking about how Catholic faith connects to poverty, foreign policy, other issues of the day." He noticed, though, that the discussion kept circling back to one topic. Kennedy "was deeply conflicted on abortion," said Wallis, "feeling kind of trapped by the liberal side, frankly."

Navigating the abortion minefield had always been particularly painful for Catholic Democrats. Buffeted as they were on one side by the Church and on the other by party donors, the best they could hope for was to minimize the flak they took from either side. But as the defeat of Kerry—and, in South Dakota, Senator Tom Daschle—demonstrated in 2004, those efforts weren't always enough. Many of Daschle's Catholic colleagues blamed his loss on local Catholic leaders who had aggressively criticized his abortion position. In hushed tones, they brooded over whether one of their own could ever again be elected president.

By early 2005, the hushed tones had turned to angry growls. In February, Wallis again met with some frustrated Catholic Democrats, this time at a breakfast hosted by Congresswoman Rosa DeLauro at the home she shared with her husband, Democratic pollster Stanley Greenberg. Seated in DeLauro's brightly colored living room, Wallis realized that his role that morning was not so much that of preacher as of spiritual comforter. These Catholics were hurting; their faith was being questioned by the Church that had formed them.

They were also fed up with their party. DeLauro and others such as Anna Eshoo of California and David Obey of Wisconsin worried about the steady flow of once-staunch Democrats such as Catholic union members and social justice advocates away from the party. The Catholic pols believed the outflow had accelerated as opposition to partial-birth abortion had come to define Democrats on the abortion issue. Never mind a Catholic president. The party wouldn't be electing *any* president until it won back their disaffected brothers and sisters. Others in the party would say it wasn't possible to win back those voters without compromising support for *Roe*. But Catholic Democrats knew those voters. For that matter, they were those voters. And they weren't willing to be written off.

More important, they were no longer willing to take untenable positions on abortion at the command of special interest groups. "I'm sick and tired of fucking NARAL writing our legislation," one congressman grumbled. No solutions came out of that early-morning venting session. Certainly, no one suggested writing their own legislation. But within a few months, a new generation of Catholic Democrats would take the initiative and show their colleagues a way out of the abortion minefield.

For thirty years, abortion politics has required Americans to choose sides. You are either pro-choice or pro-life. If a politician supports a partial-birth-abortion ban, he or she is labeled pro-life by abortion rights supporters. But if the same political leader also opposes a parental notification law, the antiabortion side will tag him or her as unacceptably pro-choice. American politics has no vocabulary for a middle position on abortion.

That's unfortunate, because polling consistently shows that more than two-thirds of Americans fall into that middle area, believing that abortion should be available in some, but not all, circumstances. Despite this, voters have largely aligned themselves with either the pro-choice or pro-life position, not as a way of signaling that they think one side is more likely to solve the issue of abortion, but because—in the face of a seemingly intractable problem—choosing a label is simply a way of making a statement. In this binary world, *pro-choice* means you support women; *pro-life* means you think a potential person is more than just a choice.

Of course, there have always been political figures who bristled at these confining categories, wondering why it was necessary to choose sides at all. But until recently these dissenting voices had little to no say in their party's approach to abortion. They were up against powerful forces—people who may genuinely have been motivated by respect for life or respect for women, but who also saw the political value of using abortion to spur fund-raising and rally the troops at election time. Screaming matches about whether abortion was a sin or a God-given right drowned out suggestions that might, for example, actually reduce abortion rates, something both sides theoretically support.

That unyielding approach to the abortion issue hurt Democrats when voters went to the polls. Forced to make a stark choice, more Americans opted to express their disapproval of abortion rather than their support for the right to choose. It didn't help that while Republicans were making an effort to at least project an image of moderation on the issue, Democrats had backed away from the popular "safe, legal, and rare" formulation. The result was predictable: in the November election, George W. Bush won one-third of the pro-choice vote, but John Kerry picked up only 24 percent of pro-life voters.

Despite the obvious urgency of the problem, changing the Democratic playbook was easier said than done. On one side were the pragmatists—primarily elected Democrats—who were tired of taking positions that won them pro-choice money but cost them votes. They thought the party needed to do more than simply declare its undying devotion to the *Roe v. Wade* decision. On the other side, the interest groups and the ideological purists they represented looked at those 2004 numbers and concluded that Democrats hadn't done a good enough job of reminding voters that they were one Supreme Court justice away from seeing *Roe* overturned. They favored a strategy that highlighted the "extremism" of the Republican Party, conjuring up images of family-planning-clinic bombings and back-alley abortions.

John Kerry was one of the first to wade into the intramural debate. In the aftermath of the election, Kerry scrutinized the exit polls with the kind of stone-cold lucidity that only defeat can bring. On issue after issue, from the economy to health care to the environment, voters had agreed with him. But they had voted for his opponent anyway. The senator became convinced that the blame lay with his own inadequately stated abortion position and, more broadly, with the public perception of Democrats as "pro-abortion." He was damned if he was going to let the party repeat the costly mistake. One month after the election, Kerry told a closed meeting of Democratic activists that they needed to "welcome more pro-life candidates into the party."

There were audible gasps of horror at the suggestion. "If we try to be fake Republicans," fumed Diana DeGette, cochair of the House pro-choice caucus, "that's not going to work." The last thing they needed was to be lectured by John "Tiptoe Around Abortion" Kerry, the man who had cost them the opportunity to safeguard the Supreme Court. "He did *not* help the cause," Planned Parenthood president Gloria Feldt observed of his comment.

It wasn't long, however before other Democrats chimed in. In late January 2005, Hillary Clinton used a speech before New York family-planning-service providers on the anniversary of *Roe v. Wade* to assert that abortion was a "sad, even tragic choice." The speech was consistent with Clinton's previous comments on this issue. But because she was widely presumed to be a candidate for the Democratic nomination in 2008, the media covered Clinton's address as if the point were to take pro-choice activists to task. More than a few pundits referred to it as her Sister Souljah moment.

In early 2005, the election of a new Democratic Party chairman served as a proxy battle between the pragmatists and the purists. Most years, the selection of a Democratic National Committee chair is a formality in which state party leaders rubber-stamp a figure selected by national party leaders. But by early 2005, Democrats had no party leaders. The congressional leadership was gone—Dick Gephardt had retired to Missouri and Tom Daschle had lost his Senate seat. Outgoing DNC chair Terry McAuliffe was too tainted by defeat to designate a successor. And with no Democrat in the White House, most prospective 2008 candidates were content to play defense, making sure no one else installed "their" man at party headquarters but not maneuvering to install their own.

The power vacuum put the decision squarely in the hands of local party activists, the kind of people who spend their days running county Democratic clubs. They are among the most liberal members of the party (as one Democratic politician puts it, "There are Democrats, there are liberal Democrats, and then there are DNC voters"). They were none too pleased when Nancy Pelosi and Harry Reid—the incoming House and Senate leaders—enlisted Tim Roemer to run for the position. Roemer, a former Indiana congressman and 9/11 Commission member, ran on a platform of restoring the party's national security credibility. But his pro-life views became the only issue anyone cared about.

Pro-choice activists had not opposed the election of the pro-life Reid to be Senate minority leader. But the Democratic National Committee chairmanship was another matter. "They said someone with pro-life views shouldn't be allowed to represent the entire party," Roemer recalled later. Some were even willing to put financial pressure on the party to oppose him. "I heard from party chairs," Roemer said, "who told me, 'Listen, I've gotten calls from some of these special interest groups and they say if I vote for you, they will cut off every single penny that they give to the Democratic Party.'"

In the end, Roemer couldn't survive the determined campaign against him. He withdrew, leaving Howard Dean as the default choice to head the DNC. But the purists' victory would be short-lived. Dean was pro-choice, but he had already adopted the Kerry and Clinton line about making the Democratic Party more welcoming for pro-life voters. On December 12, 2004, before he was even officially elected to the DNC post, Dean went on *Meet the Press* and declared that his party needed to change. "I have long believed that we ought to make a home for pro-life Democrats," Dean told host Tim Russert. "The Democrats that have stuck with us, who are pro-life, through their long period of conviction, are people who are the kind of pro-life people that we ought to have deep respect for."

Pro-choice activists became frantic. In their minds, the upshot of all this rhetorical openness would be a slate of socially conservative candidates who would push to criminalize abortion. Their fears seemed to be justified when, later that spring, Chuck Schumer—a reliable liberal and the new head of the Democratic Senatorial Campaign Committee—recruited Bob Casey Jr. to run against Rick Santorum in the Pennsylvania Senate race. Pro-choice activists had been relishing the chance to knock off Rick Santorum, perhaps the Senate's most relentless abortion opponent. Casey, who shared the pro-life views of his famous father, was not just a disappointment. He was a slap in the face.

The fatwa soon went forth: Casey would get no support from women's groups. Powerful donors were encouraged to refrain from giving to his campaign. Kate Michelman, former president of NARAL, even contemplated challenging him as a third-party candidate. For some, the Pennsylvania campaign would be a chance to make a statement. Surely no Democrat stood a chance of defeating the well-funded Santorum without pro-choice money. As if to underline the point, NARAL then took the unusual step of endorsing Senator Lincoln Chafee, Republican of Rhode Island, a full year and a half before the 2006 election. The message was clear: a pro-choice Republican is always preferable to a pro-life Democrat.

As summer arrived, a few pro-choice leaders began to lash out publicly at those Democrats who would try to muzzle them. At the Take Back America conference in June—an annual Washington gathering of liberal activists—National Organization for Women president Kim Gandy called out Kerry and Dean by name: "If that's what it means to have a big tent, if it means abandoning the core principles of our party, if it means throwing women's rights overboard like so much ballast . . . then I say, let's keep the skunk out of the tent." Ellen Malcolm, the head of EMILY's List, one of the biggest sources of financial support for many Democratic candidates, echoed Gandy's cry of betrayal. "We fought like mad to beat back the Republicans," Malcolm complained. "Little did we know that we would have just as much to fear from some within the Democratic Party."

The two sides seemed trapped in a vicious cycle. As pragmatic Democrats pursued a strategy of reaching out to pro-life voters, purists felt their position in the party more and more threatened. Their response was to retreat to increasingly dogmatic positions, which in turn alarmed the pragmatists. The low point came at a day-long meeting, titled "Abortion, Morality, and Responsibility," for pro-choice activists hosted by the Center for American Progress in March 2006. The opening session featured a panel of journalists, moderated by CNN's Bill Press, who sat at the front of a long, narrow room facing women from NARAL, Planned Parenthood, the National Women's Law Center, and other organizations that support abortion rights. When the discussion changed to a question-and-answer session, Rachel Laser, who runs the Culture Project at the centrist-Democratic think tank Third Way, stood to make a comment. There were 1.3 million abortions each year in the United States, she said. "Polls show that a majority of Americans think that abortion is morally wrong some or all of the time," Laser continued. "We have to address that."

After Laser spoke, Press turned to the audience and asked who among them thought that 1.3 million abortions per year were too many. He was greeted by raised eyebrows, a few scowls, and Laser's lone hand raised in the air.

The pragmatists sighed at reports like that; they had been through these fights time and again in the years since the *Roe* decision and knew how hard it was to make progress. But just as they were despairing of ever becoming the majority party again, a Democrat who bore no battle scars from those earlier struggles stepped in with a plan to break the deadlock.

*   *   *

It would be tempting to assume that Tim Ryan is too young to know better than to jump headfirst into the abortion debate. On a sunny afternoon in the fall of 2006, Ryan hobbles around his office on the second floor of the Cannon House Office Building, having injured his knee in a flag-football game the previous week. (The congressman played quarterback under legendary Ohio State coach Jim Tressel at Youngstown State.) Falling back into his chair with a grimace, Ryan digs the heels of his palms into his eyes, looking for all the world like a frat boy recovering from a wicked hangover instead of a late-night congressional vote. Halfway through an interview, he picks up the phone to call in an order to one of his aides: "Dude . . . I really need some coffee. Thanks, brother."

Even in his injured and caffeine-deprived state, the thirty-three-year-old congressman from Niles, Ohio, is decked out in a sage-colored suit far too fashionable to have come from any of his colleagues' closets—much less Niles, Ohio. On his left wrist he sports a white band from Bono's One Campaign. A beaded bracelet from a trip to Tibet is on his right. But despite the easy smile and the jock good looks, Ryan's colleagues have learned that he is a formidable politician.

He's also a rising star who could be spotted towering behind Nancy Pelosi on the victory podium the night Democrats took back Congress. And Ryan has become an Internet hero for repeatedly pummeling the Bush administration during the House's daily chorus of one-minute speeches. (Newt Gingrich used the same venue in the late 1980s to build a loyal following among conservative C-SPAN viewers.) The bloggers who enthusiastically pass around YouTube links of Ryan's speeches—"Democrat Tim Ryan kicks Bush's ass!"—might be surprised to know their new favorite politician is also a pro-life Catholic who is leading the charge to change the way his party thinks about abortion.

Ryan spent much of the 2004 campaign working in his home state on behalf of another Catholic Democrat, John Kerry. His own reelection, in a district that covers Youngstown and part of Akron, was never in doubt. But Ryan was troubled by his constituents' discomfort with Kerry's abortion position. Wherever he went, Ryan ran into voters who pledged their support to him, but said, "I just can't vote for John Kerry—he's for abortion."

*For* abortion? Ryan knew that even if he and Kerry didn't always vote the same way on the issue, the senator from Massachusetts was hardly an advocate of abortion. So why did his fellow Ohioans—and much of the country—believe otherwise? Perhaps it was because Kerry, like so many Catholic Democrats of his generation, maneuvered about the abortion landscape with all the finesse and ease of a water buffalo. Kerry's attempt to express his support for abortion rights while also communicating his ambivalence about the procedure itself ended up sounding both tortured and calculating. In an interview with Peter Jennings of ABC News, for example, Kerry said that although he believed unborn children were "a form of life," they were "not the form of life that takes personhood in the terms that we have judged it to be in the past." And his abortion answer during the second presidential debate—so carefully crafted and rehearsed— pleased no one.

Born after Vatican II, Ryan grew up with an altogether less complicated relationship with the Church than his older Democratic colleagues did. It has an ease and loving irreverence that eludes Catholics of Kerry's generation. Ryan is no less devoted to his faith—he was deeply influenced by the Catholic grandparents who helped raise him, and his grandfather laid the cornerstone at Our Lady of Mt. Caramel, where Ryan completed twelve years of school. But unlike pre–Vatican II Catholics, Ryan doesn't quake at the idea of questioning Church authority when he thinks it is in error.

And he does indeed think the Church is in error in its teaching against the use of contraception. "I know the Church's teaching on all of this," he says firmly. "But there is no way to have a significant reduction in the abortion rate without a strong prevention effort." His challenge to the Church is to stop being an obstacle to lowering the number of abortions. Yes, that's right, an obstacle. "When i leave

Congress, I don't want to sit back and think that there were 1.3 million abortions each year and I didn't do anything about it."

It's hard to listen to Ryan without wondering what would have happened in 2004 if those words had come out of John Kerry's mouth. Or if Kerry had responded to criticism from Catholic bishops in the way that Ryan deals with blowback from the Church. In the summer of 2006, the U.S. Catholic Conference sent Ryan a letter to communicate its "disappointment" with his leadership on abortion reduction efforts that include contraception. Ryan's reaction? "Well, I love my church, but I'm used to making nuns and priests mad." He shrugs. "I got a lot of practice during my twelve years of Catholic school."

What has the Catholic Church unhappy with Tim Ryan is that he is heading up the Democrats' effort to thread the needle on abortion. In the fall of 2006, Ryan introduced the most serious legislative attempt to reduce abortion rates without outlawing abortion that Congress has ever seen. To get to that point, Ryan had to patch together an unlikely team of allies.

At the beginning of the 109th Congress, veteran pro-life and pro-choice leaders in the Democratic caucus continued to view each other warily, each feeling somewhat betrayed by the other. But as a second-term congressman, Ryan was untainted by the lingering resentments of past debates. And so, taking advantage of his gee-whiz demeanor and preternatural charm, he barreled straight into politics' most controversial debate with a why-the-hell-not attitude.

Ryan wet his toes with a bill created by the group Democrats for Life, which they called "95-10," after the unlikely claim that it would reduce abortions by 95 percent within ten years. The congressman and his staff were intrigued, but a quick look through the legislation revealed a glaring problem. The plan included no mention of contraception, relying solely on abstinence education and efforts to persuade pregnant women to have their babies, including expanded adoption tax credits and free home visits by registered nurses for new mothers.

Ryan was convinced that any effective abortion-reduction strategy had to include efforts to both support pregnant women *and* to avoid unwanted pregnancies in the first place. At the Democrats for Life national conference in June 2006, he told the assembled members that their approach wasn't good enough: "You cannot have significant numbers of abortions reduced without birth control." But the board, which included a number of conservative Catholics, wouldn't budge. Ryan told Democrats for Life that he was sorry, but they were going to have to find someone else to introduce their bill.

Ryan took much the same approach with the pro-choice community. Early on, he invited in representatives from Planned Parenthood and NARAL to let them know what he was doing. They weren't opposed to his idea, but they already supported a Senate bill and didn't see the need for another one. Their preferred legislation, called Prevention First, was the pet project of Harry Reid, another pro-life Democrat. Unlike Ryan's effort, however, the Senate bill focused exclusively on preventing unintended pregnancies, with no attention to the needs of women who had already conceived and were continuing their pregnancies.

Although Ryan understood the importance of prevention, he insisted that there were important substantive and political reasons to go further. For one thing, a balanced approach would help attract pro-life members. Pro-life Democrats had always been uncomfortable with conservatives who seemed to condemn women for the mistake of having sex, and with liberals who seemed to condemn women for not "fixing" the mistake of an unplanned pregnancy by having an abortion. Ryan also knew that high on the list of reasons women gave for having an abortion was the concern that they couldn't afford to raise a baby. If Congress could make it easier for women to care for the babies they wanted to have by expanding child-care subsidies and food stamps, as well as providing nursing support to first-time mothers, Ryan believed it should. But he also saw an opportunity to put Republicans on the defensive by focusing attention on the wide array of programs to help pregnant women that had been slashed by the GOP Congress.

With both pro-life and pro-choice groups underwhelmed by his plan, Ryan set his shoulders and headed out to lobby his colleagues. Pro-life Democrats—particularly those who didn't rely on endorsements from the National Right to Life Committee to survive in conservative districts—were most amenable to the idea. They were tired of feeling like traitors when voting for Republican abortion bans and were eager to embrace a Democratic alternative for lowering abortion rates. Their pro-choice colleagues, however, were a tougher sell. They were queasy at the mere thought of collaborating with abortion opponents. Many still associated the *pro-life* label with right-wing bogeymen such as Republican congressman Henry Hyde and Senator Rick Santorum. They were impressed with Ryan's earnestness, but wanted to make sure this wasn't a stealth effort to make abortions less accessible.

Ryan realized that he needed a cosponsor with unassailable pro-choice credentials and the motivation to depoliticize the abortion debate. He thought he'd found just the right person in Rosa DeLauro: seven-term congresswoman from New Haven, devout Catholic, and the original executive director of EMILY's List. In addition to being one of the House's most outspoken Catholics, DeLauro had recently assumed a leading role in reestablishing lines of communication between her fellow Democratic Catholics and national Catholic leaders.

After Pope John Paul II died on April 2, 2005, DeLauro traveled to Rome with fellow representatives David Obey and Anna Eshoo to represent the Democratic caucus at the pontiff's funeral. As the three sat in a roped-off section for dignitaries in St. Peter's Square and waited for the start of the funeral mass for their beloved Holy Father, they were overcome. "I looked at them," DeLauro recalled, "and said, 'We can't let them keep us away from our church.'" Not long after they returned to the States, DeLauro led a delegation of Catholic Democrats to meet with Theodore McCarrick, the archbishop of Washington. The conversation was emotional; according to several participants, McCarrick was clearly moved by the depth of feeling in the room. "He recognized," said DeLauro, "that the Church had to be engaged in a dialogue with us."

When Ryan cornered her on the House floor after a vote in the spring of 2006, DeLauro saw an opportunity to further that dialogue by exploring a new approach to the abortion issue. At the same time, she was emphatic about the importance of protecting abortion rights. DeLauro told Ryan that she was intrigued, but she was noncommittal. Undeterred, Ryan spent months lobbying the Connecticut congresswoman, making changes to the bill after hearing her concerns about the absence of funding for Title X, which provides family planning services including contraception and counseling, but not abortion. He waited patiently while she conferred with organizations such as Catholics for a Free Choice to make sure that the legislation wouldn't roll back abortion rights.

After six months of discussion, DeLauro agreed to join Ryan as an original cosponsor, with one request: the name of the bill needed to be changed. *The Abortion Reduction Act,* while succinct and message-worthy, made pro-choice groups uncomfortable. They thought it would stigmatize women who got abortions by implying that there should be fewer of them. ("Um, that's the point," a supporter of the effort later said.) Ryan didn't bat an eye, changing the name to the less-than-melodious *Reducing the Need for Abortion and Supporting Families Act.*

Symbolic and substantive concerns behind him, Ryan moved quickly to introduce the bill. On September 14, the Abortion Team, as Ryan called them, gathered in the basement of the U.S. Capitol for a press conference. The assembled congressional representatives looked not unlike an intramural sports team. In the hallowed Washington tradition of congressional softball, Republicans are known for stacking their lineups with heavy hitters while Democrats are more "democratic." They typically give even the weakest member playing time, no matter how many pitches they're likely to whiff. Here, the diminutive DeLauro leaned over to chat with wheelchair-bound Jim Langevin while Rahm Emanuel stood on one foot pulling up his socks and cracking jokes with Stephanie Herseth. Completing the team atmosphere, Harold Ford stage-whispered a "Good job!" to each speaker after his or her brief remarks. Catholic, Baptist, Jewish, pro-choice, pro-life, they formed a previously unimaginable tableau.

"No one celebrates abortion," DeLauro declared once the cameras were rolling. Indeed, anyone tuning in would have heard a very different message from the "defend *Roe* at all costs" line to which Democrats usually cling when abortion is the topic. The party's support of abortion rights would not—and should not—change, they insisted. But it was long past time to get serious about cutting abortion rates, finally addressing the *rare* in *safe, legal, and rare.* It was what Americans wanted. "Outside Washington," said Emanuel, "many more people are 'yes, but' or 'no, well' than are interested in absolutes."

That attitude may be taking root inside Washington, as well. As soon as the press conference was over, Ryan's phone started ringing off the hook. Democratic colleagues in the Senate were on the line. They were curious, impressed by Ryan's feat. And they wanted more information—they might just want to develop something similar over on their side of the Hill. The politicians most fascinated by the abortion-reduction approach were, perhaps not surprisingly, all Catholics.

In many ways, Bill Ritter, the current Democratic governor of Colorado, is not so different from those Catholic senators. Raised in the Church, he has always been personally opposed to abortion. He has also always been a Democrat, drawn to the party that embodied the values he absorbed as a young student of Catholic social teaching. Unlike so many of his Catholic colleagues, however, Ritter is not willing to call himself pro-choice simply to pass a party litmus test. And that was a problem for Democratic leaders in Colorado.

This first became vividly apparent late in the summer of 2005, as Ritter stood in a Denver living room surrounded by almost sixty tearful women. Ritter, the city's former district attorney, had recently launched his campaign to be the Democratic candidate for governor. The women, a group of key Democratic donors and operatives, had come to hear his views on abortion. If he wanted a shot at the nomination, he would have to find a way to set them at ease. Bringing them to the end of their emotional tether didn't seem like a good place to start.

The ordeal had actually begun a few weeks earlier when Ritter contacted several key Democratic women and asked them to host a small campaign event at which he could meet their friends. One of the women was a former colleague; another, the wife of Tom Strickland, the man who had twice tried and failed to unseat U.S. senator Wayne Allard. Ritter was following the first maxim of campaigns: start with your friends and family, and build support from there. But already there was a problem. The women were deeply uncomfortable with his abortion position.

Ritter, a Catholic who had spent three years as a missionary in Zambia, dislikes the label *pro-life,* saying simply that he is "opposed to abortion." But that's still not exactly music to the ears of the women who form the Colorado Democratic Party's base. Before Ritter had even finished asking Ann Frick, who had worked with him in the DA's office, to host a coffee, the two were embroiled in a debate about the issue. Frick liked and respected Ritter, though, so she offered an alternative: she and Beth Strickland would host an event, but it would be an open question-and-answer session. They could not promise him anything other than the opportunity to explain his position directly to the women whose support—and open wallets—he would need to become governor.

So, early that September morning, the pro-choice women packed into Strickland's spacious living room in the Congress Park neighborhood of Denver, spilling into adjoining rooms and hallways. Some perched on chairs, nibbling fruit salad and brioche. But as Ritter stood at the far end of the room in front of a piano and surveyed his audience, he saw that many more of them stood leaning against the walls, arms crossed and minds apparently already set.

Even allowing for the emotional nature of the abortion debate, it would be hard to find anyone less likely to make people cry than Bill Ritter. He is tall and handsome, with the broad shoulders of a man who laid metal piping to put himself through college and law school, and the unnaturally large head of a newscaster. He has an open smile that doesn't leave his face when he hops back onto the campaign bus, settling in for the ride through Glenwood Canyon and grabbing an aide's cell phone to get an update on his beloved Broncos. As the bus pulls into a town known for its hot springs, Ritter's thirteen-year-old daughter, Tally, half-jokingly asks if she can skip the rally and hang out in the warm water instead. "But you'd miss my speech!" Ritter mock-protests. Without missing a beat, his daughter rolls her eyes: "Dad, I could *give* your speech." Ritter throws back his head and laughs.

When Ritter was Tally's age, the sixth of twelve children growing up on the Eastern Plain of Colorado, his father left the family. The next year, Ritter won a scholarship through his church to attend a Catholic seminary in San Antonio for his freshman and sophomore years of high school. The oblate priests he met there made a deep impression on him; two decades later, Ritter was a rising star in the Denver district attorney's office, but he left his job and moved with his wife and young son to Africa for three years to run a nutrition center—part of a mission the priests had inherited in western Zambia. It was an unorthodox move for an aspiring politician, to say the least. "When I left for the mission," Ritter remembers, "people told me, 'You could have a political future, you could be DA someday. You're ruining your career by going to Africa.'"

AIDS was just beginning to ravage the continent—"At the army compounds near us," he says, "eighty-five percent of the soldiers were HIV-positive." In response to the epidemic, Ritter took a radical position for a devout Catholic: he started teaching condom use to the women who came to his facility. But he remained opposed to abortion. In 1993, when Governor Roy Romer appointed him to fill a DA vacancy, these views won Ritter some grief from NARAL, which opposed his appointment.

Elected to the position in 1996 and 2000, Ritter was a popular DA who implemented innovative crime-prevention strategies, requiring his prosecutors to "adopt" public schools and to consider treatment alternatives instead of incarceration for drug offenses. Ritter considered a run for U.S. Senate in both 2000 and 2004, but he was chastened by Harry Reid's warning that he could expect to lose "a third of your money" because of his pro-life views. The political picture became even more complicated in the presidential election year, as some Catholic leaders in Colorado told voters that they could be denied Communion for supporting a pro-choice candidate. But, once again, Ritter took an unusual stance. When the U.S. Conference of Catholic Bishops held their annual meeting in Denver that year, Ritter penned a harsh article rebuking the Church's politicization of abortion. If it continued, he warned, the result would be fewer Catholics in public office.

Term-limited, Ritter stepped down as DA at the end of 2004 and began to put together his campaign for governor, relying on a standard Democratic platform of education, health care, and economic development. But he wasn't getting any traction with the pro-choice activists and donors who control the Democratic primary process. That's when he contacted Strickland and Frick and asked them to host a small campaign event.

At political meet and greets, an unwritten etiquette is observed: someone may push a candidate on a particular issue, but always with a smile and never too far before circling back to safe ground. On that morning in Strickland's living room, however, all rules were off. From the start, the hosts of the event made clear that they were not endorsing their invited guest. And the questions were aggressive and emotional. "Don't restrict women's right to choose," the women begged. "Why do you allow exceptions for rape or incest but not when a fetus has severe abnormalities?" others asked. One woman looked at Ritter with tears in her eyes and asked him why he didn't trust women to make their own choices.

Facing the gathered women, Ritter had two options. He could take the Cuomo/Kerry approach and allow that, while he opposed abortion personally, that position wouldn't influence his views as governor. Or he could stand firm, explain what he believed, and hope they respected him for it. The first option would be tempting for anyone in Ritter's situation and was a familiar straddle—most Catholic Democrats who had been elected in the eighties and nineties had opted for some version of this position. But it carried political risks as well. To win the governorship, Ritter would need to capture the exurbs that went to both Bush and Democratic senator Ken Salazar in 2004. Voters in counties such as Larimer and Arapahoe have little patience for clever positioning. What they likely heard in Kerry's convoluted abortion explanation was that he wanted credit for being opposed to abortion, but he wasn't so Catholic that it meant anything to him.

Ritter went with the second course. "I told them I could not commit to any of the hypotheticals they were presenting because of my opposition to abortion." But he gave it an important twist. There was a clear distinction, he told the women, between being pro-life and *pro-life*. As governor, he would not actively seek to tighten abortion restrictions. To the contrary, he would overturn an executive order issued by Republican governor Bill Owens disqualifying women's health clinics from getting state funding for teen pregnancy prevention programs if they also provided abortions. He would sign legislation allowing emergency contraception, a bill that Owens had vetoed. His goal would be lowering abortion rates through prevention, not restriction.

However, Ritter didn't shy away from admitting that if an abortion ban including exceptions for the life of the mother, rape, and incest crossed his desk, he would sign it. (Later, influenced by the exchange, he added fetal abnormalities to the list.) There was no doubt in his mind that abortion was wrong. The question for him was how to lower abortion rates without putting women at risk or throwing doctors in jail.

The candidate's answers didn't satisfy all, or even most, of the women at the breakfast. Some were still crying as they left. But others were impressed that he had shown up, listened carefully to them, and stood his ground. "Some people came out of the meeting," said Ann

Frick, "and said, 'He and I don't see eye to eye, but he'll be thought-ful and take our concerns into account.'" It was something they never thought they'd say about a pro-life politician.

The frosty tension between pro-life and pro-choice Democrats has thawed considerably since the days following the 2004 election. That isn't to say that Tim Ryan and Bill Ritter will be getting engraved invi-tations to the annual NARAL dinner anytime soon. But the idea that liberals need to talk about preventing unwanted pregnancies just as much as they do about defending *Roe* is, with some exceptions, accepted wisdom.

Taking the lead is the National Campaign to Prevent Teen Preg-nancy, the most visible player in an astounding ten-year effort that cut teen pregnancy and abortion rates by one-third. Although it will require a name change, the group is expanding its mission to address the cohort that now has the highest rate of abortion: twentysomething women.

This would have prompted outcries a few years ago—nearly every-one can agree that teenagers should be spared the question of whether to give birth or have an abortion. But to many, the implication that adult women should change their behavior to avoid unplanned preg-nancies smacks of paternalism. These are brave new days, however, when it is becoming okay to suggest that planned pregnancies are a goal everyone should strive for.

Democratic leaders are also beginning to recognize that they don't need to turn exclusively to pro-life candidates such as Bob Casey to win back pro-life voters. In 2006, candidates running statewide races in Michigan and Ohio demonstrated impressive support from moderate Catholics and evangelicals (Michigan governor Jennifer Granholm and Ohio gubernatorial candidate Ted Strickland each split the evangelical vote in their states)—far outpacing the modest gains Democrats made nationally—without altering their pro-choice positions. The only change they made was to use the language of *abortion reduction* in addi-tion to *choice,* and to proactively bring up the issue instead of avoiding it or reacting defensively. There is a new, if still wary, openness to pro-life candidates in the Democratic Party. But just as important, the realization that pro-life *and* pro-choice candidates can win with the same approach to abortion reduction has eased the fears of Democrats who foresaw a future in which the party simply became pro-life.

It's one thing, however, to stomach a pro-life candidate for a statewide race that helps Democrats win back the Senate. Or to tolerate a losing presidential candidate while he vents his frustration. It would be quite another for abortion rights activists to sit quietly by—or even applaud—while a Democratic nominee endorsed abortion reduction efforts from the podium at a national convention. That will be the real test of whether the abortion détente holds. Already there are signs of regression.

After her big speech in early 2005, Hillary Clinton backed away from strong public statements about abortion reduction, although she has worked behind the scenes with Harry Reid on the Prevention First bill. EMILY's List endorsed her less than three hours after she announced her White House candidacy in early 2007; whether she will be constrained by that affiliation or seize the opportunity for a Nixon-to-China moment remains to be seen. More troublesome for the pragmatists who support the Ryan-DeLauro approach has been the way choice groups have worked behind the scenes in attempts to torpedo abortion-reduction efforts.

In late July of 2007, Ryan and DeLauro succeeded in getting some of the provisions of their legislation into an appropriations bill that went before the House of Representatives for a vote. In their eyes, it was a perfect opportunity to press the issue. If Republicans defeated the bill, they could be accused of standing in the way of reducing abortion rates. And if the bill passed, Democrats could claim credit for taking real steps toward making abortion rare.

Several of the leading abortion rights organizations, however, continued to fear that a successful abortion-reduction effort would hurt their overall cause and make women feel guilty about having abortions. They couldn't publicly oppose the bill without giving ammunition to the critics who charged that they were pro-abortion. But they did quietly made the rounds on Capitol Hill to meet with pro-choice Democrats. Sitting down with each representative, lobbyists from Planned Parenthood and the National Women's Law Center argued that polling showed the abortion-reduction message alienated Democratic and independent voters. If Democrats took a leading role on the issue, they insisted, it wouldn't help them at the polls—it would actually lose them voters.

In fact, their polling said no such thing. Just as previous polls had reported, a survey commissioned by Planned Parenthood found that substantial majorities of Americans supported reducing the need for abortions. When they tested the goals of "reducing the need for abortions" and "reducing the number of abortions," it was true that respondents were less comfortable with the latter. But Planned Parenthood's own materials in support of the Prevention First legislation (the Senate effort focuses exclusively on expanding access to contraception) laud that "the bill would work to reduce the number of abortions in America—a goal we all share."

The lobbying failed to frighten pro-choice Democrats into removing the abortion-reduction language from the appropriations bill or opposing the final legislation. When it came time to vote, all but seven Democrats cast votes in support. The bill was approved by the House of Representatives, with 139 Republicans voting in opposition.

"Mr. Cellophane"—the tune from the musical *Chicago* about a man who is used to being ignored—could have been the theme song for Bill Ritter's primary campaign. "From the beginning," he remembers, "people began to buzz about who's going to run. They would hear about me and say, 'Who else?'" Each time another Democrat opted out of the race, the Denver and Boulder newspapers reflected the party's desperation, if not exactly the reality of the situation. "Democrats Still Casting About," read one headline nine months into Ritter's campaign, at a time when poll numbers showed him drawing strong support from all corners of the state.

Despite the near-constant news coverage of the Democrats' frantic search, Ritter plowed ahead, answering queries about his abortion position, he says, "in about five out of six phone calls I made for money." Over and over, he patiently answered the same questions that had been put to him by the women at Beth Strickland's house that fall morning. Eventually, he convinced the donors and leaders of the party establishment that his opposition to abortion could really be focused on preventing unwanted pregnancies without putting women at risk. Ritter faced no opponent in the primary.

Having endured the rigors his own party put him through, Ritter found the general election surprisingly smooth sailing. One reason for his appeal across party lines, he found, was that his approach to abortion defused its power as a divisive issue. Ritter took the traditional Catholic Democratic line and improved upon it, essentially saying, "I am personally opposed to abortion, *and* I intend to use my position to lower the abortion rate." By reducing abortion rates through prevention, not restriction or criminalization, Ritter promised to let his faith inform his politics without imposing his beliefs on citizens. It gave him credibility when he said of his faith, "I won't check it at the door of the governor's office." It also allowed him to move on to other issues, a luxury many Catholic Democrats never enjoy.

On a late-fall day, with the campaign winding down and the cushion of a double-digit lead, Ritter addressed the Rotary Club of Colorado Springs. It was not his natural constituency—a roomful of businessmen in one of the state's more conservative areas. El Paso County boasts just one elected Democrat (the cheerfully named state representative Mike Merrifield), and only 20 percent of the registered voters there share his party affiliation. Between the Air Force Academy, defense contractors, and conservative Christian organizations (in addition to Focus on the Family, more than one hundred Christian groups have their headquarters in Colorado Springs), most liberals found reason to leave long ago. The few who remain like to reminisce about the last time one of them won a countywide office, a few decades back.

The cars in the parking lot outside the Rotary meeting are covered with stickers for Ritter's opponent, GOP congressman Bob Beauprez. So it isn't surprising that the questions that follow Ritter's stump speech are less than welcoming. One man notes that Beauprez spoke to the group the previous week: "Why should we support you instead?" Another wants to know Ritter's stand on illegal immigration (most in the group are opposed) and civil unions (ditto). Ritter doesn't bat an eye, but works the room as if he were addressing a jury. "I predict there are people in this room who disagree with me," he says, prompting some chuckles. (He gets the same response later that afternoon from some liberal college students who don't agree with his opposition to legalizing marijuana.)

With abortion off the table, though, Ritter has room to maneuver. He keeps returning to his pet issues—health care, education, and economic development. Having passed the cultural threshold with some of the voters, he finds they are with him on his core agenda. When Ritter finishes one answer, noting that "public policy has to interact with reality," a little white-haired lady in the back who later describes herself as a "very conservative Republican" pipes up, "Amen!" By the time the lunch ends with the clanging of the Rotary bell, and Ritter makes his way out the door, she's been converted, mouthing to her tablemates, "I like him! I like him a lot!"

She wasn't the only one. On Election Day 2006, Ritter won with 58 percent of the vote statewide, including an unheard-of 40 percent in El Paso County. That total was double the percentage the previous Democratic gubernatorial candidate chalked up in the county, and significantly higher than the 32 percent John Kerry tallied in 2004. The first confident attempts at ending the abortion stalemate and making politics safe for Catholic Democrats had borne fruit. Elsewhere in the party, another beleaguered faction faced an equally daunting challenge. Evangelical Democrats were trying to chisel into the GOP bloc Karl Rove had created and bring their born-again brothers and sisters back to the Democratic fold.

# CHAPTER 7

# "WHERE HAVE YOU BEEN?"

## THE DEMOCRATS DISCOVER EVANGELICALS

The town of Holland, Michigan, with its shops full of wooden shoes, city parks featuring historic windmills, and streets filled with thousands of klompen dancers during the annual Tulip Time festival, can feel more like an Epcot exhibit than a Midwestern burg. The smallish city on the shore of Lake Michigan in the western half of the state was founded in the mid-nineteenth century by a group of Dutch Calvinists fleeing religious persecution, and their descendants still dominate the area today. It's nearly impossible to walk down the sidewalk on Eighth Street without running into a Vanderploeg, Vanderzwaag, or Vanderjagt. Holland is the sort of place where the biggest public nuisance is the proclivity of local teenagers to cruise the boulevards on spring evenings with their car doors open to decapitate the town's famous flowers.

Nearly everyone in town belongs to either the Reformed Church in America (RCA) or the Christian Reform Church (CRC), two evangelical denominations whose headquarters are just down the road in Grand Rapids. In that respect, Holland is more representative of western Michigan than it first appears. Since this part of the state has experienced rapid growth over the past decade, Holland, Grand Rapids, and the surrounding counties are starting to rival metropolitan Detroit for political influence.

Because of the auto industry, labor unions have been the traditional power brokers in Michigan state politics. But in western Michigan—where foreign cars are just as prevalent as Detroit exports—it is religious conservatives who can influence the outcome of an election. Largely for that reason, Democrats long ago wrote off this half of the state as unwinnable. The WHAT WOULD JESUS DO? bracelets that gained popularity in the late 1990s were launched in Holland. To many in the area, it seemed clear that Jesus would not vote for a Democrat.

So it was with no small amount of skepticism that a handful of conservative pastors from Holland churches found themselves in a vestry room in the fall of 2005, sitting across the table from Mark Brewer, the head of the Michigan Democratic Party. It was hard for anyone to remember the last time a Democrat had asked to meet with them. As everyone sipped coffee to take off some of the Michigan chill, the pastors suspected the meeting was just a formality, something Brewer had to check off on his political to-do list—"Met with evangelical wackos." After all, it wasn't exactly a secret that the party was worried about its poor showing among religious voters in 2004. Or that Governor Jennifer Granholm's likely Republican opponent in her 2006 reelection race would be a Christian Reform Church member from western Michigan, Dick DeVos.

It came as a surprise, then, when Brewer opened the meeting not by talking at them but by asking for their thoughts. What did they think was the appropriate role for faith in the public square? What frustrated them about the Democratic Party? Did they have any advice for Democrats? He didn't have to ask twice.

An hour and a half—and many earfuls—later, Brewer ended the meeting, telling the group that he would soon be back. Oh, and if they wouldn't mind, he'd be grateful if they could help draft a statement about faith for the Michigan Democratic platform. Shaking his head in bewilderment, one of the pastors turned to Brewer and asked him the question they all shared: "Where have you been this whole time?"

For most of the last three decades, Democratic operatives and activists believed they were living on a different planet from evangelicals—

born-again Christians who emphasize a personal relationship with God and the authority of Scripture, particularly the Gospel. That, at least, was when they thought about evangelicals at all. The growth of evangelical culture seemed to take place in a parallel universe, only intruding on the Democratic consciousness via the occasional televangelist scandal or biannual headlines about the return/disappearance of the religious right.

The election of George W. Bush shone a brighter spotlight on evangelicals. But it also underscored existing liberal stereotypes about them—that they were conservative, Republican, irrational, and intolerant. A low-grade resentment of evangelicals simmered throughout much of Bush's first term, mainly expressed in the form of caustic comments about "religious nuts" and "Jesus freaks." After the Democratic defeat in 2004, liberals fell into a serious postelection depression that left them looking for someone to blame. Evangelicals fit the bill perfectly.

Early interpretations of the 2004 exit polls mistakenly concluded that the top issue that drove voters was "moral values," a vague term that was nonetheless assumed to include only the hot-button issues of abortion and gay marriage. In fact, the percentage of voters who named national security or the war as their top issue swamped "moral values" voters (by a margin of 34 to 22 percent). But that scarcely seemed to matter. Pundits promptly cemented the spin that "values voters" had decided the election. Just as quickly, "values voters" became shorthand for "opponents of abortion and gay marriage," which was in turn shorthand for "evangelicals."

The focus on social conservatives wasn't completely unfounded. Postelection analyses may have exaggerated the pivotal role of "values voters," but ballot initiatives to ban gay marriage batted 1.000 that year, passing in twelve states around the country. White evangelicals turned out in record numbers, with 3.5 million more of them heading to the polls than in 2000. And 78 percent of white evangelicals cast their votes for Bush, making them the most reliable Republican constituency (except for Mormons, a tiny group by comparison). Whether or not abortion and gay marriage were the top issues motivating voters, socially conservative voters had an undeniable impact on the outcome of the election.

Perhaps most frightening for many liberals was the fact that they hadn't seen this coming. In newsrooms around the country, journalists tried to figure out how they could have missed the importance of value-driven issues. One such meeting took place at the National Public Radio offices in downtown Washington early on the morning after the election. A crowd of stunned producers and editors packed into a conference room to debate where they had gone wrong. One problem, they decided, was that most of them didn't actually know any evangelicals. Others dismissed the idea that the election results represented any widespread cultural concerns. "I think it's just these Bible-thumping Republicans who are shoving this stuff down people's throats," complained a producer. When a colleague suggested that this was perhaps an unhelpful stereotype, the producer stared at her. "Sometimes," she snapped, "stereotypes are true."

The evangelicals-as-poor-deluded-saps line was common in liberal corners, fed by the book *What's the Matter with Kansas?* Why, liberals wondered, would these people—who were usually assumed to be poor or working class—vote against their economic interests? Couldn't they see that Democrats were the ones who had their real concerns in mind? Lost on these liberals was the fact that wealthy Democrats routinely elevated values above their own economic interests on Election Day. They insisted that working-class voters would behave differently, that these voters would set aside their values and vote Democratic if only the party made an even stronger appeal to their wallets.

And if that didn't work, well, forget evangelicals. If they were so interested in imposing their morality on everyone else, then let them suffer economically under Republican rule. One of the most popular Internet graphics following the election—which Democrats e-mailed one another in consolation—was a map showing the "United States of Canada," encompassing all of Canada, along with Washington, Ore-

gon, California, New York, and New England, with "Jesus Land" fill-
ing up all the other states. It was a stark image, but it perfectly captured
the "us versus them" mind-set of liberals at that moment. Bar the door,
Martha! The evangelicals are coming!

A series of best-selling books and documentaries—from Kevin
Phillips's *American Theocracy* and Michelle Goldberg's *Kingdom Coming* to Heidi Ewing and Rachel Grady's Oscar-nominated *Jesus
Camp*—only deepened the siege mentality. Evangelicals, these works
argued, were growing in number and embracing a right-wing theology that was rapidly gaining political traction. For the average liberal
with little prior knowledge of evangelicals, the warnings were indeed
alarming. One scene from *Jesus Camp* showed adults at a right-wing
Pentecostal church encouraging young children to bless a life-size
cutout of George W. Bush; the film then instructed viewers that more
than one-third of American adults are evangelical. That's true, but a
small fraction of those evangelicals are Pentecostals or fundamentalists. And a full 40 percent of them are politically moderate, a fact that
both liberal and conservative activists go out of their way to obscure.

The fear and anger directed at evangelicals reached such a fever
pitch that when a postelection *Los Angeles Times* poll asked Democrats
whether they would be willing to vote for an evangelical to be president, only a bare majority (53 percent) answered yes. The odds are
high that the Democrats who balked at the idea of an evangelical
president had actually already cast a vote for an evangelical candidate—
at least if they had voted for Jimmy Carter or Bill Clinton or Al Gore.
But with George W. Bush and James Dobson casting enormous shadows over the religious label, it was easy for Democrats to forget the
evangelicals in their midst.

Even John Kerry was prone to that mistake. Walking through
Dulles Airport on his way out of Washington not long after the election, Kerry was stopped by a supporter. The man shook Kerry's hand
and told the senator he was an evangelical. "I voted for you," he said,
"and so did a lot of evangelicals. But you could have gotten more of us
if you'd tried." Kerry was floored. *Evangelical Democrats?* He hadn't met

with any white evangelicals during the campaign; his staff had largely assumed they were all Republican voters. It was suddenly much easier to understand why Kerry fared worse among evangelical voters than any other Democratic presidential nominee in modern history. To speak directly to a constituency, the candidate needs to at least know it exists.

No one needed to tell Eric Sapp about the existence of evangelical Democrats. He saw one every morning when he looked in the mirror. Tall and sandy-haired with a near-permanent grin, Sapp entered politics after earning degrees in both public policy and theology at Duke University. He had worked for Democrats in both the House and the Senate and was used to getting strange reactions when colleagues learned that he was an evangelical and an ordained minister. Questions about how it was possible to be a Christian *and* a Democrat were actually useful opportunities to clear up stereotypes. The occasional "Isn't *evangelical Democrat* an oxymoron?" was a tolerable, if unoriginal, jab. But sometimes the suspicions had more corrosive implications.

At one point during Sapp's tenure on the staff of the Senate health and education committee, colleagues pulled him off work on genetic-testing legislation because they assumed he was pro-life and therefore unacceptably conservative on the issue. He's not. Sapp did not subscribe to the GOP talking point that evangelicals were persecuted by a secular culture or a hostile Democratic Party. But he did find it endlessly frustrating that some liberals overlooked political allies simply because they were evangelical.

During the 2004 presidential campaign, Sapp began to worry that Democratic ignorance about evangelicals was more than just a personal annoyance. That fall, Sapp took off a few weeks from his job as legislative director for Congressman David Price to volunteer with the Democratic campaign effort in North Carolina's Research Triangle. There he encountered a disturbing number of Democrats, particularly evangelicals, who felt increasingly alienated from the party. Even the volunteers in the campaign office were torn—they couldn't vote for

Bush, but they weren't sure they could pull the lever for Kerry, either. For the most part, Sapp remembers, "It wasn't even about the party's position on social issues so much as the language and the absolutism. They hear the way liberals talk—'If you don't like abortion, don't have one.' That so dismisses their view."

Sapp wasn't surprised by the Democrats' poor showing on Election Night, or by the record-low support the party received from white evangelicals. It became clear to him that the party needed an organized, intense effort to repair its relationships with religious Americans. But how? It wouldn't be easy to cut through conservative spin about godless Democrats or through liberal stereotypes about who religious voters were.

Sapp was still brainstorming ideas when he met Mara Vanderslice, the former religious outreach director for the Kerry campaign and a fellow evangelical. Vanderslice was making the postelection rounds in Washington, testifying to anyone who would listen about the targeted religious outreach she had road tested during the last weeks of the campaign. Every Kerry constituency staffer had headed off to a swing state to help local campaigns in the lead-up to Election Day, and Vanderslice had ended up in Michigan. The state's large Catholic population worried Michigan campaign director Donnie Fowler, the son of former Democratic National Committee chair Don Fowler and a South Carolina native who had little experience with Catholics. If Kerry was going to take Michigan, Fowler knew, the campaign would have to do something to change the candidate's image as a "bad" Catholic.

Within hours of Vanderslice's arrival, Fowler let her loose on winning over undecided Catholic voters, giving her staff, resources, and free rein. After six months of beating her head against the wall in the Kerry campaign's headquarters, Vanderslice could hardly believe her luck. The first thing she did was write a new script for the campaign's phone banks. The campaign had been on the defensive answering questions about abortion, but Vanderslice wanted to be proactive with language that volunteers could use to talk to undecided voters about lowering abortion rates. She also reached out to groups of Catholic nuns, traditionally a far more liberal constituency than priests. The sisters were enthusiastic campaign workers, canvassing key neighborhoods in their sturdy shoes. Catholic voters who were still up in the air by October got used to the shock of picking up the phone and hearing, "This is Sister Mary Alice calling to ask you to support John Kerry for president." The final piece of Vanderslice's strategy was a direct-mail piece that framed Kerry's policies as efforts to improve the "common good," a resonant phrase from Catholic social teaching.

It wasn't much, but Vanderslice's innovations chipped away at the "godless" reputation of Democrats. And they got results. On November 4, Michigan was a rare bright spot on an otherwise disappointing list of election returns. Nationally, Kerry became the first Democratic nominee in sixteen years to lose the Catholic vote, by a margin of 47 to 52 percent. In Michigan, however, he edged out Bush 50 to 49, enough to put him over the top there. More remarkable was Kerry's support from weekly-mass-attending Catholics, the voters thought most likely to vote Republican. His showing among this group was a full fifteen points higher than in Ohio and Pennsylvania, states with similar Catholic populations. Weekly attenders in Michigan even voted for Kerry in higher numbers than their peers in his home state of Massachusetts.

"What was I doing in Washington that whole time?" Vanderslice asked herself. She was convinced that these targeted outreach efforts could be replicated in other races—and with other religious constituencies. Armed with the results from her pilot project in Michigan, Vanderslice met with officials at the Democratic National Committee and the party campaign committees to pitch her services. She found them far more encouraging than the Kerry campaign, but still unsure if religious outreach was a good investment. When the inevitable "thanks, but no thanks" came in, Vanderslice turned to Sapp and his boss, Congressman Price, for advice. The congressman encouraged her to go outside the party structure and start her own consulting group to work with individual candidates. Within weeks, Vanderslice founded

Common Good Strategies and brought on Sapp as her partner for the 2006 cycle. A new breed of Democratic consultant was born.

While the national party wasn't yet ready to invest significant resources into religious outreach or to develop a broad strategy for reaching "values voters," the 2004 results troubled them. Nothing quite focuses the mind like a thumping at the polls, and leading Democrats were soon at least sitting down to figure out why the party seemed to have a problem talking about values and communi-cating with religious voters. Minority Leader Nancy Pelosi asked Representative James Clyburn, a preacher's son from South Car-olina, to put together a Faith Working Group that would help educate the Democratic caucus about religious issues and constituencies.

Encouraged by evangelicals on their own staffs, some Democrats even began to venture out into evangelical communities. When the popular motivational preacher Joel Osteen moved his Lakewood Church into the former Compaq arena in Houston, the better to accommodate his forty-two-thousand-plus congregation, Pelosi was there for the opening service. In a 180-degree turn from his presiden-tial campaign, Howard Dean started telling Democratic audiences they needed to make room for evangelicals in the party and even appeared on Pat Robertson's *700 Club* television show in May 2006. As for John Kerry, his Dulles Airport encounter prompted a yearlong tutorial in evangelicalism that included a budding friendship with megachurch pastor Rick Warren and a meeting with congregants from Ted Haggard's Colorado Springs church.

Not everyone was happy about the idea of Democrats courting evangelicals. Or rather, almost everyone was unhappy about it. Most Democrats fell into one of two groups: those who were uncomfort-able with reaching out to evangelicals but were willing to try anything to win; and those who believed evangelicals were a lost cause and that efforts to woo them would actually hurt the party. The best-case sce-nario envisioned by the latter group was that Democrats would end up pandering to evangelicals, faking religious sentiment, threatening the separation of church and state, and pretending to be more conservative than they really were. At worst, the party would actually move to the right, sacrificing its core principles, and leaving both abortion and gay rights unprotected.

*Washington Post* columnist Ruth Marcus voiced the concerns of many on the left in a May 2006 column titled "The New Temptation of Democrats." Marcus wrote that the strategy of winning over evangelicals was "a long shot" for Democrats that posed "dangerous temptations" for the party. "By all means," she warned, "let Democrats woo evangelicals and cast the message in a way that speaks to religious voters. But in so doing, keep in mind: What does it profit a party to gain a demographic but lose its soul?"

As it turns out, Democratic efforts to reach out to evangelicals were about to benefit from seismic changes taking place within the broad evangelical community. Evangelicals had supported Republican candidates in record numbers in 2004. But it soon became clear that they intended their votes as a sign of disapproval of Kerry more than support for Bush and the GOP. The victory parties were barely over before the marriage of convenience began to dissolve.

Once it did, keeping track of evangelicals' many grievances against the administration required a scorecard. Conservative evangelicals were angry with Bush for spending his political capital on Social Security privatization instead of efforts to ban gay marriage or abortion. They were offended when Harriet Miers's nomination to the Supreme Court was badly bungled after being peddled to them as a way to put one of their own on the bench. The scandal involving Republican lobbyist Jack Abramoff, who tricked religious right leaders into doing the bidding of the gambling interests he represented— while at the same time referring to evangelicals as "wackos" in e-mails with colleagues—only deepened their suspicion that Republicans were just using them for their electoral strength.

For their part, moderate evangelicals—who account for four out of every ten evangelicals—were angry at Republicans for abandoning "compassionate conservatism." These believers are not tied to controversial figures such as Pat Robertson or Jerry Falwell, but to shared cultural touchstones such as the *Left Behind* book series or Michael W. Smith concerts. They are just as likely to send their children to public schools as their nonevangelical neighbors, and many throw back beers on a Saturday night just as happily as they attend church the next morning—often at so-called megachurches, which have rapidly expanded in the suburbs, reflecting the spread of evangelicalism up the rungs of the socioeconomic ladder and into the mainstream.

Although theologically conservative, this group is politically independent; moderate evangelicals supported Clinton in 1996 and Bush in 2000. They are fairly conservative on social issues—most are pro-life, although they are not single-issue abortion voters—and express particular concern about popular culture. In the past decade, they have broadened their areas of concern, paying attention to such causes as the environment and third-world poverty. After the 2004 election, they became increasingly frustrated with Bush. Moderate evangelicals began to suspect that business interests—and not religious constituencies—were the real power players in the Republican Party, and that big business would always win out when its interests collided with religious concerns.

It was hardly a new tension in the Republican coalition. In 1984, Sidney Blumenthal wrote an article in the *New Republic* detailing the efforts of Reagan's political advisers to sideline the religious conservatives who had vaulted them into power. A "strategy of repressive tolerance," he wrote, was the work of economic conservatives who found the agenda of the religious right inconvenient and often embarrassing. The battle plan sounds familiar to those who have closely observed the Bush White House: the religious right rallied its followers around such issues as abortion and school prayer; the White House offered "insincere gestures of support" while instructing congressional leaders to place relevant legislation in permanent limbo; and White House aides made sure the religious right constituency was "maintained in a state of permanent mobilization."

Evangelicals and big business clashed again in the mid-1990s over extending China's most-favored-nation trading status. Religious conservatives, led by evangelicals, argued that the United States should not trade with a country that had little respect for human rights. They were particularly upset by China's persecution of Christians. But their concerns lost out to pressure from multinational corporations that lusted after China's vast, largely untapped market. Similarly, Bush's Justice Department sided with telecommunications companies instead of religious leaders in the spring of 2006 on whether to regulate the transmission of pornography over wireless devices.

Adding to the friction was a power struggle within the evangelical community itself. On one side were the old guard of the religious right, figures such as James Dobson and Jerry Falwell and James Kennedy (the Florida-based televangelist and founder of Coral Ridge Ministries), who had cast their lot with the Republican Party decades earlier and, while now disillusioned, were loath to give up the perks of the alliance and the access to power. Challenging their claim to speak for evangelicals were individual megachurch pastors, authors, and political leaders whose livelihoods didn't depend on sowing "culture war" fears that could be harvested in regular fund-raising drives. The new guard wasn't necessarily any less theologically or socially conservative. But it sought to expand the universe of issues that evangelicals considered Christian priorities beyond the traditional political hobbyhorses.

Randy Brinson was not an obvious candidate to start the movement of moderate evangelicals away from the Republican Party. A lifelong Republican from Montgomery, Alabama, Brinson was a gastroenterologist who decided in 2003 to use his own money to start a religious version of MTV's Rock the Vote that would register young evangelicals and get them involved in politics. Redeem the Vote was an astounding success, partnering with more than thirty Christian music acts and summer concerts such as Creation East and Spirit West Coast (the Christian equivalents of Lilith Fair or Lollapalooza). By the time the 2004 election rolled around, Redeem the Vote had registered more voters than all of the efforts of the religious right heavyweights—Focus on the Family, the Southern Baptist Convention, the American Family Association, and the Family Research Council—combined.

Suddenly, Brinson was on the radar of national media such as the *Washington Post* and *Nightline,* and catching the eye of fellow conservatives. When a who's who of the religious right convened at the Hay-Adams Hotel in Washington a few weeks after the election, Brinson was invited. He showed up expecting a celebratory atmosphere, but instead found a hostile group intent on punishing its enemies. Topic A was how to oust pro-choice senator Arlen Specter from his position as chair of the Senate Judiciary Committee. That, Brinson said, "was my first inkling that I wasn't one of them."

Like many evangelicals, Brinson had always assumed that the Republican Party was the only option open to a good Christian. Now he saw that this calculation had led the old guard of the religious right to become Republicans first and Christians second. Brinson was determined to avoid that trap. So when congressional Democrats—who had heard about his success reaching young voters—came calling, he told them bluntly that he didn't have any interest in being used by Democrats, either. What he did want was to find politicians of either party who could deliver on a broad range of evangelical concerns, such as protecting programs to help the poor, supporting public education, expanding health care, and, yes, reducing abortion rates. The response from Democrats? We can do that.

In quick succession, Brinson found himself meeting with advisers to Nancy Pelosi and Harry Reid, field directors at the Democratic Congressional Campaign Committee, and aides to Howard Dean at the Democratic National Committee. When they even managed to agree on the importance of a strategy to lower abortion rates, Brinson, who is staunchly pro-life, realized that Democrats might just make for more reliable partners. As for the Democrats, they recognized that Republicans had done them an enormous favor. "Listening to [Brinson] talk," a leadership aide said later, "I thought, 'These guys bitch-slapped him, and he's willing to play ball.'"

He wasn't the only one. While Brinson was learning that Christians didn't burst into flames when they entered the Democratic National Committee headquarters, another prominent evangelical was having his own road-to-Damascus moment. Richard Cizik, vice president for governmental affairs at the National Association of Evangelicals (NAE), was a frequent subject of profiles on "kinder, gentler" evangelicals in outlets such as *Newsweek* and *USA Today*. What set him apart from the religious right crowd was his work trying to get evangelicals invested in what he called "creation care," the idea that God made it their responsibility to tend to the earth when He told Adam, in Genesis 2:15, to "watch over" the Garden of Eden "and care for it." In a sly allusion to the evolution debate that occupied the attention of many of his colleagues, Cizik was fond of saying that when he died, God wasn't going to ask him, "Rich, how did I create the earth?" but, "Rich, what did you do to protect that which I created?"

An evangelical who argues that global warming is a critical problem doesn't endear himself to the Republican Party. In 2005, Cizik was occupied with convincing his organization to take a stand on climate change, a move that would place considerable political pressure on the Bush administration to take the issue seriously. The NAE represents fifty-two denominations with forty-five thousand churches and 30 million members across the country. Getting them all to agree on something is no easy task, but Cizik had made impressive strides and was optimistic. Even so, he knew that the White House wasn't happy about his creation-care work and would probably prevail upon the more pliable figures of the religious right to push back.

Cizik was right. On the morning of the National Prayer Breakfast in the winter of 2006, Cizik opened up his *Washington Post* to find an article based on a letter the old guard had sent his boss, then president of the NAE Ted Haggard. (In the fall of 2006, Haggard resigned his position after allegations surfaced that he had frequented a male prostitute in Colorado.) The letter writers—Dobson; Prison Fellowship founder and former Nixon hatchet man Charles Colson; Donald Wildmon, head of the conservative American Family Association; and the rest—suggested, in the way that Tony Soprano makes suggestions, that the NAE back off its plan to take a public position on global warming. "Bible-believing evangelicals," they argued, "disagree about the cause, severity and solutions to the global warming issue." The leaked letter was a blatant attempt to torpedo Cizik's efforts, and it worked. The NAE would take no stand on climate change.

But while the old guard had succeeded in shutting down Cizik in one area, their triumph was short-lived. While they were busy spinning creation care as the project of a lone renegade, something interesting was happening at the grass roots. A survey released that same month, in February 2006, by the Evangelical Environmental Network (EEN) told a very different tale. Sixty-three percent of evangelicals said that global warming was an immediate concern; half went even further, agreeing that immediate government action was needed to reduce global warming, even if it meant a high economic cost for the country. Released with the survey was a statement signed by more than eighty-five evangelical leaders—including megachurch pastor and best-selling author Rick Warren, and thirty-nine presidents of Christian colleges—that asserted global warming was real and demanded immediate attention. Even James Dobson's bullying tactics had lost their punch. When he tried to pressure Haggard to fire Cizik because the environmental efforts were a "distraction," Haggard refused. "The last time I checked," he shot back at Dobson, "you weren't in charge of the NAE."

The expansion of the evangelical agenda to include concern for the environment—as well as other issues such as the war in Iraq, poverty, and AIDS in Africa—was not an entirely new phenomenon. It had a firm foundation in the teachings and traditions of evangelical churches. Over the past few decades, it's true, sermons that touched on politics tended to revolve around social issues such as abortion and homosexuality. But that's not all evangelicals hear in church. They learn their Gospel stories backward and forward, and the parables of Jesus are filled with radical messages about equality and peace and caring for the poor. They sing about Jesus' love for all the children of the world, "red and yellow, black and white." And more recently, the role of the career missionary has been replaced by lay congregants who take mission trips of several weeks or several months at a time. If they had wondered whether the kind of poverty the Bible talked about still existed, these trips allowed them to see suffering and inequality with their own eyes.

Political observers have always associated evangelicalism with more conservative political beliefs. And, indeed, a 2003 survey by the Pew Forum on Religion and Public Life showed evangelicals expressing high support for both the war in Iraq and efforts to restrict abortion (support for the war has since dramatically dropped). But in the same survey, evangelicals favored universal health care and increased spending on welfare programs by large margins. Among Republicans, evangelicals were far more likely than their nonevangelical peers to support such "liberal" causes. They had just rarely seen people within the evangelical community taking the lead on these issues.

That changed after the 2004 election. Immediately after the election, the right-of-center magazine *Christianity Today* ran an editorial declaring that "single-issue politics is neither necessary nor wise." One-third of the students and faculty at conservative Calvin College in western Michigan signed a full-page ad protesting Bush's Iraq policy when he gave a commencement address there in June of 2005. The Christian rock band Jars of Clay founded a nonprofit organization to build clean-water well systems throughout southern Africa and started challenging its audiences to help eradicate water-borne illnesses. Even a few Republicans, such as Kansas senator and GOP presidential candidate Sam Brownback, got involved, calling on evangelicals to focus on such problems as sex trafficking and prison reform.

Without question, however, the most important convert to this new world of political evangelicalism was Rick Warren. The founding pastor of Saddleback, a megachurch in Southern California, Warren came to national prominence when his inspirational book *The Purpose-Driven Life* sold more than 25 million copies. As late as the 2004 election, Warren—who was named "the most influential evangelical in

America" by *Time* magazine in 2006—seemed to be a more low-key, but no less politically conservative, version of James Dobson or Jerry Falwell. Two weeks before the election, Warren sent out his list of "non-negotiable" issues that Christians should consider when casting their votes: abortion, stem-cell research, gay marriage (or "marriage"), human cloning, and euthanasia.

By early 2005, Warren was already undergoing a change of heart. He went to the annual conference of the World Economic Forum in Davos, Switzerland, and met Jim Wallis. The two stayed up late talking about biblical admonitions about the poor. He started a campaign to end global poverty, admitting, "I went to Bible school and seminary and got a doctorate. How did I miss two thousand verses in the Bible [about the poor]?" The next year, Warren signed onto joint statements with Wallis and other evangelical leaders calling for action on global warming and the situation in Darfur, and condemning the torture policy of the United States.

The new Rick Warren didn't go over terribly well with his old friends on the religious right, who warned him that these ventures were a bad use of his time and ministry. When Warren hosted a summit on HIV/AIDS in December of 2006 and invited Democratic senator Barack Obama to address the gathering about AIDS in Africa, it was the last straw. A dozen leaders from the most conservative organizations—the American Family Association, Eagle Forum, the National Clergy Council—issued a scathing letter demanding Warren rescind the invitation. "You cannot fight evil while justifying another," they wrote, arguing that Obama's support for abortion rights made him an unfit ally on any issue. Warren responded by welcoming Obama to the stage with one of his famous bear hugs.

With evangelicals broadening their list of priorities and putting themselves up for grabs politically, it seemed inevitable that a shrewd Democrat would reach out to disillusioned evangelical voters. The first Democratic state party leader to take on the challenge, however, wasn't a longtime Baptist from Alabama but a battle-hardened party hand from Michigan who describes himself as "not really religious." On a humid afternoon in early August of 2006, Michigan Democratic Party chair Mark Brewer tries to explain, in between swigs from a water bottle, what led him to court the conservative evangelicals that his party had long ago written off. With a round, jowly face and hair that sweeps across his forehead, Brewer has the unmistakable look of a campaign lifer who lives off delivery pizzas and never has time to get a haircut.

Indeed, he's been with the state party for more than twenty years, working as assistant general counsel until he was elected chairman in 1995. In that time, Brewer has seen Michigan go from a solidly Democratic state dominated largely by labor unions to a toss-up when those Catholic union members responded to Ronald Reagan's cultural appeals in 1984 and became the original "Reagan Democrats." Democratic candidates have carried the state in the last four presidential elections thanks to the party's strength in three metropolitan Detroit counties (Wayne, Oakland, and Macomb). But with autoworkers steadily losing their jobs in that area, and the blistering growth of conservative western Michigan—Grand Rapids is now the state's second-largest city; its dozen-odd Christian publishing houses and denominational headquarters make it a kind of mini–Colorado Springs—the state's long-term demographic trends favor the GOP. Brewer realized his party needed to adapt to this new reality.

After the 2004 election, Brewer started to puzzle over ways that Democrats might make inroads among white evangelicals. The way he saw it, Democrats didn't need to win over every evangelical in the state to give themselves some breathing room at election time. "In a state like this," he explains, "if I can get two or three percent of evangelicals to either be independents or to vote Democratic, that's a huge shift." After all, he points out, Republicans managed the same feat in 2004 with African-Americans. That year, African-Americans—who represent 11 percent of the electorate—cast 88 percent of their ballots for Democrats nationally. But Bush was able to get those numbers down to 84 percent in such key states as Ohio and Pennsylvania—and he kept the White House as a result. The GOP didn't need a strategy to sway the entire black community; it just needed to pick off enough votes to put the party over the top. Brewer was convinced that Democrats could poach a similarly decisive percentage of evangelicals if they just tried.

As Brewer talks in the conference room of the stunning redbrick, nineteenth-century Queen Anne house that serves as the Michigan Democratic Party's headquarters in Lansing, he is joined by one of the two religious outreach staffers he's hired for the 2006 campaign. No other single constituency has as many people—or as great a share of the party chair's attention—devoted to it this cycle. It's a testament to Brewer's powers of persuasion that he was able to gather the party leadership around the long, polished table in this room more than a year earlier and convince them that an intense religious outreach program would be a good use of their money.

There was only one problem: neither Brewer nor anyone else in the state party then had any contacts with white evangelical leaders or databases of evangelical voters. He did, however, remember the work of a young Kerry campaign worker named Mara Vanderslice, who, in just a few weeks in the fall of 2004, had increased Democrats' share of the Catholic vote in Michigan. In November 2005, Brewer signed a contract with Vanderslice and her partner, Eric Sapp, hiring them to develop and help implement an evangelical outreach plan for the state party.

In this era of microtargeting and Internet databases, the phone book isn't the most obvious place to go trolling for potential votes. But given that Sapp and Vanderslice were starting from scratch, they didn't have much in the way of alternatives. "I don't ever want to go through that again," Sapp says, grimacing at the memory. "We literally went through the yellow pages, looking up names of churches and pastors in the cities where we wanted to set up meetings. And then we cold-called them." Sometimes they went one better than that, stopping by churches in person to ask startled church secretaries whether the pastor was in. Sapp paid special attention to evangelical strongholds such as the Grand Rapids/Holland area, whose booming populations posed the biggest risk to state Democrats.

From the beginning, the Common Good strategists decided that a major problem for Democrats was that evangelicals had as many suspicions about them as they did about evangelicals. If evangelicals believed Democrats were insincere and uninterested in faith and values, no amount of targeted mailings or advertising or clever sound bites would win them over. But if Democrats could meet with a significant number of leaders in the evangelical community, giving them a chance to ask tough questions and to share their concerns, it might just be possible to dissolve some of those stereotypes. Hillary Clinton had done something similar when she first ran for the Senate in 2000, holding "listening meetings" around New York State. One of the unexpected benefits of being demonized and attacked by conservatives for more than a decade turned out to be that voters were surprised and relieved when the real Hillary Clinton didn't come across as shrewish or manipulative. Sapp and Vanderslice thought they might benefit from a similar dynamic.

In each city, Sapp tried to find a pastor who would be willing to host a meeting, assuming that other ministers would respond more positively to an invitation from a colleague than a direct request from the Democratic Party. Each sit-down kicked off with a meaty, but introspective, question: "What is the proper place for faith in public life?" Vigorous debate ensued, but it rarely broke down along partisan lines. Conservative pastors disagreed among themselves about the answer to the question, and some found themselves agreeing with their more moderate peers. Importantly, once the group had turned the philosophical question over, they had a framework for discussions about more controversial topics. The Democrats could acknowledge the importance of allowing religious communities to make moral distinctions about right and wrong while also suggesting that policy debates had to operate under different rules.

This concession proved critical when the discussion eventually turned to specific issues, particularly abortion. It allowed Sapp to steer the conversation past the moral debate between "pro-life" and "pro-choice," where the sides would never agree, and toward a consideration of real-world policies, through which both sides wanted to reduce the abortion rate.

"Okay," Sapp would allow. "Let's say we do overturn *Roe v. Wade.* We know that at least forty states will still allow abortion, and in the ones that wouldn't, it's already pretty hard to get an abortion. So at most, we're looking at a ten percent reduction in the abortion rate as a result of overturning *Roe.*" Already, heads started to cock as pastors thought this through. Then Sapp would point out that the primary reason women give for having abortions is that they can't afford to raise a child. Going through a list of programs cut by the Republican Congress that would have provided economic support to pregnant women, he would mention that Democrats have a plan to make it easier for women to choose to have babies instead of abortions. But, Sapp would add, the most effective way to lower abortion rates is to make sure that unplanned pregnancies don't occur in the first place. And that can't happen without increased access to contraception.

Then he'd unleash the kicker: "So if Democrats do all that—restore programs to support pregnant women and make it easier to avoid unplanned pregnancies—abortion rates would decrease by thirty percent. Does that still make Republicans the pro-life party?" At this point, even the most combative and suspicious of pastors would settle back into their chairs, slightly stunned. They'd never heard Democrats sounding so reasonable before.

The religious leaders also had something to say about a concern Vanderslice had raised during the Kerry campaign. In the absence of any stated concern for the rights of religious people—even something as costless as an occasional nod to "freedom of religious expression"—most religious people understood "separation of church and state" as a code for removing any trace of religion from public life. This alarmed religious voters. The Constitution only forbids state sanction of a particular religion; it doesn't prevent, say, politicians from discussing their faith. What's worse, Democrats clearly didn't intend this scenario. But with the GOP hammering home the argument that Democratic politicians seek to discriminate against religious communities, it was easy to see how religious voters might get the wrong idea. Democrats had done nothing to persuade them that the charge wasn't true. Until then.

Over nearly a year, Brewer sat down with more than five hundred pastors and lay leaders around Michigan using the same format. After hearing at every stop that no one knew what Democrats stood for, Brewer saw an opportunity to do more than just talk. He had already asked several of the pastors he'd met to draft language about faith communities that would be inserted into the Michigan party's platform in the fall of 2006. But Brewer decided to go further, asking a group of evangelicals to help draft a preamble for the platform that would lay out Democratic values and principles. "As we talked to folks in these meetings," he says, "it became clear that this was a way to make a statement, it was a way to say that we wanted these voters in our party." What they came up with was more than he could have hoped for:

> There was a time when Americans were challenged to ask not what their country could do for them, but what they could do for their country. America has always been at its best when Americans ask not "what's in it for me," but "what can I do to give back?" The Michigan Democratic Party understands this basic principle. That is why Democrats in this state are seeking the Common Good—the best life for each citizen of this state. The orphan. The family. The sick. The healthy. The wealthy. The poor. The citizen. The stranger. The first. The last.

Once the language was approved by the state platform committee, Brewer printed up fifteen thousand copies of a mailer based on the preamble and the faith statement and had them distributed in religious communities around Michigan. Several months before the election, Brewer knew that not all of the pastors he'd met with had been convinced. But he was okay with that. "You just have to take the edge off," explained Brewer. "Now that they've met me, they can see I don't have two horns and a tail. You're less likely to demonize

someone if you've met with them, shared a meal, shared a prayer."
Prior to Brewer's listening campaign, the typical pastor would likely
have climbed up to the pulpit in the weeks before the election to tell
his flock that a Christian's duty was to vote against Democrats. That
many of these pastors wouldn't be performing this ritual in 2006
constituted a major step forward.

Vanderslice and Sapp also worked with candidates in half a dozen
other states in 2006. They replicated the listening meetings that had
worked so well in Michigan for their other clients. But in addition, the
two consultants test-drove some strategies so obvious that at times
they wondered why Democrats hadn't thought of them earlier. Their
favorite was the "sweet as pie" tactic, which they used to disarm and
neutralize hostile conservative evangelicals in Pennsylvania. In that
state, state treasurer Bob Casey was challenging incumbent U.S. senator Rick Santorum, whose vigorous opposition to abortion rights
made him a favorite of religious conservatives. That distinction was
diminished somewhat because Casey was a pro-life Democrat. But
Santorum's campaign expected to get an added boost from the Pennsylvania Pastors Network, a group of right-wing evangelical pastors
who had come together during 2004 as part of the RNC's effort to
organize clergy and churches.

In the spring of 2006, the Pennsylvania Pastors Network asked
Santorum to speak at one of the group's monthly meetings. But it did
not extend a similar invitation to Casey. A nonpartisan organization that
gives a platform to one candidate but not another risks losing its tax-
exempt status. In the past, the reflexive Democratic response would
have been to huff and puff about the improper political interference of
a religious organization, with complaints to the Internal Revenue
Service and Federal Election Commission thrown in for good measure.
The reaction often succeeded in forcing faith groups to play by the
rules, but it reinforced the stereotype of secular Democrats opposed to
religion in the public square. The Casey campaign, advised by Common Good Strategies, took a different approach.

"We're so thrilled that you're interested in the Senate race," Casey's advisers told the organizers of the Pennsylvania Pastors Network. "Our candidate would love to come address your group as well. Which month would work best for your schedule?" The conservative clergy were taken aback. They didn't want to host Casey. But now that he had specifically asked to address their members—and because Santorum had already sent a videotaped message to one of their meetings—they couldn't very well deny Casey's request. They could, however, simply stop holding meetings. The Pennsylvania Pastors Network couldn't violate any election laws if there weren't any monthly gatherings for Casey to speak at.

For the Casey campaign, that was a victory. The polite request effectively shut down all Pennsylvania Pastors Network meetings until late summer of 2006, when the group relented and allowed Casey his turn to meet with them. At that gathering in Altoona, Casey didn't convert many of the pastors into Democratic voters. But he did impress them enough to dampen their enthusiasm for giving Santorum the kind of support they had devoted to the Bush campaign in 2004.

The Pennsylvania Pastors Network ran into similar problems with its Web site, which had featured details about Santorum and his policy positions. Again, the Casey campaign called. "We'd be happy to send you our information and have you feature that on your Web site as well," they told the pastors. Rather than face legal stickiness by promoting only one candidate, the Pennsylvania Pastors Network removed Santorum's photo and campaign platform from its Web site. For the Casey campaign, it was a double victory. They prevented the Pennsylvania Pastors Network from lending an extra boost of support to the Santorum campaign *and* did so not by threatening to call on government investigators but by offering up sweetness and light to the evangelical pastors.

In many of their races, the Common Good strategists also made use of advertising on Christian radio. The price of ads in that medium was far lower than in secular radio, usually costing one-quarter as much for a thirty-second spot. The novel advertising approach allowed Democratic candidates to deliver targeted messages to an audience that hadn't often heard from them. In at least one race, it dispelled a myth about the supposed brilliance of GOP candidates in reaching out to religious constituencies.

In Ohio's Fifteenth District, seven-term Republican congresswoman Deborah Pryce ran for reelection in 2006 against Democratic opponent Mary Kilroy, a Common Good client who spent part of her campaign working to connect with religious voters. Pryce, who had coasted to victory in her previous campaigns, suddenly found herself fighting for voters she had always taken for granted. In a play to hang on to those votes, Pryce ran a spot of her own on Christian radio: a negative ad.

Christian radio stations pride themselves on providing programming that is family-friendly and "safe for little ears," as the clean-cut announcers remind listeners every quarter hour. Those radio hosts, such as the Washington-area duo "Brandon and Becky," take seriously their responsibility to ensure that those tuned to their station will "hear no evil" because they "speak no evil." When anything threatens that solemn vow—such as a negative campaign spot—the Brandons and Beckys issue a disclaimer. In Pryce's case, that meant that before her ad played on a Christian radio station, the announcer first informed listeners in a sorrowful tone that the Federal Communications Commission required their station to allow candidates to buy ad time and did not allow them to edit content. That meant, he explained, that what listeners were about to hear broke the station's family-friendly promise and might not be safe for little ears.

On Election Day, Pryce held on to her congressional seat. But instead of the twenty-five-point margin she had enjoyed on average in her three previous races, Pryce eked out a victory, garnering just 1,055 more votes than Kilroy. Her Christian radio gambit had backfired, turning off the very voters Pryce was struggling to keep within Republican lines.

Vanderslice and Sapp also proved that a Democratic candidate didn't need to be pro-life like Casey or a minister like Ohio gubernatorial candidate Ted Strickland to engage evangelical voters. He didn't even need to be from a Judeo-Christian background. In Kansas, a former Clinton White House aide named Raj Goyle ran against a conservative evangelical Republican for a state senate seat in Wichita. Although Goyle was Hindu, he used Common Good's faith outreach strategies to win over the white evangelical Christians who made up a significant part of his district and helped him unseat his opponent.

It was both a satisfying and exasperating discovery for the Common Good duo to find that even the most basic of strategies to reach religious voters threw their Republican opponents off-balance. Even before road testing their ideas in the 2006 campaign, both Sapp and Vanderslice had suspected that the GOP was getting the support of some religious voters by default. When Republican candidates were the only ones talking about values or talking to faith constituencies, they were guaranteed to win some religious votes, no matter how inept their efforts or right-wing their appeals. But when Democrats challenged them on the same turf, as Common Good candidates did in 2006, Republicans were sent scrambling to develop a better religion strategy, not just *a* strategy. It was simple, effective, and yet revolutionary. The consultants couldn't help wondering: why had it taken two campaign novices to develop a game-changing plan for Democrats?

On a Friday afternoon in Holland two weeks before the 2006 elections, Michigan governor Jennifer Granholm came to Hope College, a school affiliated with the Reformed Church in America, to give a speech. It had not quite been a year since Mark Brewer's first get-to-know-you meeting with local pastors, and western Michigan was still considered the home turf of Granholm's opponent, the Grand Rapids–born Amway heir Dick DeVos. Inside Dimnent Chapel, an old stone church with a 120-foot tower in the middle of campus, a crowd of more than seven hundred flowed over into hallways and the balcony. When Granholm took the pulpit to speak, the contrast of her bright red suit against a stained-glass wall of blue and turquoise formed a striking image.

She was there to give what evangelicals would call her testimony. "I come here as a politician to speak of faith, hope, and love," began the governor, after some opening acknowledgments. Weaving together references to her military chaplain brother and to the way her faith moved her to address poverty and inequality, she called for a "new sense of morality." A churchgoing Catholic whose husband considered the priesthood before they met, she drew on Catholic social teaching, telling her listeners, "We are all God's children charged to seek the common good." The way Granholm talked about her own faith sounded rather unlike any Democrat who had come this way in years. "Long before I was governor and long after I am done," she said, "it will be my faith that makes me who I am and, frankly, whose I am."

But Granholm's address wasn't the most remarkable part of the afternoon. That had come when the crowd gave her a standing ovation on her way *into* the chapel. Before the governor even said a word, the students at this conservative Christian campus were on their feet to applaud her. Although it was looking like a good year for Democrats, Granholm had once been among the most vulnerable incumbents in the country, endangered by the steep decline of the U.S. auto industry, which had left Michigan's economy the worst of any state not recently devastated by a hurricane. Now, largely on the strength of the groundwork Brewer and others had already laid, even Granholm's most conservative constituents were willing to give her the benefit of the doubt.

And on Election Day, they were willing to vote for her. Granholm's share of the evangelical vote that fall was 47 percent, representing a thirty-six-point improvement on Kerry's showing among Michigan evangelicals in 2004. She bettered her own 2002 performance in the most conservative western counties by an average of eight percentage points. By contrast, a late campaign appearance by DeVos at Hope drew just a fraction of the crowd that greeted Granholm, and his electoral showing wasn't much better.

It was a good year for Democrats all around. Yet at the national level, the party didn't gain much ground among evangelical voters. Although the Democratic share of the white evangelical vote increased by 4 percent over the previous election, the accomplishment faded under inspection. After all, 2004 had been a low-water mark for the party, so the "gain" was really just a return to still-not-terribly-impressive 2000 levels. What's more, Democrats made gains of between 3 and 5 percentage points among nearly every subgroup in 2006 as the rising partisan tide lifted all demographic boats. All it proved was that in an extraordinary election year, some white evangelicals would switch their votes to Democratic candidates, just like members of every other group.

The handful of Democratic races that boasted high levels of support from evangelical voters all featured Common Good candidates—the consultants went seven for seven in 2006. In Ohio, the victorious Democratic candidate for governor, Ted Strickland, actually took half of the evangelical vote, something that hadn't happened for Democrats since before the era of the religious right. Former NFL quarterback Heath Shuler earned a North Carolina congressional seat in a district that no one had fingered as a Democratic pickup. But the biggest winners of all were those Democrats who had argued in favor of reaching out to evangelicals. Now instead of theories and anecdotal evidence, they had empirical proof that the investment of time and resources paid off. Evangelicals would vote for Democrats after all. They would even vote for pro-choice liberals such as Granholm and Strickland. The climate was indeed changing.

CHAPTER 8

# A LEVEL PRAYING FIELD

## CONCLUSION

On a June evening in 2007, nearly three years after my Baptist pastor got my attention by insisting that good Christians could not vote for Democrats, I once again sat in a religious audience listening to a discussion about faith and politics. On this typical Washington summer night, with the humidity hanging wet and heavy in the air, I was grateful to be in the cool comfort of George Washington University's Lisner Auditorium. This time, the occasion was a presidential forum on faith and values, sponsored by a coalition of progressive religious organizations led by Jim Wallis's Sojourners. The event was beamed across the country by CNN in a live broadcast. And in a sign of how much had changed in the few years since the 2004 election, the leaders doing the talking were the three front-runners for the Democratic nomination: John Edwards, Barack Obama, and Hillary Clinton.

The 2008 campaign was in full swing, with Democrats raising record amounts of money and taking advantage of a churning desire on the part of Democratic voters to take back the White House. But where once Democratic politicians would have worried that God-talk during the primary season would alienate or scare off their base voters, these leading candidates were unabashedly embracing the subject of religion. Each had hired a director of faith outreach, and all were engaging Catholics, evangelicals, and other religious voters in key states. The candidates and their advisers had calculated that answering personal questions about religion in front of a national television audience wouldn't hurt their efforts—and might just help them.

Edwards went first, fielding a question from CNN morning anchor Soledad O'Brien, the forum's moderator, about "the biggest sin you've ever committed." For the candidate who once pointedly refrained from talking about his faith, it wasn't 2004 anymore. The former North Carolina senator's reply was true to his evangelical upbringing: "If I've had a day in my fifty-four years where I haven't sinned multiple times, I would be amazed. I sin every single day. We are all sinners. We all fall short, which is why we have to ask for forgiveness from the Lord."

During his turn, Obama was asked by O'Brien whether he agreed with George W. Bush's rhetoric about good and evil. "I do think there's evil in the world," said the Illinois senator. But, he warned, returning to a theme he had explored in a seminal address to a Sojourners audience in June 2006, "The danger of using good-versus-evil in the context of war is that it may lead us to be not as critical as we should be about our own actions." Obama made the case for a humbler version of faith than the country has seen in George W. Bush, who subscribes to a syllogistic doctrine of presidential infallibility: God works through Christians; I am a Christian; I have decided to do X; therefore, X is God's will.

But it was Hillary Clinton, the Bible-study-attending former first lady, who perhaps most surprised the television audience, discussing intimate details about her religious life in a perfectly relaxed manner. When the CNN anchor asked how Clinton's faith helped her deal with "infidelity in your marriage," the crowd hissed in disapproval of the prying question. Clinton didn't miss a beat, responding, "Well, I'm not sure I would have gotten through it without my faith." O'Brien followed up by asking Clinton what she prays for. The candidate laughed. "It depends upon the time of day," she said, earning appreciative chuckles from the audience. By the time her fifteen minutes were up, Clinton had gone on to talk about the "prayer warriors" who support her, to admit that her instinct as a lifelong Methodist is to avoid wearing her faith on her sleeve, and to say of abortion: "I have tried to talk . . . about abortion being safe, legal, and rare. And by *rare,* I mean *rare.*"

If the candidates seemed infinitely more at ease discussing faith than John Kerry had in the previous election, something was also noticeably different about the individuals they'd selected to advise them on religion. When the Kerry campaign turned over religious outreach to the political newbie Mara Vanderslice and her unpaid intern, it sent a clear signal that faith voters were an afterthought at best. In contrast, the 2008 candidates had decided to focus on faith, carefully choosing their religion advisers and giving them senior positions in the campaign. In the second row of Lisner Auditorium sat David Bonior, Edwards's campaign manager. The pro-life former congressman had studied to become a Catholic priest before he entered politics, and he handled the campaign's religion portfolio among his other duties. Joshua DuBois, Obama's director of religious outreach and a member of a Pentecostal Assemblies of God church, chatted up reporters in the spin room after the forum. Unlike Vanderslice in 2004, the veteran political aide enjoyed the critical advantage of having his candidate's ear—and a candidate who had an ear for the language of faith. Like Bill Clinton, Obama often wrote or ad-libbed his own speeches, especially those to religious audiences, and the chapter he wrote on faith for his book *The Audacity of Hope* is one of the most revealing and thoughtful explorations of religion and politics by an officeholding politician.

Backstage, Clinton conferred with Burns Strider, a gregarious Southern Baptist from Grenada County, Mississippi, and a former missionary. Strider was one of the handful of evangelical congressional aides who took on more visible roles following the 2004 election, advising both Nancy Pelosi and South Carolina congressman James Clyburn on faith issues. He had already proven to be the most strategic of the new breed of religion advisers. To target evangelicals who might be open to dialogue with the Clinton campaign, for instance, Strider identified those Baptist churches that directed a significant portion of their offerings to the Cooperative Baptist Fellowship, which funds global antipoverty missions. And he had help from some special guests in heavily Catholic Iowa. Melanne Verveer, who had helped President Clinton reach out to Catholic leaders, and Elizabeth Bagley, the Democratic fund-raiser who was frustrated in her attempts to advise John Kerry during 2004, hit the early caucus state to meet with and energize Catholic voters.

Although Bill Clinton benefited from the religious instincts of experienced campaign hands during his White House runs, this level of sophisticated religious outreach was unprecedented in Democratic politics. Never before had a Democratic presidential campaign—much less three—hired advisers at such a senior level to provide strategic advice about religious constituencies. Nor had anyone in Democratic politics ever focused so seriously on religious voters in the party primaries. The received wisdom that such a strategy would drive away the supposed secular base of the party had been shattered.

In addressing matters of religion early and often, Edwards, Obama, and Clinton were following the successful model used by candidates in the 2006 midterm elections who worked with Common Good Strategies, the Democratic religious consulting firm. It was an approach pioneered by Virginia Democrat Tim Kaine, who won the governor's seat in 2005 after a campaign that highlighted his faith. In the past, Democratic candidates had resorted to religious references only in the final weeks of a campaign, making them vulnerable to charges that God-talk was the electoral equivalent of throwing up a Hail Mary pass. But Kaine, an observant Catholic who'd spent time working as a missionary in Honduras, spoke about how his faith had inspired him to enter public service in his very first campaign ad, making religion a natural and consistent part of his appeal.

The Democratic front-runners at the CNN forum knew that if they wanted to avoid John Kerry's fate in November 2008, they needed to follow Kaine's lead and gear up their religious operations before the party primaries. But they were also encouraged by the renewed visibility and enthusiasm of religious progressives who were intent on making their voices heard in the party. The unexpected success of Jim Wallis's book *God's Politics: Why the Right Gets It Wrong and the Left Doesn't Get It* following the 2004 election had catapulted the evangelical activist to the prominent media position that had eluded him for most of his three-decade-long career as a political agitator. It also brought a much-needed infusion of financial support for Wallis's organization.

By 2006, Wallis was able to hire a team of political organizers, fund-raisers, and communications specialists to expand Sojourners' work. The staff moved out of crumbling quarters and into a shiny new headquarters outfitted with a recording studio and flat-screen televisions. The CNN forum was the marquee event for the organization's annual conference, a gathering that just a few years earlier barely attracted the attendance of a lone congressman or two.

Now, in the summer of 2007, I had to crane my neck to take in the religious progressives from Sojourners and other affiliated organizations who packed every seat in Lisner Auditorium up to the top row of the balcony. They whooped and hollered, celebrating their return to relevance as much as their support for the candidates on the stage. In the VIP section down front, a reunion of religious Democrats giddily embraced and seemed slightly stunned that their once-quixotic cause was now the subject of an hour-long nationally televised special. During a commercial break, I watched as former Clinton White House press secretaries Dee Dee Myers and Mike McCurry, both members of Sojourners' advisory board, chatted in the center aisle. A few feet away, Clinton-family friend and evangelical liaison Linda Lader worked the crowd, greeting old friends and those new to the cause.

Making my way through the audience, I came upon a row where Common Ground religion consultants Eric Sapp and Mara Vanderslice were joined by a collection of young Catholics who had served on Vanderslice's religious advisory squad during the 2004 campaign and were now benefiting from the Democratic Party's changing approach to religion. John Kelly had just been hired as the Democratic National Committee's first Catholic-outreach coordinator. Alexia Kelley, who'd served as the DNC's religious liaison for the last few months of the

2004 race, was now the executive director of Catholics in Alliance for the Common Good, a progressive Catholic organization.

At the end of the row was Tom Perriello, a young Catholic activist and consultant who had spent the years since the election mobilizing religious Americans on topics ranging from Darfur to torture. Perriello had recently decided to enter the congressional race to unseat Virginia Republican Virgil Goode, who had made an ignoble name for himself earlier in the year by criticizing Keith Ellison, the first Muslim to serve in Congress. In the first four weeks of his candidacy, Perriello raised more than $117,000, largely in individual contributions from religious voters, and bested Goode's take for the entire third quarter of 2007 by nearly $8,000. More important, the young Virginian's campaign represented a new step for the generation of religious Democrats who had stepped up after the defeat in 2004. A few years before, they would have been thrilled just to focus attention on the fact that Goode's ugly comments did not represent the views of all Christians. Now one of their own was looking to capture the congressional seat and provide a new model of a politician shaped by religious faith.

The young Democrats were beaming. "Who would have thought?" Vanderslice asked, looking up at the bright television lights on the stage and the enormous banners labeled FAITH, VALUES, and POVERTY. "Three years ago, who would have thought?"

The Democrats' turnabout in the 2008 campaign has been all the more remarkable because the Republican presidential candidates have been the ones struggling with religious questions. Arizona senator John McCain, who was already infamous in conservative religious circles for calling Pat Robertson and Jerry Falwell "agents of intolerance" during his race for the 2000 GOP nomination, managed the impressive feat of alienating religious voters with his religious outreach operation. In the spring of 2007, two McCain aides who had been hired to spearhead religious outreach quit and then went public with their complaints about a campaign that, they said, "had contempt for Christians." Describing an experience that sounded eerily like Vanderslice's time on the Kerry campaign, the two prominent religious right activists complained that senior McCain advisers ignored their phone calls and e-mail messages and contacted them only to demand church directories.

The twice-divorced, pro-choice Rudy Giuliani sounded like a Democratic candidate not just when outlining his positions on social issues, but also in his answers to questions about faith. On a number of occasions, the former New York City mayor simply refused to talk about his Catholicism, arguing that it was private. In August 2007, Giuliani told the New York *Daily News,* "My religious affiliation . . . and the degree to which I am a good or not-so-good Catholic, I prefer to leave to the priests," and he declined to say if he attends church. When Archbishop Raymond Burke, the same Catholic prelate who went after John Kerry in 2004, said that Giuliani should be denied Communion as well, the mayor tartly responded, "Everybody has a right to their opinion." And his attempts to make his position on abortion palatable to social conservatives by insisting that policymakers should focus on reducing abortion rates instead of outlawing abortion sounded precisely like Hillary Clinton's approach to the issue, though perhaps not as eloquent.

Former Massachusetts governor Mitt Romney, who appeared to be the strongest contender for the GOP nomination as the candidates entered the summer campaign season, found his candidacy challenged on the basis of his Mormon faith. A few decades ago, a Mormon might have been able to run as a Republican presidential candidate without his religious views becoming a key issue. But the modern Republican Party has both elevated the importance of a candidate's religiosity and increased the power of conservative evangelicals in its base. With many conservative evangelicals believing that Mormonism is a cult, those twin developments caused problems for Romney on the campaign trail. At the August 2007 GOP straw poll in Ames, Iowa, a group of conservative pastors based in Council Bluffs on the Nebraska border distributed flyers urging voters not to support Romney. "Mitt Romney represents Mormonism which is counterfeit Christianity, a cult," read the leaflets. In early August, Romney debated Jan Mickelson, a popular Iowa conservative radio talk-show host, about the impact of his religious beliefs on his political positions. Their heated exchange quickly made its way to YouTube.

The religion tribulations of the GOP front-runners created an opening for Mike Huckabee, a Southern Baptist minister and former Arkansas governor. At the Family Research Council's Values Voters Summit in October 2007, Huckabee greeted the crowd "not as one who comes to you, but as one who comes from you." And he delivered what has to be the first ever presidential candidate shout-out to Shadrach, Meshach, and Abednego while making the case for himself over his more established, better-funded opponents. The point was not lost on the audience of Sunday school veterans: the Bible is, after all, jam-packed with stories of the seemingly weak who triumph, heroes who shock the naysayers. On the strength of his fiery sermon, Huckabee won the event's straw poll among voters who cast their ballots on-site, and by late fall he had shimmied up the polls from long shot to front-runner.

But while Huckabee won over evangelical voters in the pews, most of the Christian Right's old guard refused to get behind him, splitting their endorsements between Romney, Giuliani, and former Tennessee senator Fred Thompson. Huckabee, whose more progressive stands on education policy and immigration reflected the changes going on within the broader evangelical community, was, they complained, "too liberal."

Ongoing changes within the evangelical community continue to shift the electoral landscape in Democrats' favor. Particularly distressing for the GOP has been the loosening of its lock on evangelical voters. Between November 2004 and February 2007, the percentage of white evangelicals who self-identified as Republicans declined from roughly 50 percent to 44 percent. The shift accelerated as the year progressed. By July 2007, the percentage had dropped another four points to 40 percent.

The change has largely been driven by a movement of younger

evangelicals away from the GOP. Even more than secular universities, Christian colleges have become centers of political activism. In a throwback to the young evangelical days of the 1960s, students at Wheaton, Calvin, and elsewhere are mobilizing to oppose the war, support children's health insurance, and lobby their campuses to "go green." On overseas mission trips during January-semester or spring breaks, their eyes are being opened to global poverty with an immediacy that could never be achieved by watching slide shows put together by visiting missionaries.

After years of hearing from religious leaders who preached about hot-button social issues, young evangelicals also now hear a more nuanced message. In the years following the 2004 election, Jim Wallis toured nearly three dozen Christian campuses and challenged the students he met. "Yes, four thousand abortions take place every day," he'd say. "But nine thousand people will die from HIV/AIDS today. Thirty thousand children will die of malnutrition or from diseases spread by unclean drinking water. How can I say that abortions are more important than anything else? We need to broaden what 'life' issues are." Wallis is joined by evangelical preacher Rick Warren, whose religious and political agenda is now light-years away from what it was when he sent the preelection e-mail in 2004 narrowly defining the "non-negotiable" issues as abortion, gay rights, stem-cell research, euthanasia, and human cloning. When I asked Warren in September 2007 about that e-mail, he stopped me before I could finish the question. "I absolutely regret that," he said. "It was wrong."

It is, however, far too soon for Democrats to begin celebrating. Evangelicals may be leaving the Republican Party, but most are not becoming Democrats just yet. For now, evangelicals fleeing the GOP are labeling themselves independents. That's because influential segments of the Democratic Party remain either conflicted about or opposed to efforts to court religious voters.

For the most part, the leadership of the Democratic Party is on board with directing resources to the mission of establishing and cultivating relationships with religious voters. Even Howard Dean, who once dismissively described the GOP as the "white Christian party," has taken a lead role as chair of the Democratic National Committee to force hesitant Democratic activists to get over their squeamishness about religion.

Of course, the DNC's first baby steps toward reaching out to religious constituencies were wobbly and accident-prone. In the summer of 2005, an unnamed party official explained Democratic outreach to evangelicals by telling *U.S. News & World Report,* "We're dealing with a serious bloc of people, not just crazies with big Bibles." Dean further blundered in a May 2006 interview with Pat Robertson's Christian Broadcasting Network. "[Democrats] have an enormous amount in common with the Christian community," he said, "and particularly with the evangelical Christian community." To many, the statement sounded as if he were Ambassador Dean dispatched to liaise with creatures from Planet Christian. But to his credit, Governor Dean would not give up, and the DNC did improve on its learning curve. By the fall of 2007, the party organization had developed a database to identify voters by religious affiliation, among other characteristics. And Dean's schedule was filled with appearances at black churches *and* religious colleges populated by those "white Christians" he had once associated only with the GOP.

However, for many Democratic activists and operatives, the phrase "white Christians" still conjures up images of finger-wagging priests and Scopes-era fundamentalists. The fear and disdain it inspires is what leads campaign advisers to declare "white churches" out of their purview or Catholic campuses off-limits, even if those statements effectively wall the party off from a full three-quarters of the electorate.

In a small but influential segment of the media and the Democratic Party, the targeting of religious conservatives for criticism and ridicule has become either sport or habit over the past three decades. The genuine mystification that greeted Jimmy Carter's revelation in 1976 that he was born-again has been replaced by a moral superiority that tries to pass as cleverness. While it may entertain fellow liberals, it often alienates potential allies in the religious world. During the Lewinsky investigation in the late 1990s, for example, *New York Times* columnist Maureen Dowd took on Kenneth Starr, the widely unpopular independent counsel, by skewering him for humming hymns while he jogged. In the same vein, when John Kerry's brother, Cam, made an appeal to a gathering of Orthodox Jewish leaders in 2004, he led off by criticizing then attorney general John Ashcroft not for eroding civil liberties or for the declining rate of civil rights prosecutions during his tenure, but for Ashcroft's habit of starting his work day with private prayer. (It was a particularly ill-conceived comment for a room full of people who begin each day with prayer.) Even Dick Gephardt sought to apologize for his previous pro-life position in a 2003 speech to pro-choice activists by blaming it on his being raised Baptist. Going after a conservative based on his private religious practice or seeking absolution for political apostasy by blaming a faith tradition appeals to an unattractive strain of intellectual superiority among liberals. It also draws an unnecessary line between secular liberals and the religious voters who often share their values.

In the fall of 2007, a liberal Democrat named Tim Burgess, who also happens to be an evangelical, ran for the Seattle city council. Although Burgess's campaign platform consisted of reliably liberal positions, he was surprised when local Democrats began to target him with attacks that played on fears about his faith. "He doesn't share our values," his Democratic primary opponent charged at a public forum, accusing Burgess of being a closet conservative. "He's backed by evangelical money," complained a critic online. Similarly, in the weeks leading up to the 2006 midterm elections, the Democratic Congressional Campaign Committee (DCCC) sought to generate support by exploiting concerns about conservative Christians. Staffers at the DCCC drafted a fund-raising appeal to be sent out under the names of former Clinton campaign advisers James Carville and Paul Begala that told donors they needed to combat the influence of churches organizing congregants to vote in the upcoming election. Begala balked, reminding the staffers that progressive churches often did the same thing. "I can't criticize them for organizing churches," he said. "I don't know about you guys, but that's what I used to do for a living." When I talked to him the next day, he was still frustrated: "They want to say, 'Republicans are going to churches!' and scare Democrats into giving money to the party. It might work, but it also alienates a lot of voters."

The Democratic operatives who write these fund-raising appeals or reflexively criticize candidates like Burgess assume that attacks on evangelicals and religious conservatives can't hurt them, that those voters are lost to Democrats from the start. But they forget that 10 million white evangelicals voted for Al Gore in 2000, that 40 percent of evangelicals are politically moderate, and that Hispanic and African-American voters are disproportionately religious.

When John Edwards's campaign hired Amanda Marcotte, a popular and aggressively liberal blogger, to author its campaign blog in February 2007, the operation considered her outspokenness an asset. The discovery that Marcotte had criticized Catholics in sometimes offensive terms on her personal blog, ridiculing pro-life views with statements like "What if Mary had taken Plan B after the Lord filled her with his hot, white, sticky Holy Spirit?" didn't seem to bother secular liberals. If anything, the fact that conservatives were the first to take issue with Marcotte's writings seemed sufficient to convince many of her blogging peers to rally around not just her right to express herself but the political wisdom of the Edwards campaign in hiring her. Just as many liberals turned against faith-based initiatives once conservatives began trumpeting them, so did conservative attacks on Marcotte lead them to dismiss as "irrelevant" any concerns about her anti-Catholic sentiments.

Catholic Democrats were outraged but quickly found themselves on the outside of the circle. These Catholics were dismayed that Marcotte's writing hadn't triggered alarms within the Edwards campaign. But they were shocked and hurt when liberal activists declared that anyone who objected to Marcotte's statements was an intolerant right-winger in cahoots with Bill Donahue, the blustery head of the

Catholic League. "They are no different than the religious right they pretend to oppose," wrote one prominent blogger. Marcotte resigned from the campaign after less than a week, and her departure was loudly bemoaned in the liberal blogosphere. "Sadly, the inhuman still rules the world of American politics," despaired Chris Bowers, another leading liberal blogger. "We will all be a lot better off when there is a more prominent place for someone like Amanda Marcotte in our public discourse." For Catholic Democrats, that expression of a hoped-for future was discomforting.

These examples aren't widespread throughout the party. For the most part, they're limited to a few opinion journalists, a cadre of operatives, and activists who have weathered decades of fights against a religious right movement that sometimes seemed like an unbeatable monolith. But the comments are important because they feed an existing suspicion that Democrats are cultural elitists who consider themselves intellectually superior to religious believers. Republicans and conservative evangelical leaders have gotten years of mileage out of a 1993 front-page article in the *Washington Post* that conflated followers of Jerry Falwell and Pat Robertson with evangelicals in general, and then described them as "poor, uneducated, and easy to command."

Every additional statement like this becomes ammunition for the GOP. Like an abusive boyfriend, Republicans keep religious voters in the party coalition by alternately painting their options as bleak and wooing them with sweet talk. *You can't leave me—where are you going to go? To them? They think you're stupid, they hate religion. Besides, you know I love you—I'm a compassionate conservative.* The tactic works as long as the faithful don't call the GOP's bluff and as long as Democrats can be viewed as hostile to religion.

Finally, there are strategists within the Democratic Party who genuinely believe that engagement with faith communities and voters is a politically dangerous proposition. They assume that Democrats could never find areas of substantive agreement with religious voters, and so dismiss outreach efforts as pure pander. If it's nothing more than spouting Bible verses, they say, Democrats will only look inauthentic and morally adrift. And they would be correct—if that's all that Democrats were doing. Others argue that demographic trends make religious outreach a waste of time and resources, that the ranks of secularists in the United States are rapidly increasing. In fact, that growth is far slower than was previously thought. When surveys such as a 2006 Baylor University study ask Americans for details about their religious practice and beliefs, a surprising number of those who say they have no faith tradition report attending worship services or praying. Describing oneself as "religious" seems to have become less popular over the past few decades; but Americans haven't lost faith at the same time.

Some skeptical Democrats also express serious concern that the only way Democrats can successfully woo faith voters is by running actively religious candidates. They rightly recoil at the idea of an implicit religious test. The example of the 1980 election, in which the Southern Baptist Sunday school–teaching Carter was defeated by Ronald Reagan, a man who didn't attend church, should prove that personal piety is neither a required nor sufficient quality in a candidate. The Democratic politicians who have been able to reach across the aisle to religious voters haven't been those who majored in Jesus talk. They have been the ones who were willing to sit down and talk, period. It's not complicated, says Ted Olsen, the managing editor for online journalism at *Christianity Today,* the most widely read evangelical magazine: "Evangelicals aren't necessarily looking for a candidate who is like them. They're looking for a candidate who *likes* them."

The initial shock I felt in the summer of 2004 after hearing Pastor Mike's declaration that my faith was in question because of my political leanings didn't drive me away from the First Baptist Church. But the incident did spark my curiosity about the evangelicals I considered family—and it inspired me to do some witnessing of my own. If the people I had once worshipped with had such negative views of Democrats and political liberals, I decided, it was because too many religious Democrats had not followed the instructions of one of our favorite Sunday school tunes, "This Little Light of Mine." We had kept our lights hidden underneath our bushels, not sharing our faith with our secular brothers and sisters, nor the moral passion behind our politics with our friends in the pew next to us.

I include myself among that group of the forgetful and the meek. For nearly fifteen years, I had also made the mistake of conflating evangelicalism with political conservatism. I shunned the label and nearly convinced myself that I really belonged in a more socially acceptable denomination, among the Methodists or Presbyterians. At times I felt an ache, when I missed the pure joy of evangelical worship, the support of peers who unabashedly talked about their personal faith. But like many people I meet at liberal gatherings who admit they grew up in an evangelical environment, I described myself as a former Baptist. There is a certain cachet, it seems, to being from that world and yet bragging that you now of course know better.

It wasn't until I traveled to the middle of Washington State in July of 2006 to cover a Christian music festival that I realized I wasn't a former evangelical at all. Creation Fest takes place on an enormous concert ground overlooking the Columbia River, which cuts a gorge so beautiful it looks as if the Good Lord fashioned it personally. After the sun set, the Southern rock band Third Day (as in "on the third day, He rose again") took the stage and led the crowd in a version of "Blessed Assurance." It's a hymn I've sung hundreds of times in the Baptist Church, but I was surprised to find that I still knew the words by heart. *This is my story, this is my song, praising my Savior all the day long.* Much of the crowd and I might not have shared the same political opinions—earlier in the day, a teenager ran past me yelling, "High-five! Not aborted!"—but we had a strong personal faith in common. I didn't realize how much I had missed that fellowship until my eyes started welling up as I stood in the dark surrounded by nearly fifteen thousand candle-holding evangelicals. Just like me.

There's nothing conservative or political in singing about Jesus at the top of your lungs. So when I visited my congregation at the Baptist church in Michigan just a few days after the CNN presidential faith forum in June 2007, for the first time in a long while I was there not to see friends or take anthropological notes, but to worship. After the service, Reverend Younge, the retired minister who has become my conversation partner, found me to ask about the book that he knew I was writing. He teased me about it, asking if the title was going to be *Democrats Without a Prayer.* As I mock-protested, reminding him of all the changes in the political and religious landscapes over the previous three years, Pastor Mike walked by. He had heard Reverend Younge's comment. Without breaking stride, he turned and said, "Both parties need our prayers right now," then moved on to greet a group of parishioners. I stood speechless for a moment. But then I looked at Reverend Younge and we both smiled. It wasn't a level praying field yet. But it was a start.

# APPENDIX A

The Catholic Vote for presidential party candidates,
1960–2004

|       | Democrats | Republicans |
|-------|-----------|-------------|
| 1960  | 78%       | 22%         |
| 1964  | 76%       | 24%         |
| 1968  | 59%       | 41%         |
| 1972  | 41%       | 59%         |
| 1976  | 57%       | 43%         |
| 1980  | 42%       | 49%         |
| 1984  | 39%       | 61%         |
| 1988  | 49%       | 51%         |
| 1992* | 44%       | 35%         |
| 1996  | 54%       | 31%         |
| 2000  | 50%       | 46%         |
| 2004  | 46%       | 52%         |

*Perot captured 21% of the Catholic vote in the 1992 election.

# APPENDIX B

The White Evangelical Vote for presidential party candidates,
1960–2004

|        | Democrats | Republicans |
|--------|-----------|-------------|
| 1960   | n/a       | n/a         |
| 1964   | n/a       | n/a         |
| 1968   | n/a       | n/a         |
| 1972   | n/a       | n/a         |
| 1976   | 58%       | 42%         |
| 1980   | 33%       | 63%         |
| 1984   | 22%       | 78%         |
| 1988   | 18%       | 81%         |
| 1992*  | 23%       | 62%         |
| 1996   | 32%       | 61%         |
| 2000   | 28%       | 72%         |
| 2004   | 22%       | 78%         |

*Perot captured 15% of the white evangelical vote in
1992.

# ACKNOWLEDGMENTS

It would be an exaggeration to say that I took on this project in order to have an excuse to write the acknowledgments. But only a slight one.

My gratitude properly starts with my parents. For more years than anyone should, they have provided me with material and emotional support, not to mention regular care packages filled with the world's best molasses and sugar cookies. My mom has encouraged my writing career since the earliest days, using her glue gun to create bound copies of the "books" my sister and I authored and her demanding eye to proofread my essays on Shakespeare. My dad has only occasionally suggested that I find a more reliable field—all the while bragging about me throughout most of southeast Michigan. As the years pass, I realize that their true gift to me has been the increasingly rare combination of a fierce respect for politics and a solid spiritual faith. They are idealists of the best kind.

I have also been blessed with a trio of mentors who have been more than generous with their time, counsel, and instruction. Marvin Kalb set the bar for care and professionalism that I strive to meet in my work. E. J. Dionne has never hesitated to take time out of his absurdly busy schedule to dispense advice, and he is a valuable reminder that grace and humility can coexist with talent and influence. Paul Glastris is the toughest, smartest editor I'll ever work with. It is thanks only to years of writing six, eight, ten drafts until a story met his standards that I can even think of setting off on my own.

Others have contributed immeasurably to my formal and informal education. Nancy Koppin, Kathy Thompson, and Cyndi Burnstein endured my often overwrought high school prose and somehow saw a writer there. Tom Daschle started me down the road of exploring how religion and politics intersect by sharing his very personal struggles as a Catholic Democrat. My professors and fellow students at Harvard Divinity School nurtured that interest and convinced me it was worth pursuing. I owe particular thanks to Father Bryan Hehir, for whom I wrote the term paper that became Chapter 3 of this book.

I continue to benefit from the support of my former colleagues at the Pew Forum on Religion and Public Life, including Luis Lugo, Melissa Rogers, and Sandra Stencel, and from the Washington Monthly family, especially Paul and Kukula Glastris, and the legendary Charlie Peters. I owe a debt to the Sociology Department at Princeton University, and particularly to Robert Wuthnow, for training me as a social scientist. It took me three semesters to realize that the professors who told me I wrote "like a journalist" didn't mean that as a compliment—but they were right. Special thanks is due to John Huey, Rick Stengel, and Priscilla Painton at *Time,* who have given me a wonderful opportunity at the magazine and who have displayed amazing understanding in allowing me to promote the book during a hectic election season.

While I was still working at the *Washington Monthly,* Gail Ross bullied me into writing the proposal for this book—and I have been grateful ever since for that nudge. As both an agent and a friend, she has shepherded me through the book-proposal and writing process. My one regret about the book is that I never got the chance to work with Lisa Drew, who believed in the idea from the very beginning but left for a much-deserved retirement before the project began.

I am enormously grateful to Nan Graham at Scribner, who generously agreed to take on the book upon Lisa's departure and made a personal commitment to producing a book of the highest quality. Samantha Martin was patient, insightful, patient, kind, and patient throughout all stages of the project, and the book benefitted greatly from her eye. Steve Boldt was a superb copy editor and saved me from numerous embarrassing mistakes.

# ACKNOWLEDGMENTS

Every author should be so lucky as to have the Brookings Institution for a home base. For the better part of a year, thanks to the munificence of Strobe Talbott and Pietro Nivola, I worked out of an office in the Governance Studies program and was warmly welcomed as a colleague. Bill Galston was especially helpful—if I could have simply downloaded his thoughts into my hard drive, the book would have taken far less time to write and would have been far more insightful. Erin Carter, Korin Davis, and Bethany Hase helped make me at home in the program, and Elisabeth Jacobs was a constant source of good cheer.

Although all errors in the book are my own, I owe an enormous debt to those who read, reviewed, and suggested changes to the manuscript. Chuck Mathewes generously hosted a seminar at the Center for Religion and Democracy at the University of Virginia that provided me with invaluable feedback at a crucial stage in the writing process. Various ideas in the book were first explored in previously published material, and I am grateful for the keen editing eyes of Emily Bazelon, Frank Foer, Jim Rice, Peter Scoblic, Wen Stephenson, and Joan Walsh. In addition, I am enormously lucky to have smart friends who are also editors: Nancy Gibbs, Kate Marsh, Molly Marsh, and Ben Wallace-Wells all read portions of the book. Paul Glastris read every word.

Special thanks go to D. W. Pine, *Time*'s tremendously talented art director, who created my dream cover design at the last minute. Jeff Sheler, a very smart observer of evangelicals, provided invaluable assistance for Chapter 2. Jerry Mayer came up with the original idea for the article that led to this book. I will always be grateful for Holly Lebowitz Rossi and Amy Potter Hetletvedt, two true friends who made sure I didn't get lost in the course of writing.

I beg the forgiveness of those I've forgotten to thank, but among others who provided shelter, friendship, counsel, and book-title suggestions are Colleen Rost-Banik; Peter Beinart; Monica Belmonte; Jon Chait; Isaac Chotiner; Jon Cohn; Judy Coode; Michelle Cottle; Erin Cross; Melissa Deckman; Jeff and Kim Dolan; Sid Espinosa;

## ACKNOWLEDGMENTS

Ryan Harbage-Fisher; Jen Frahm; Tom Frank; Danny Franklin; Matt Gaffney; Carol Guthrie; Matt and Jeana Hoyt; Robby Jones; Brent Kendall; Rachel and Rob Kimbro; Lisa Konick; David Kuo; Michael Lindsay; Marsha Moseley; Jennifer Noricks; Michael Norman; Christine Rosen; Jake Rosenfeld; Kimberlee Salmond; Peter Scoblic; Lee Seese; Christian Sinderman; Gretchen Stanford; Jennifer Coulter Stapleton; Faith Hoyt-Sullivan; Erik Thompson; Patricia Tolbert; Diane Winston; Michael Sean Winters; Amy Zapf; Sacha Zimmerman; the congregations of St. Columba's Episcopal Church in Washington, D.C., and the First Baptist Church of Plymouth, Michigan; and my friends from the Grassmere Group.

Dalia and Howard Scheiber have welcomed me into their family, and I am grateful for their encouragement. My brother-in-law, Kwasi Mitchell, consistently struck the right balance between nagging, cheerleading, and bribery to get me through the writing of each chapter.

Male authors tend to thank their wives for maintaining their lives and homes while they write. I'm not sure how women who don't have sisters manage to write books. My sister, Katie, is a close friend and provided me with food, clothing, shelter, pedicures, and moral support. She may also be one of the only other people who can understand the dual identity of growing up in a home where portraits of Bobby Kennedy and Jesus hung on the wall.

Finally, this book simply would not exist without Noam Scheiber. I am beyond lucky to have such a talented writer and sharp political mind as my in-house editor. Every portion of the book has been improved by his editing hand, as well as his near-limitless patience for conversations about structure and ideas. More than that, his steadfastness, love, and humor sustained me, particularly during the last months in which I juggled the demands of a new job all day and the drafting of chapter revisions all night. I can never thank him enough.

# NOTES

This book is based on original reporting and research. It would not be possible without the cooperation of dozens of individuals who generously shared their time, memories, and thoughts with me. When a statement in the book appears in quotation marks, it is because at least one source remembered hearing those words. When I describe a character's thoughts, it is because the character told me what he or she remembered thinking. Memories do not always perfectly capture events and conversations—I have tried my best to confirm what sources told me.

I am grateful to the following people who took time to speak with me, sometimes on numerous occasions: Kim Baldwin, Diana Butler Bass, Paul Begala, Mark Brewer, Randy Brinson, Leslie Brown, Jeff Carr, Jimmy Carter, Shaun Casey, Richard Cizik, Paul Contino, Rosa DeLauro, Nathan Diament, Elise Elzinga, Ann Frick, Barbara Bradley Hagerty, Tony Hall, Pat and Kristin Headley, Mark Hulsether, Michael Kazin, Alexia Kelley, John Kerry, Ron Klain, Kate Kooyman, David Kusnet, Rachel Laser, Jen Lynch, Martin Marty, Flo McAfee, Mike McCurry, Eric McFadden, John McGreevy, David Obey, Laura Olson, Ricken Patel, Tom Perriello, Sam Popkin, Bill Ritter, Tim Roemer, Melissa Rogers, Tim Ryan, Eric Sapp, Yonce Shelton, George Stephanopoulos, Burns Strider, David Swartz, Romal Tune, Mara Vanderslice, Melanne Verveer, Kirk Wager, Jim Wallis, and Bob Wuthnow. Absent from this list are a handful of sources who spoke to me on the condition that I would not use their names.

## CHAPTER 1: JESUS BUMPS AND GOD GAPS

3 *"hearing from the Lord"* "Robertson: God Says It's Bush in a 'Blowout' in November," *USA Today,* January 2, 2004.

3 *or else leave the congregation* Andre Rodriguez, "Members Say Church Ousts Kerry Supporters," *Asheville Citizen-Times,* May 7, 2005.

8 *"I'll never lie to you"* Jimmy Carter, *I'll Never Lie to You: Jimmy Carter in His Own Words* (New York: Ballantine Books, 1976).

8 *"turn the White House into a Billy Graham Bible class"* Quoted in Kenneth L. Woodward, "Carter's Cross to Bear," *Newsweek,* June 7, 1976, p. 56.

9 *"I can endorse you"* Peter Goldman, "The Battle of the Button," *Newsweek,* September 1, 1980, p. 18.

10 *register their evangelical neighbors* Dan Gilgoff, *The Jesus Machine: How James Dobson, Focus on the Family, and Evangelical America Are Winning the Culture War* (New York: St. Martin's Press, 2007), p. 189.

## CHAPTER 2: "THE GODDAM CHRISTIANS"

14 *"the social and political injustice of our nation"* The full text of "The Chicago Declaration on Evangelical Social Concern" may be found at the Web site of Evangelicals for Social Action: http://esa-online.org/Display.asp?Page=About.

15 *"at the YMCA hotel on S. Wabash"* Quoted by Joel A. Carpenter, "Compassionate Evangelicalism," *Christianity Today* 47, no. 12 (December 2003): pp. 40–42.

16 *"the Moral Majority would be the result"* Ron Sider, interview, June 20, 2007.

17 *and not just in one's words* President Theodore Roosevelt's second State of the Union address, December 2, 1902. The text may be seen at the American Presidency Project Web site: http://www.presidency.ucsb.edu/ws/index.php?pid=29543.

17 *"in the fire of a religious awakening"* Letter of greeting to the United Methodist Council, January 17, 1938. John Woolley and Gerhard Peters, *The American Presidency Project* (Santa Barbara: University of California [hosted], Gerhard Peters [database], http://www.presidency.ucsb.edu/ws/?pid=15671).

17 *"God's work must truly be our own"* President John F. Kennedy's first Inaugural Address, January 20, 1961. The text is available in *"Let the Word Go Forth": The Speeches, Statements, and Writings of John F. Kennedy 1947 to 1963* (New York: Delta, 1991), p. 15.

17 *"and to every rank of society"* Alexis de Tocqueville, *Democracy in America* (New York: Penguin Classics, 2003), p. 342.

17 *its character was overwhelmingly evangelical* For a detailed description of the cultural influence of evangelical Protestants during this period, see Jeffrey L. Sheler, *Believers: A Journey into Evangelical America* (New York: Viking, 2006), pp. 50–52.

17 *all hallmarks of classic evangelicalism* Characteristics of evangelicalism are summarized by British historian David Bebbington in *Evangelicalism in Britain: A History from the 1730s to the 1980s* (London: Unwin Hyman, 1989), pp. 2–17.

18 *"are identified with the kingdom of God among men"* Quoted by George M. Marsden, *Fundamentalism and American Culture,* new ed. (New York: Oxford University Press, 2006), p. 11.

18 *"their faith to be the normative American creed"* Ibid.

19 *"hardly looked like the precincts of Zion"* Randall Balmer, *Thy Kingdom Come: How the Religious Right Distorts the Faith and Threatens America* (New York: Basic Books, 2006), p. xv.

21 *"Liberalism continued to grow"* Marsden, p. 104.

23 *"man as taught in the Bible"* The text of the Butler Act, enacted on March 21, 1925, appears in full at the "Scopes Trial Homepage" at the University of Missouri–Kansas City School of Law Web site: http://www.law.umkc.edu/faculty/projects/ftrials/scopes/tennstat.htm.

24 *"You insult every man of science and learning"* From the Scopes trial transcript, http://www.law.umkc.edu/faculty/projects/ftrials/scopes/scopes2.htm.

27 *"there is no room"* Carl F. H. Henry, *The Uneasy Conscience of Modern Fundamentalism* (Grand Rapids, Mich.: Eerdmans, 1947), p. 35.

28 *everyone from journalist Walter Lippmann to Supreme Court justice Felix Frankfurter* For a complete history of the magazine *Christianity and Crisis,* see Mark Hulsether,

*Building a Protestant Left: Christianity and Crisis Magazine, 1941–1993.* (Knoxville: University of Tennessee Press, 1999).

28 *"Mainline churches always have the advantage"* Martin E. Marty, *A Nation of Behavers* (Chicago: University of Chicago Press, 1976), p. 71.

29 *"merely an offering of pious words"* Richard Quebedeaux, *The Young Evangelicals* (New York: Harper & Row, 1974), p. 37.

30 *about his fundamentalist upbringing* Information about activism on Christian college campuses in the 1960s and 1970s is drawn from David R. Swartz's terrific dissertation-in-progress, tentatively titled "Left Behind: The Young Evangelicals and the Politicization of American Evangelicalism, 1965–1985," University of Notre Dame.

30 *address students and faculty in the campus chapel in 1972* Ibid.

31 *"Nowhere are we commissioned to reform externals"* Falwell quotes himself several decades later in Jerry Falwell, *Strength for the Journey: An Autobiography* (New York: Simon & Schuster, 1987), p. 290.

31 *deeply offended by such actions* For a discussion of class differences in Catholic reactions to the Vietnam War and the civil rights movement, see Mary Hanna, *Catholics and American Politics* (Cambridge: Harvard University Press, 1979).

32 *the national mission board contributed $10,000 to Angela Davis's defense fund* A history of the United Presbyterian Church's troubles is recounted in John R. Fry, *The Trivialization of the United Presbyterian Church* (New York: Harper & Row, 1975).

33 *"I had lacked something very precious"* Martin Schram, *Running for President: A Journal of the Carter Campaign* (New York: Pocket Books, 1978), p. 111.

34 *"not something out of the ordinary"* Quoted in William Martin, *With God on Our Side: The Rise of the Religious Right in America* (New York: Broadway Books, 1996), p. 150.

34 *"really didn't know what an evangelical was"* Ibid., p. 149.

35 *"his initials are the same as our Lord's"* Myra MacPherson, "Evangelicals Seen Cooling on Carter," *Washington Post,* September 27, 1976, A1.

35 *"he found no contradiction"* James David Barber, *The Pulse of Politics: Electing Presidents in the Media Age* (New York: W. W. Norton, 1980), p. 203.

35 *"Jimmy Carter has found it"* Kenneth L. Woodward, John Barnes, and Laurie Lisle, "Born Again," *Newsweek,* October 25, 1976, p. 68.

35 *"Surely the Lord sent Jimmy Carter"* Martin, p. 154.

36 *"I kept striking that out in every draft"* Stuart Eizenstat interview, Miller Center, University of Virginia, Jimmy Carter Presidential Oral History Project, January 29–30, 1982.

37 *"God forgives me"* Quoted in "Trying to Be One of the Boys," *Time,* October 4, 1976.

37 *"screw is just not a good Baptist word"* MacPherson.

38 *"who professed to be a Christian"* Martin, p. 189.

39 *"the Democrats were secular"* Jim Wallis, interview, July 27, 2006.

40 *"it is often apt to make you puke"* See Edward Plowman, *The Jesus Movement in America: Accounts of Christian Revolutionaries in Action* (New York: Pyramid, 1971).

40 *four-fifths who did so a few decades earlier* See "Fading Big Five," *Time,* March 8, 1976.

41 *quickly quashed the proposal* See "Higher Education's Missing Soul," *Christian Science Monitor,* May 25, 2007.

42  *he was summarily fired* See "Do You Know Where Your Church Offerings Go?" *Readers' Digest,* January 1983, and archived at the Web site of the Material History of American Religion Project at Vanderbilt University Divinity School: http://www.materialreligion.org/documents/july99doc.html.

42  *"the greatest tract of virgin timber"* Republican activist Morton Blackwell, as quoted by Martin, p. 191.

42  *"men and women of Christian faith"* Falwell, p. 334.

43  *He spoke admiringly of the Bible* "A Tide of Born-Again Politics," *Newsweek,* September 15, 1980, p. 28.

44  *"my finest hour"* Quoted in Frances Fitzgerald, *Cities on a Hill* (New York: Simon & Schuster, 1986), p. 189.

44  *"There'd be many more Democrats among them"* Jeffrey L. Sheler, "Nearer My God to Thee," *U.S. News & World Report,* May 3, 2004, p. 59.

46  *"deep down, he is shallow"* Quoted in Warren Goldstein, "The New Evangelists," *Yale Alumni Magazine,* November/December 2006, p. 45.

46  *"What the fuck would it take?"* Ibid.


## CHAPTER 3: "KEEP YOUR ROSARIES OFF MY OVARIES"

51  *just 13 percent of the delegates had been women* See Mark Stricherz, "Goodbye, Catholics," *Commonweal* 132, no. 19 (November 4, 2005).

52  *"I wonder if he knows the cause"* Quoted in "The Battle for the Democratic Party," *Time,* July 17, 1972.

54  *a relatively small, underfinanced, and understaffed body* For a useful history of American Catholic institutions in the early– to mid–twentieth century, see Mary Segers, "The American Catholic Church in Contemporary American Politics," in *Church Polity and American Politics,* ed. Mary Segers (New York: Garland Publishing, 1990), p. 7.

55  *"the salvation of souls requires it"* Gaudium et Spes: The Pastoral Constitution on the Church in the Modern World, written during the Second Vatican Council and promulgated by Pope Paul VI in December 1965. The text can be found in David O'Brien and Thomas Shannon, ed., *Catholic Social Thought: The Documentary Heritage* (Maryknoll, N.Y.: Orbis Books, 1992), p. 219.

56  *"the system is a social sin"* Quoted in Hanna, p. 16.

56  *"It just wasn't the kind of thing they did"* This quote comes from one of several dozen not-for-attribution interviews that Mary T. Hanna, a political scientist at SUNY-Binghamton, conducted with Catholic clergy and lay leaders in the early- to mid-1970s for her 1979 book, *Catholics and American Politics.* Quoted on p. 20.

56  *"normal Christians to become involved"* Ibid.

57  *"to draw principles of reflection"* From *Octogesima Adveniens: A Call to Action on the Eightieth Anniversary of Rerum Novarum,* released by Pope Paul VI in 1971. Quoted in O'Brien and Shannon, p. 266.

58  *"Our defense of human life"* The full text of the statement issued by the National Conference of Catholic Bishops on April 22, 1970, can be found at http://www.priestsforlife.org/magisterium/bishops/70-04-22statementonabortionnccb.htm.

59 *Justice Douglas was even more hostile* See John T. McGreevy, *Catholicism and American Freedom: A History* (New York: W. W. Norton, 2003), p. 263.

59 *"We're not going to shut up"* Quoted in Hanna, p. 150.

59 *"bad logic and bad law"* Quoted in George Marlin, *The American Catholic Voter: Two Hundred Years of Political Impact* (South Bend, Ind.: St. Augustine's Press, 2004).

59 *the official support of his church* Ibid.

59 *"beyond a doubt to our fellow citizens"* Quoted in Timothy Byrnes, *Catholic Bishops in American Politics* (Princeton: Princeton University Press, 1991), p. 57.

59 *"the most detailed and explicit proposal"* Segers, p. 10.

60 *"we see a moral imperative for such political activity"* Quoted in the November 25, 1975, issue of *Origins,* a Catholic News Service publication that prints Catholic documents ranging from encyclicals to pastoral letters to diocesan policy statements.

61 *94 percent of adults in a* Washington Post *poll* See Alan Cooperman and Claudia Deane, "In Poll, Pope Lauded, Views Are Questioned," *Washington Post,* October 16, 2003, A3.

62 *"an effort to enact theological positions into law"* McGreevy, p. 261.

63 *"You just don't know what would reach them"* Quoted in William Prendergast, *The Catholic Voter in American Politics: The Passing of the Democratic Monolith* (Washington, D.C.: Georgetown University Press, 1999), p. 157.

64 *advice on how to tackle the abortion question* Ibid., p. 170.

64 *"intense reaction among pro-abortion lobbying groups"* Quoted in McGreevy, p. 280.

64 *to the party's position on abortion* Quoted in the *Syracuse Post-Standard,* July 20, 1976.

65 *"many of whom are Catholics"* Prendergast, p. 170.

65 *Bernardin declared himself* Quoted in McGreevy, p. 284.

65 *"a clear signal of support for Ford"* See "On Abortion, the Bishops vs. the Deacon," *Time,* September 20, 1976.

65 *pro-lifers chanting, "Life! Life! Life!"* Ibid.

66 *cost Ford the White House* See Marlin, p. 291.

66 *"free of that inordinate fear of communism"* Ibid., p. 295.

66 *Carter was booed* Ibid.

66 *Mondale simply passed up the dinner* See Prendergast, p. 189.

67 *a candidate's abortion position* Ibid.

68 *"there is no leeway"* Quoted in Richard Jensen, "The Media and the Catholic Church v. Geraldine Ferraro," in *Oratorical Encounters: Selected Studies and Sources of Twentieth Century Political Accusations and Apologies* (New York: Greenwood Press, 1988), p. 260.

68 *the archbishop refused to rule it out* Marlin, p. 300.

68 *"step out of his spiritual pulpit"* Quoted in Prendergast, p. 187.

68 *he personally considered abortion to be "sinful"* From "Religious Belief and Public Morality: A Catholic Governor's Perspective," Mario Cuomo's address at the University of Notre Dame on September 13, 1984. The full text can be found in Mario Cuomo, *More than Words: The Speeches of Mario Cuomo* (New York: St. Martin's Griffin, 1994), pp. 32–50.

70 *a candidate who favored abortion* Prendergast, p. 189.

70 *"from their planned campaign strategies"* Ed Magnusonith, "Pressing the Abortion Issue," *Time,* September 24, 1984.

70  *"teaching which are not true"* Quoted in Marlin, p. 300.

70  *Her car moved swiftly past locals* See Magnusonith, September 24, 1984.

71  *"threatens the hard-won understanding"* See "A Faith to Trust," *New York Times,* September 15, 1984.

71  *"You cannot beat an incumbent President in peacetime"* Quoted in Peter Goldman and Tony Fuller, *The Quest for the Presidency 1984* (New York: A Newsweek Book/Bantam Books, 1984).

72  *"There are other issues"* Quoted in Hanna, p. 154.

73  *"applications of this broader attitude"* See, for example, Kenneth Briggs, "Bernardin Asks Catholics to Fight Both Nuclear Arms and Abortion," *New York Times,* December 7, 1983, A1, and "Excerpts from Cardinal Bernardin's Appeal for a 'Consistent Ethic of Life,'" *New York Times,* December 7, 1983, B8.

73  *expand the national Catholic conversation* For the text of the letters on disarmament and on economic justice, see *The Challenge of Peace: God's Promise and Our Response* (U.S. Catholic Conference, 1984), and *Economic Justice for All: Pastoral Letter on Catholic Social Teaching and the U.S. Economy* (U.S. Catholic Conference, 1986).

73  *capitalism and Catholicism could go hand in hand* See, for example, Michael Novak, *The Catholic Ethic and the Spirit of Capitalism* (New York: Free Press, 1993), and George Weigel and Robert Royal, *Building the Free Society: Democracy, Capitalism, and Catholic Social Teaching* (Grand Rapids, Mich.: Eerdmans, 1993).

74  *state constitutions mandated it* William Saletan, *Bearing Right: How Conservatives Won the Abortion War* (Berkeley: University of California Press, 2003), p. 14.

74  *Democratic women all over the state* McGreevy, p. 280.

74  *"higher order than the right to life"* Jesse Jackson, "How We Respect Life Is the Overriding Moral Issue," *Right to Life News,* January 1977.

74  *"I intend to remain steadfast on this issue"* Dick Polman, "For Gephardt, Iowa Is Must-Win State," *Philadelphia Inquirer,* January 16, 2004.

75  *he had changed his views* Bill Lambrecht and Deirdre Shesgreen, "Abortion Stance Shows Wider Shift on Social Issues," *St. Louis Post-Dispatch,* July 6, 2003, A9.

75  *"must be warned"* John Elson, "Bishops, Politicians, and the Abortion Crisis," *Time,* February 19, 1990.

75  *"in danger of going to hell"* Ibid.

76  *a vote for the Democratic candidate for Senate* Bruce Nolan, "Sin at the Polls Debated by Clergy," *Times-Picayune,* November 9, 1996.

76  *were unwelcome at church events in his diocese* Teresa Malcolm, "Pennsylvania Governor Warned on Abortion Stand," *National Catholic Reporter,* December 4, 1998.

76  *"by leading others into serious sin"* See *Living the Gospel of Life: A Challenge to American Catholics* (National Conference of Catholic Bishops, 1998), IV, p. 29.

76  *"an attempt to intimidate"* Hanna Rosin and Thomas Edsall, "Catholics Open Major Campaign Against Abortion," *Washington Post,* November 19, 1998.

77  *"would prompt the archbishop to decertify the institution"* Rosa DeLauro, interview, December 7, 2006.

77  *"a big shouting match with the good monsignor"* David Obey, interview, December 22, 2006.

78  *"Harris Wofford would have lost"* Mary McGrory, "Smooth Sailing," *Washington Post,* July 9, 1992.

79 *"the number of abortions should be reduced"* Quoted in David Rosenbaum, "Party's Quest for a Middle Road: A Liberal Stance in Business Suits," *New York Times,* July 15, 1992.

79 *the first woman to defeat an incumbent governor* Cathryn Donohoe, "Other Pro-life Democrats Got the Cold Shoulder at the DNC," *Washington Times,* August 31, 1992.

79 *"to let him give the speech"* Nat Hentoff, "Governor Casey Silenced—Again," *Washington Post,* October 24, 1992.

79 *"Governor Casey, go away!"* Ibid.

## CHAPTER 4: ISAIAH 40:31

82 *mainline Protestants, black pastors, and Jewish leaders* My description of this faith breakfast comes from David Lauter, "Clinton Voices Concern U.S. May Be Too Secular," *Los Angeles Times,* August 31, 1993, and Susan Trausch, "Politics and Faith," *Boston Globe,* September 3, 1993, and from off-the-record interviews with participants and planners.

83 *"change from the inside out"* "Remarks by President Bill Clinton at Prayer Breakfast at the White House State Dining Room," *Federal News Service,* August 30, 1993.

84 *"the so-called religious right"* See "God and the Oval Office: Clinton's Reflections on Values and Religion Should Trigger Worthy Debate," *Los Angeles Times,* September 5, 1993.

84 *"evangelical Protestantism and Roman Catholicism"* George Weigel, "A Prayer for Clinton's Redemption," *Los Angeles Times,* September 10, 1993.

85 *why the party had lost its appeal* Prendergast, p. 193.

85 *"the Democratic party left him"* Ibid., p. 222.

86 *"not the party of self-discipline"* See Michael White, "Party Must Adjust Policies to Fit American Family, Democrats Told," Associated Press, April 5, 1986.

87 *were long gone* For an excellent exploration of the progressive evangelicalism of William Jennings Bryan, see Michael Kazin's excellent 2006 biography of the three-time presidential candidate, *A Godly Hero: The Life of William Jennings Bryan* (New York: Knopf, 2006).

87 *"ill-conceived housewife hobby project"* Quoted in Betty Cuniberti, "Tipper Gore: Activist, Mother, Soon-to-Be Potential First Lady?" *Los Angeles Times,* April 3, 1987.

87 *"without a federal guidance counselor"* Dave Barry, "Setting the Record Straight on Some Really Bweep! Lyrics," *Chicago Tribune,* December 15, 1985.

88 *"None of us is very religious"* Quoted in Garry Wills, *Under God: Religion and American Politics* (New York: Simon & Schuster, 1991), p. 55.

88 *Americans were pragmatic and secular* Ibid., p. 52.

88 *"You all ever heard of Jesus?"* Quoted in Marjorie Williams, *The Woman at the Washington Zoo* (New York: Public Affairs, 2005), p. 81.

89 *all invitations to appear at Catholic universities* See Prendergast, p. 194.

90 *his stepfather would approve* Bill Clinton, *My Life* (New York: Knopf, 2004), p. 39.

90 *considered becoming a Jesuit* Ibid., p. 76.

90 *favorite undergraduate course was* Melanne Verveer, interview, April 6, 2007.

91 *"the guidance of God in this job"* Peggy Wehmeyer, "President Clinton and Religion," *ABC News World Tonight,* March 22, 1994.

91 *"a grave scandal against the Church"* Barry Horstman, "Bishop's Intrusion into Senate Race Stirs Debate," *Los Angeles Times,* December 3, 1989.

92 *"safe, legal, and rare"* Samuel Popkin, interview, September 27, 2006.

92 *"I am pro-choice"* See Clinton's acceptance speech at the 1992 Democratic National Convention, "Transcript of Speech by Clinton Accepting Democratic Nomination," *New York Times,* July 17, 1992, A14.

93 *"a homily to the converted"* Gwen Ifill, "Clinton Says Foes Sow Intolerance," *New York Times,* September 12, 1992.

93 *"more than talk about family values"* Ibid.

94 *"going back to its founding"* Patricia Zapor, "Clinton Says Laws on Parental Notice for Abortion Would Be OK," Catholic News Service, October 21, 1992.

95 *"lines of communication into the evangelical community"* Bill Clinton, p. 405.

96 *a moralizing shrew* Michael Kelly, "Saint Hillary," *New York Times Magazine,* May 23, 1993.

96 *his pastor back in Little Rock* Bill Clinton, p. 532

96 *she was in the White House* See Hillary Rodham Clinton, *Living History* (New York: Scribner, 2003), pp. 167–68.

98 *She regularly defended Clinton to her classmates* Fred Barnes, "Rev. Bill," *New Republic,* January 3, 1994.

98 *"God flooded his heart with love"* Ibid.

98 *to call him when he was in Washington* See Ted Olsen, "Why Clinton Likes Him," *Christianity Today,* January 2003.

100 *"Obviously, there was disagreement on an issue"* Verveer, April 6, 2007.

100 *"They had no idea the depth of his convictions"* Ibid.

101 *"someone was straightening my tie"* Richard Cizik, interview, April 8, 2007.

101 *"That was incorrect"* Bill Clinton, p. 661.

102 *the establishment of the IRF office* A fascinating discussion of U.S. policy on international religious freedom took place around the tenth anniversary of the IRF office, hosted by the Pew Forum on Religion and Public Life. A transcript of the debate, involving two former heads of the office, is available at http://pewforum.org/events/?EventID=139.

103 *a trio of religious leaders* Hillary Rodham Clinton, p. 460.

103 *"Clinton was composing his speech"* George Stephanopoulos, *All Too Human* (New York: Little, Brown, 1999), p. 22.

104 *"That's the one I'll use"* From Michael Waldman, *POTUS Speaks: Finding the Words That Defined the Clinton Presidency* (New York: Simon & Schuster, 2000), p. 118.

106 *"a large Bible under his arm"* Remarks are from "Kerry, Bush, and the Faith Factor," a May 3, 2004, event at the National Press Club. A full transcript is available at http://www.eppc.org/programs/religionandmedia/conferences/eventID.82,programID.37/conf_detail.asp.

106 *"He must be really chuckling over this"* Quoted in Rich Lowry, "Clinton's Revelation—How and Why Clinton Needs to Appeal to Southern Baptists," *National Review,* March 7, 1994.

107 *his eight years in office* In their August 2006 paper for the Guttmacher Institute, "Estimates of U.S. Abortion Incidence, 2001–2003," Lawrence B. Finer and

Stanley K. Henshaw note that the annualized decline in the abortion rate between 1992 and 1996 was 3.4 percent, and between 1996 and 2000, it was 1.2 percent. During the years of the Clinton administration, then, the total decline in the U.S. abortion rate was approximately 18.4 percent.

108 *"He blew it"* Mary McGrory, "Clinton Vetos Catholic Voters," *Washington Post,* April 14, 1996.

108 *"There wasn't a single restriction"* Paul Begala, interview, August 22, 2006.

109 *please don't boo him* Tony Hall, interview, November 10, 2006.

109 *He prayed with the first lady* Hillary Rodham Clinton, p. 470.

109 *"this man does not deserve grace?"* Olsen, January 2003.

110 *"a fancy way to say that I have sinned"* John F. Harris, "For Clinton, a Day to Atone but Not Retreat," *Washington Post,* September 12, 1998.

110 *public statements of contrition* See "Scholars Criticize Calls to Forgive Clinton," *Christian Century,* December 2, 1998.

110 *"evokes religious sentiments"* Gabriel Fackre, ed., *Judgment Day at the White House: A Critical Declaration Exploring Moral Issues and the Political Use and Abuse of Religion* (Grand Rapids, Mich.: Eerdmans, 1998).

110 *"to gain cheap forgiveness"* Joe Fitzgerald, "President Hasn't Paid Price for True Forgiveness," *Boston Herald,* February 6, 1999.

110 *"It's a message sent to us"* Ibid.

111 *"And again and again"* Florence McAfee, interview, March 28, 2007.

111 *Many political observers were startled* Maureen Dowd, "Playing the Jesus Card," *New York Times,* December 15, 1999.

113 *"The Lord said unto Gideon"* See Donna Brazile, *Cooking with Grease: Stirring the Pots in American Politics* (New York: Simon & Schuster, 2004), p. 215.

113 *"rally the armies of compassion"* Richard Benedetto, "Bush Pledges Tax Breaks to Aid the 'Armies of Compassion,'" *USA Today,* July 23, 1999.

113 *Gore himself had endorsed* See Jacob S. Hacker, "Faith Healers," *New Republic,* June 28, 1999.

114 *a White House conference on philanthropy* Jennifer Moore and Grant Williams, "Clintons Vow to Strengthen Philanthropy," *Chronicle of Philanthropy,* November 4, 1999. See also Hillary Clinton's remarks on December 17, 2001, at Abyssinian Baptist Church; transcript available at http://pewforum.org/events/?EventID=19.

## Chapter 5: "We Don't Do White Churches"

118 *"Geez not high priority"* Quoted in Steven Waldman and John C. Green, "Freestyle Evangelicals: The Surprise Swing Vote," Beliefnet.com, http://www.beliefnet.com/story/129/story_12995_2.html.

118 *"an issue about nothing"* From Howard Dean's address to the annual NARAL dinner on January 21, 2003. The full transcript is available at http://www.gwu.edu/~action/2004/interestg/nara1012103/dean012103spt.html.

119 *"How the fuck did you get hired?"* Mara Vanderslice, interview, August 8, 2006.

120 *"What good is it, my brothers"* Quoted in Karen Tumulty and Perry Bacon Jr., "A Test of Faith," *Time,* April 5, 2004.

121  *they would support in the election* Dan Balz and Richard Morin, "Bush Poll Numbers on Iraq at New Low," *Washington Post,* May 25, 2004, A1.

121  *pro-choice politicians for criticism* "Archbishop to Dissenting Politicians: Stop Receiving Communion," Catholic News Service, May 5, 2004.

122  *"stance violates church teachings"* "Kerry Takes Communion on Mother's Day," Associated Press, May 10, 2004.

123  *"The Eucharist must not become"* "Archbishop Martin Disagrees with Vatican over Eucharist," *Irish Times,* April 27, 2004.

123  *their president to be a man of faith* See "Religion and Politics: Contention and Consensus," a survey report from the Pew Forum on Religion and Public Life, July 24, 2003.

124  *The media frenzy* Credit for the term *Wafer Watch* goes to Religion News Service journalist Adelle Banks, who coined it in the spring of 2004 to describe the intensity with which her colleagues in the mainstream press shadowed Kerry's every move during visits to Catholic churches.

124  *"It never crossed our minds"* Christine Stanek, interview, February 26, 2007.

125  *"We weren't looking for a fight"* John Kerry, interview, January 10, 2007.

125  *"Mary Beth was terrified of the politics"* Anonymous Kerry friend, September 1, 2006.

127  *"director of religious outreach"* Walter Shapiro, "Religion on the Stump Could Add a New Dimension to Election," *USA Today,* June 10, 2004.

128  *"for Fidel Castro, not John Kerry"* Press release, "Kerry's 'Religion Outreach' Director Is a Gem," Catholic League for Religious and Civil Rights, June 14, 2004.

129  *Within three days of the first release* See Robert Marus, "Democratic Religious Liaison Resigns Under Fire from Catholic Group," Associated Baptist Press, August 6, 2004.

130  *"there was no one who could do that"* Mike McCurry, interview, September 19, 2006.

130  *"We didn't have networks"* Vanderslice, August 8, 2006.

131  *One longtime Capitol Hill aide* Anonymous Senate aide, interview, October 3, 2006.

133  *"Here I am. Send me!"* From President Bill Clinton's address to the 2004 Democratic National Convention, July 26, 2004. Transcript is available at http://www.cnn.com/2004/ALLPOLITICS/07/26/dems.clinton.transcript/.

133  *"We worship an awesome God"* From Barack Obama's keynote address to the 2004 Democratic National Convention, July 27, 2004. Transcript is available at http://www.washingtonpost.com/wp-dyn/articles/A19751-2004Jul27.html.

133  *"In this campaign, we welcome people of faith"* From John Kerry's acceptance speech at the 2004 Democratic National Convention, July 29, 2004. Transcript is available at http://www.washingtonpost.com/wp-dyn/articles/A25678-2004Jul29.html.

134  *When Vanderslice submitted* Vanderslice, August 8, 2006.

134  *"We want a minister of color"* For the full story of Eddly Benoit's experience with convention organizers, see Ari Lipman, "Losing Faith," *Boston Review,* April/May 2005.

136  *"doing good works in the community"* Vanderslice, August 8, 2006.

137  *"I did it on my own"* From President George W. Bush's remarks at the Faith-Based and Community Initiatives Conference in Los Angeles, California, March 3,

2004. A full transcript is available at http://www.whitehouse.gov/news/releases/2004/03/ 20040303-13.html.

138 *"wonder-working power"* From Bush's 2003 State of the Union, January 28, 2003. Transcript is available at http://www.cnn.com/2003/ALLPOLITICS/01/28/sotu.transcript/.

140 *"He was constantly wrestling with the question"* Ron Klain, interview, June 29, 2006.

140 *"'What's your response to the letter?'"* Ibid.

142 *"fundamental teaching and belief of faith"* See John Kerry's responses in the third presidential debate, October 13, 2004. A full transcript is available at http://www.debates.org/pages/trans2004d.html.

143 *"if they can't afford it otherwise"* Ibid.

144 *"a bit less concerned about ourselves"* Pat and Kristin Headley, interview, September 30, 2006.

147 *"George Bush the second time around"* McCurry, September 19, 2006.

148 *In a sad illustration* Press release, "NCC's Edgar Urges U.S. to Accept Responsibility for Uighur Chinese Refugees at Guantánamo," November 1, 2004.

149 *Catholics for Kerry rally in Columbus* Eric McFadden, interview, August 21, 2006.

149 *"We don't do white churches"* Alexia Kelley, interview, August 30, 2006.

149 *his faith was carefully calculated* Mike Allen, "Kerry Seeks Support in Black Churches," *Washington Post,* October 11, 2004.

150 *an audiotape of the speech* Barbara Bradley Hagerty, interview, August 29, 2006.

150 *"Jesus tells us"* Barbara Bradley Hagerty, "The Faith of Senator John Kerry," *NPR's Morning Edition,* October 6, 2004.

151 *"what our life will mean"* From John Kerry's remarks in Ft. Lauderdale, Florida, on October 24, 2004. A full transcript is available at http://www.gwu.edu/~action/2004/kerry/kerry102404sp.html.

## CHAPTER 6: PRO-LIFE *AND* PRO-CHOICE

153 *"we know that's not true"* Jim Wallis, interview, July 15, 2007.

154 *"feeling kind of trapped by the liberal side"* Ibid.

157 *"pro-life candidates into the party"* Debra Rosenberg, "Pro-choice Democrats Eye a More Restrictive Approach to Abortion as One Way to Gain Ground at the Polls," *Newsweek,* December 20, 2004.

157 *"that's not going to work"* Ibid.

157 *"He did not help the cause"* Ibid.

157 *"sad, even tragic choice"* Patrick Healy, "Clinton Seeking Shared Ground over Abortions," *New York Times,* January 25, 2005, A5.

158 *"be allowed to represent the entire party"* Tim Roemer, interview, December 8, 2006.

159 *"have deep respect for"* Howard Dean, *Meet the Press,* December 12, 2004.

159 *before the 2006 election* John Mulligan, "Abortion-Rights Group Endorses Chafee," *Providence Journal,* May 20, 2005, B1.

160 *"keep the skunk out of the tent"* From Kim Gandy's remarks to the 2005 Take Back America conference on June 3, 2005. Full transcript is available at http://www.now.org/press/06-05/TBA-06-03-05.html?printable.

160 *"We have to address that"* Jeffrey Goldberg, "Central Casting: The Democrats Think About Who Can Win in the Midterms—and in 2008," *New Yorker,* May 29, 2006, p. 62.

162 *"judged it to be in the past"* See John Kerry, *ABC World News Tonight with Peter Jennings,* July 22, 2004.

162 *"without a strong prevention effort"* Tim Ryan, interview, September 28, 2006.

163 *"during my twelve years of Catholic school"* Ibid.

163 *by 95 percent within ten years* The so-called 95-10 plan could never have come close to reducing the abortion rate by 95 percent, given that its focus was purely on measures to help women carry their babies to term and provide resources for motherhood. After Ryan added pregnancy prevention efforts to his legislation, Democrats for Life convinced Congressman Lincoln Davis (D-Tenn.) to introduce a version of their bill as an alternative.

165 *"keep us away from our church"* Rosa DeLauro, interview, December 7, 2006.

167 *"No one celebrates abortion"* Democratic press conference at the U.S. Capitol Building, Room HC-9, September 14, 2006.

168 *at which he could meet their friends* Ann Frick, interview, October 25, 2006.

168 *spilling into adjoining rooms and hallways* Ibid.

169 *" 'by going to Africa' "* Bill Ritter, interview, October 22, 2006.

171 *"because of my opposition to abortion"* Ibid.

171 *"Some people came out of the meeting"* Frick, October 25, 2006.

172 *without altering their pro-choice positions* In Ohio, Democratic gubernatorial candidate Ted Strickland captured 48 percent of the evangelical vote and boasted a twenty-point advantage among Catholic voters. His colleague in Michigan, incumbent governor Jennifer Granholm, won the support of 47 percent of evangelical voters in her state, as well as 56 percent of Catholics. Both support a woman's right to choose.

173 *EMILY's list endorsed her* Press release, "Statement by Ellen R. Malcolm, Endorsing Sen. Hillary Clinton for President," January 20, 2007.

174 *"They would hear about me and say, 'Who else?' "* Ritter, October 22, 2006.

175 *"phone calls I made for money"* Ibid.

CHAPTER 7: "WHERE HAVE YOU BEEN?"

179 *by a margin of 34 to 22 percent* Jay Root, " 'Values Voters' Key to Bush's Re-Election," *Star-Telegram,* November 4, 2004, A1.

179 *78 percent of white evangelicals* See John C. Green, "The American Religious Landscape and the 2004 Presidential Vote: Increased Polarization," Pew Forum on Religion and Public Life, February 3, 2005.

180 *"stereotypes are true"* Anonymous interview, October 5, 2006.

180 *"United States of Canada"* To see a map of the United States of Canada and Jesus Land, go to http://www.urbandictionary.com/define.php?term =united+states +of+canada&i=1. The creators of the map might want to pay a visit to the First Baptist Church of Plymouth, Michigan, as they appear to be under the unfortunate impression that Michigan is not actually part of Jesus Land.

181  *only deepened the siege mentality* See Kevin Phillips, *American Theocracy: The Peril and Politics of Radical Religion, Oil and Borrowed Money in the 21st Century* (New York: Viking, 2006), and Michelle Goldberg, *Kingdom Coming: The Rise of Christian Nationalism* (New York: W. W. Norton, 2006).

181  *out of their way to obscure* See John C. Green, "Religion a Strength and Weakness for Both Parties," Pew Forum on Religion and Public Life, August 30, 2005. According to Green's analysis, 40 percent of white evangelicals can be categorized as politically moderate based on their positions on political issues and/or self-identification.

181  *only a bare majority* Elizabeth Mehren, "A Mormon for President? Voters Balk," *Los Angeles Times,* July 3, 2006, A16.

181  *Kerry was floored* John Kerry described the encounter in a question-and-answer session at Pepperdine University on September 18, 2006. A video of his speech and answers can be accessed at http://www.pepperdine.edu/pr/releases/2006/september/kerry.htm.

183  *"That so dismisses their view"* Eric Sapp, interview, April 12, 2007.

183  *giving her staff, resources, and free rein* Vanderslice, August 8, 2006.

185  *Pelosi was there for the opening service* Shelby Hodge, "Her Big 5-Oh," *Houston Chronicle,* July 21, 2005.

185  *television show in May 2006* David Brody, "Howard Dean: Democrats Have Much in Common with Evangelicals," Christian Broadcasting Network, May 10, 2006.

186  *"gain a demographic but lose its soul?"* Ruth Marcus, "The New Temptation of Democrats," *Washington Post,* May 22, 2006.

187  *"maintained in a state of permanent mobilization"* Sidney Blumenthal, "The Righteous Empire," *New Republic,* October 22, 1984.

189  *"that I wasn't one of them"* Randy Brinson, interview, February 5, 2006.

190  *On the morning of the National Prayer Breakfast* Alan Cooperman, "Evangelicals Will Not Take Stand on Global Warming," *Washington Post,* February 2, 2006.

191  *a high economic cost for the country* Mark Pinsky, "Evangelicals Call for Action on Global Warming," *Orlando Sentinel,* February 9, 2006.

192  *by large margins* See "American Struggle with Religion's Role at Home and Abroad," Pew Forum on Religion and Public Life, March 20, 2002.

192  *"single-issue politics is neither necessary nor wise"* See "For Whom Would Jesus Vote?" *Christianity Today,* November 2004.

192  *a commencement address there in June of 2005* Elisabeth Bumiller, "Preaching to the Choir? Not This Time," *New York Times,* May 23, 2005.

192  *help eradicate water-borne illnesses* Kate Bowman Johnston, "So Much to Sing About," *Sojourners,* November 2005.

193  *Two weeks before the election* See Rick Warren, "Why Every U.S. Christian Must Vote in This Election," *Rick Warren's Ministry ToolBox,* October 27, 2004. The newsletter is also available at http://www.pastors.com/RWMT/default.asp?id =178&artid=7543&expand=1.

193  *"How did I miss two thousand verses in the Bible?"* Ann Rodgers, "Pastor Urges Anglicans to Unite and Care for Poor," *Pittsburgh Post-Gazette,* November 12, 2005.

193  *"You cannot fight evil while justifying another"* Hannah Elliott, "Pro-Lifers Call on

Rick Warren to Bar Obama from AIDS Summit," Associated Baptist Press, November 28, 2006.

194  *"that's a huge shift"* Mark Brewer, interview, August 7, 2006.

195  *"And then we cold-called them"* Sapp, April 12, 2007.

196  *In each city* Descriptions of the listening meetings are from interviews with Eric Sapp, April 12, 2007, and Mark Brewer, August 7, 2006.

198  *"we wanted these voters in our party"* Brewer, August 7, 2006.

198  *"The stranger. The first. The last"* The full text of the 2006 Michigan Democratic Party Platform is available at http://www.pastors.com/RWMT/default.asp?id=178&artid=7543&expand=1.

198  *"You just have to take the edge off"* Brewer, August 7, 2006.

203  *"I come here as a politician"* See "Granhom: 'Stop Using Religion to Divide,'" *Grand Rapids Press,* October 28, 2006.


CHAPTER 8: A LEVEL PRAYING FIELD

206  *"the biggest sin you've ever committed"* The full transcript for the CNN faith forum is available at http://transcripts.cnn.com/TRANSCRIPTS/0706/04/sitroom.03.html.

206  *"I would be amazed"* Ibid.

206  *"there's evil in the world"* Ibid.

206  *"without my faith"* Ibid.

207  *global antipoverty missions* Burns Strider, interview, October 8, 2007.

208  *his very first campaign ad* Mark Murray, "Test of Faith," *Washington Monthly,* October/November 2005.

210  *by nearly $8,000* Bob Gibson, "Perriello Enters Race for 5th Seat," *The Daily Progress,* October 7, 2007.

210  *"had contempt for Christians"* Dan Gilgoff, "Fired McCain Campaign Aides Sound Off," *U.S. News & World Report,* May 31, 2007.

211  *"I prefer to leave to the priests"* David Saltonstall, "Bedeviled by Faith: Rudy Dodges Questions About Whether He's a 'Good Catholic,'" New York *Daily News,* August 8, 2007.

211  *"Everybody has a right to their opinion"* Cheryl Wittenauer, "Bishop Would Deny Communion to Giuliani," Associated Press, October 3, 2007.

211  *"Mitt Romney represents Mormonism"* Lisa Wangsness, "At Straw Poll, Group Attacks Romney on Mormonism," *Boston Globe,* August 11, 2007.

212  *"I don't think he's a Christian"* Dan Gilgoff, "Dobson Offers Insight on 2008 Republican Hopefuls," *U.S. News & World Report,* March 28, 2007.

212  *admitted that he rarely attends church* Kim Chipman, "Thompson Says He Won't Tout His Religion on Trail," Bloomberg, September 11, 2007.

212  *dropped another four points to 40 percent* Nancy Gibbs and Michael Duffy, "Leveling the Praying Field," *Time,* July 12, 2007.

213  *"We need to broaden what 'life' issues are"* Jim Wallis, Pepperdine University, September 6, 2006.

214  *"white Christian party"* Carla Marinucci, "In S.F., Dean Calls GOP 'a White Christian Party,'" *San Francisco Chronicle,* June 7, 2005.

214   *"not just crazies with big Bibles"* Dan Gilgoff, "Democrats Kick Off a Multifront Campaign to Connect with Religious Voters," *U.S. News & World Report,* July 17, 2005.

214   *"the evangelical Christian community"* CBN News, "Howard Dean: Democrats Have Much in Common with Evangelicals," May 10, 2006.

215   *humming hymns while he jogged* Maureen Dowd, "Too Late for Libations," *New York Times,* April 5, 1998.

215   *starting his work day with private prayer* Anonymous Jewish leader, interview, September 14, 2006.

215   *on his being raised Baptist* Gebe Martinez, "Gephardt's Uneven History Left Behind for 2004 Run," *CQ Weekly,* May 30, 2003.

216   *"it also alienates a lot of voters"* Begala, interview, August 22, 2006.

216   *Catholic Democrats were outraged* Ben Smith, "Edwards Blogger Flap Discomforts Religious Left," *Politico,* February 9, 2007.

216   *anyone who objected to Marcotte's statements* Matt Stoller, "Step Up, Religious Left," MyDD.com, February 9, 2007, http://mydd.com/story/2007/2/9/94229/04000.

217   *loudly bemoaned in the liberal blogosphere* Chris Bowers, "Politics and the Inhuman," MyDD.com, February 12, 2007, http://mydd.com/story/2007/2/12/2324/03559.

217   *"poor, uneducated, and easy to command"* Michael Weisskopf, "Energized by Pulpit or Passion, the Public Is Calling," *Washington Post,* February 1, 1993, A1.

217   *that growth is far slower* The American Religious Identification Survey (ARIS) that is usually cited by those who see a doubling of the secular population in the United States identifies those Americans who choose "none" or "no religion" to describe their religious affiliation, which is not the same as those who self-identify as secular or atheist or agnostic. The percentage of Americans in those latter categories remains fairly low and has not increased significantly over the past decade. What the Baylor University study did was probe those "none" respondents to see if they were truly areligious. What they found is that a surprising percentage believe in God, pray frequently, and even name a religious congregation that they attend. In other words, they have some connection to faith or a religious tradition. They might be put off by the Christian Right, but they don't accurately belong in the category of people who are put off by religion in general—or who would be opposed to the Democratic Party's engagement with religious voters. In addition, many sociologists believe that increases in the percentage of secularists are largely due to a life-stage effect. They have long observed that many people fall away from their religious tradition during college but tend to return once they get married and, more often, when they have children. Because the age at which people marry and have children has risen, that cohort of unmarried and/or childless Americans has grown substantially in size. But for the most part, the life-stage effect continues: though they marry later, people are still returning to their religious traditions when they move to a more settled life stage. Their placement in the "none" category is therefore largely temporary.

217   *"They're looking for a candidate who likes them"* Ted Olson, Yale University, October 12, 2007.

# INDEX

# ABOUT THE AUTHOR

Amy Sullivan is the nation editor at *Time* magazine and a leading expert on religion and politics. She is also a contributing editor at the *Washington Monthly,* where she served previously as an editor. Sullivan, who has also worked on Capitol Hill and at the Pew Forum on Religion and Public Life, has written for a broad range of publications, including *The Boston Globe,* the *Los Angeles Times, The New Republic, Slate,* and *The Washington Post.* A Michigan native, she holds degrees from the University of Michigan and Harvard Divinity School.

29037169R00151

Made in the USA
Lexington, KY
24 January 2019